The Encyclopedia of
BASIC SEWING

A guide to the basic skills for successful
dressmaking and homemaking

Edited by Ethne Rose

Thomas Nelson Inc., Publishers
Nashville • New York

Copyright © 1979 Marshall Cavendish Ltd

All rights reserved under International
and Pan-American Conventions.
Published in Nashville, Tennessee, by
Thomas Nelson, Inc. 1979

Printed in Great Britain

Library of Congress Catalog
Number: 79-2579

ISBN 0-8407-4080-8

This book may not be sold outside the
United States of America and its territories

Library of Congress Cat. No. 79-2579

Introduction

Have you ever wished you could sew just about anything really well – from clothes for yourself and all the family to curtains, cushions, chair covers, table and bed linen and all those little things for the house done the way you want them? Then *Basic Sewing* is the book for you. How exciting it is to know that you can create beautiful and useful things for your home and family simply by following the clear and simple instructions and step-by-step illustrations. And think of the added satisfaction of the savings on your household budget at the same time.

Basic Sewing contains everything you have to know about the equipment you will need: needles, thread, sewing machines, scissors and shears, and all the other basic tools. Those tricky jobs you may dread doing – like making buttonholes or putting in zippers – are clearly and simply explained. How to work with differently textured and patterned fabrics and how to tackle many types of seams are made easy in *Basic Sewing*.

You'll be amazed at how soon you will be ready to make all the lovely things in this book. Your husband needs a new shirt; you want an evening dress; your daughter wants a pretty dress and your son a pair of tough new overalls – here's how to do it all, from measuring and making up the paper patterns to perfecting every trimming of the finished garment.

Perhaps you're considering redecorating but are not happy about the prospect of fitting your furniture into a bright, new color scheme. *Basic Sewing* unravels the mysteries of making draperies and curtains, slipcovers and, as a finishing touch, even lampshades. Use your flair and create a bedroom with the most modern look: an eiderdown, or continental quilt, in a bold designer print or solid cover, with a fitted sheet, pillowcases and dust ruffle in a complementary pattern or shade.

Don't stop here because *Basic Sewing* gives you all the foundation you will need to master commercial patterns as well as the know-how to actually create your own ideas. And even after you have mastered the essential techniques of good sewing you will find this book an indispensable reference work, useful to even the most experienced needlewoman.

Contents

Sewing Basics

Tools   6
Measurements   7
Patterns   8
Cutting out   12
Seams and stitches   17
Pressing   21

Dressmaking

Sundress   24
Fastening • Facing and hems •
Gathering and shirring • The Pattern
Mother and Daughter Aprons   38
Ruffles and Flounces • The Pattern
Toddler's Dress   45
The Pattern
Long Evening Dress   49
Darts • Pattern alterations • The Pattern
Skirt with Flare   57
Waistbands • Belts • The Pattern
Man's Sportshirt   66
Sewing jersey and stretch fabrics •
The pattern
Blouson Cover-up   71
Bias strips and rouleau • The Pattern
His 'n' Her Nightshirt   76
The Pattern
Summer Separates   80
The Pattern

Classic Shirt   88
The Pattern
Knife-pleated Skirt   92
Working with pleats • The Pattern
Unisex Jackets   99
Bound buttonholes • The Pattern
Slim-fitting Pants   106
Ajusting pants patterns • The Pattern •
Pattern for Child's Overalls

Home Sewing

Table Linen   118
Round tablecloth • Rectangular
tablecloth • Napkins and placemats
Pillows and Slipcovers   127
Flat pillow covers • Piped pillow covers • Box
cushions • Round Pillows with welt • Tie-on
cushions • Slipcovers
Window Treatments   143
Unlined draperies • Sheer draperies and curtains •
Lined draperies • Reversible draperies •
Hand-stitched pinch pleats • Café curtains •
Tie-backs • Window shades
Bed Linen   169
Throw-over bedspreads • Flounced bedspreads •
Eiderdown set
Lampshades   179
Detachable Tiffany shades • Lined lampshades
Sewing Snips   189
Lined picnic basket • Potholders • Deckchair and
windbreak • Showercap and sponge bag

Sewing Basics

Know Your Tools

A sewing machine

There are three main types: straight stitch, swing needle (zigzag), and swing needle automatic.

Straight stitch This type will sew only in a straight line. It is the least expensive and is perfectly adequate for basic sewing. It is also possible to buy attachments, such as a zipper foot for stitching close to a zipper.

Swing needle Besides doing straight stitching this machine does zigzag stitching, which is useful for finishing seams and hems, for making buttonholes, for stitching stretch fabrics, and for sewing on buttons. It is also possible to do simple embroidery stitches. Swing needle machines are in the medium price bracket.

Swing needle automatic This type of machine does embroidery as well as the stitches which the other two types offer. But this type of machine is the most expensive and rather a luxury unless you intend to do a good deal of decorative stitching and embroidery. Electronics have added a new refinement to automatic sewing machines. There are various models now on the market with electronically regulated motors. These enable the sewing speed to be very precisely controlled with no sacrifice of power even when sewing. only one stitch at a time. Electronic models are especially good whenever exact stitching is needed, e.g. for turning corners, inserting zippers, for decorative applications or for sewing through several layers of thick fabric.
Note Make sure that the machine you buy has a clear instruction book. It is also important, particularly with a more complex machine, to have it explained by an expert and if possible to take a few short lessons in its use in order to get the best possible results.

Machine needles Use size 70-90 (11-14) for lightweight fabrics, size 90

(14) for medium-weight fabrics and size 90-110 (14-18) for heavy-weight fabrics. Continental sizes are given first here, followed by Standard sizes in brackets.
Ballpoint machine needles should be used for knit fabrics to avoid cutting the thread and causing a run.
Sewing needles Use size 8 or 9 for most fabrics, size 6 or 7 for fabrics such as heavy linen and for stitching on buttons, and size 10 for fine work.

Tools you will need

Pins Use steel dressmaking pins, at least 2·5 cm (1 in) long.

Tapemeasure The fiberglass type is the best as it will not stretch. One with a metal strip attached at one end is useful, especially when taking up hems. Tapemeasures are now marked with centimeters and millimeters on one side and inches on the other. For an approximate comparison between the two standards simply look on the other side of the tapemeasure.

Thread For man-made or synthetic fibers use a synthetic thread. Linen and cotton fabrics require mercerized cotton, either 40 or 50. For woolen fabrics use either a synthetic or silk thread.
With all types of thread the higher the number given on the label, the finer the thread.

Scissors Large shears are advisable when working with heavy fabrics. The handles should comfortably fit the hand (left-handed shears are available). Small shears, 18-20 cm (7-8 in) long, are best for cutting out most fabrics as they are heavier than scissors and glide through the cloth more easily.
Small sharp scissors are useful for clipping seams and threads. Never use your dressmaking scissors for cutting any kind of paper, including patterns, because this will quickly make the blades blunt and ineffective.

Stitch ripper This is better than scissors for cutting machine-made buttonholes, and for removing buttons and snaps, as well as being useful for unpicking seams, etc. Various types are available in the notions department of most stores.

Iron It is necessary to have a good medium-weight iron with thermostatic controls. With a steam iron you should use distilled water, unless you live in an area with very soft water.

Ironing board An essential item for pressing seams flat. It should stand firmly and have a smooth-fitting cover. A sleeve board is useful.

Pressing cloth A piece of finely woven wool (for woolen fabrics), cotton or cheesecloth through which you are able to see details, 61 cm (24 in) square. Your cloth should not have holes, frayed edges or a prominent grain, as these can leave an impression on the fabric being pressed. The cloth should not contain any finish as this will stick to the iron.

Tailor's ham An egg-shaped, firmly stuffed cushion. This is useful for pressing curved areas of a garment. A pressing roll is also useful for pressing seams in narrow areas, e.g. sleeves. You can make one by covering a piece of wooden doweling with blanketing tightly rolled and stitched around.

Tailor's chalk Have two pieces for marking your fabric, white for dark fabrics and dark for light fabrics.

Tracing wheel Use this for marking pattern outlines onto fabric. One made from steel with sharp points is best.

Thimble This should fit the middle finger of your sewing hand. Choose a metal one, as the needle can penetrate a plastic thimble while sewing.

Needle & Thread Chart

Successful dressmaking depends on using the right thread because if both thread and fabric share the same characteristics, they can be laundered together, ironed at the same temperatures and will also shrink and stretch together. The natural threads are silk and cotton, the latter mercerized or unmercerized. This means it is specially treated for luster and greater strength. Silk is multi-purpose and combines strength with elasticity. The most commonly used synthetic threads are made from polyester fiber: you may also find cotton-wrapped polyester thread. The higher the number thread the finer; the most commonly used thickness is 50, but for finer fabrics 60 can be used.

Synthetic fabrics For man-made fiber fabrics, and mixtures of natural and man-made fibers, a synthetic thread should be used. This thread is usually stronger than natural thread and has a lot of stretch, which is particularly important when sewing fabrics such as synthetic knits. Cotton-wrapped polyester thread is suitable for sewing fine leather which tends to have a good deal of stretch in it as well.

Natural fabrics For cotton and linen a mercerized cotton thread is used for most purposes. Synthetic thread will melt under the heat required for pressing these fabrics. Unmercerized cotton is used for basting. Wool can be sewn with silk or mercerized cotton. Always sew silk with fine, lustrous pure silk thread.

Fabric	Fiber	Thread	Needle sizes	
			Hand-sewing	Machine-stitching
Fine	synthetic; mixtures	synthetic extra fine	9–10	9 to 11
lawn, georgette,	cotton and linen	mercerized 50	9	9 to 11
voile, chiffon,	wool	mercerized 50 or silk	9	9 to 11
organdy, net, lace	silk	silk	9	9 to 11
Lightweight	synthetic; mixtures	synthetic	8–9	11 to 14
such as poplin,	cotton and linen	mercerized 50	8–9	11 to 14
gingham, silk,	wool	mercerized 50 or silk	8–9	11 to 14
cotton	silk	silk	8–9	11 to 14
Medium-weight	synthetic; mixtures	synthetic	8–9	11 to 14
such as gabardine,	cotton	mercerized 50	7–8	11 to 14
brocade, tweed,	linen	mercerized 40	7–8	11 to 14
water-proofed	wool	mercerized 50 or silk	7–8	11 to 14
fabrics	silk	silk	7–8	11 to 14
Heavy-weight	synthetic; mixtures	synthetic	6	16 to 18
such as coatings,	cotton	mercerized 40	7–8	14 to 16
canvas, heavy home	linen	mercerized 40	6–7	14 to 18
furnishing fabrics	wool	mercerized 40 or silk	7–8	14 to 16
	silk	silk	7–8	14 to 16
Some special fabrics				
velvet	synthetic; mixtures	synthetic	8–9	11 to 14
	cotton	mercerized 50	7–8	11 to 14
	silk	silk	7–8	11 to 14
fine leather and vinyl		synthetic		14 to 18

Pinking shears Not essential but useful to give a neater finish to seams, particularly when working with knitted and non-fraying fabrics.

Yardstick or meter stick Use this for measuring hems.

Metric measurements
Instead of yards, feet, inches and fractions of an inch, metric measurements are written as meters (m), centimeters (cm) and millimeters (mm). There are one hundred centimeters in each meter and ten millimeters in each centimeter. Therefore $1\frac{1}{2}$ centimeters ($1\frac{5}{10}$) is written as 1·5 cm. Fractions of less than 1 centimeter can also be witten in millimeters, e.g. "a 5 mm seam" or "0·5 cm" instead of "a $\frac{1}{2}$ cm seam". A $1\frac{1}{2}$ cm seam is written as 1·5 cm.

The measurements in this book are written first in metric with the *approximate* Standard equivalents in brackets. Wherever possible both sets of figures have been worked out in round numbers. You must always work consistently with one or the other set.

Fabric lengths are usually sold by the meter and cut to tenths of a meter (10 cm), e.g. 1 meter 70 centimeters is

1·70 m. 10 cm is approximately 4 in and takes the place of the Standard $\frac{1}{8}$ yard. Fabric widths are sold by the centimeter as shown below.

Fabric widths
- 90 cm (36 in)
- 115 cm (45 in)
- 120 cm (48 in)
- 140 cm (54-56 in)
- 150 cm (60 in)

The measurements in this chart comply with the standard measurements used by pattern companies. Skirt lengths can be ascertained by counting the squares downward from waist to hem on the required graph pattern then multiplying by the given scale of 2·5 cm (1 in) per square.

How to take your measurements
Bust Make sure that you keep the tapemeasure well up over the shoulder blades at the back, and measure across the fullest part of the bust (fig. 1).

Waist Tie a piece of hem tape or straight binding around the waist to establish the true waistline. Then run tapemeasure around your waist over tape so that it is comfortable but not loose (fig. 2). Keep tape on as a guide for taking other measurements.

Hips This measurement should be taken around the fullest part of the hips, usually 15-20 cm (6-8 in) below the waistline (fig. 3).

Back neck to waist Measure from the small bone at the back of the neck to the waistline (fig. 4).

Back neck to hem Measure from the same bone to the hemline. Remem-

Metric measurements used on dressmaking patterns						
Size	8	10	12	14	16	18
	cm (in)	cm (in)	cm (in)	cm (in)	cm (in)	cm (in)
Bust	80 (31½)	83 (32½)	87 (34)	92 (36)	97 (38)	102 (40)
Waist	61 (24)	64 (25)	67 (26½)	71 (28)	76 (30)	81 (32)
Hips	85 (33½)	88 (34½)	92 (36)	97 (38)	102 (40)	107 (42)

1   2   3   4   5

ber to allow extra for a hem (fig. 5).

Sleeve With arm bent, measure from arm top to the wrist around the bent elbow (fig. 6).

Depth of bust It is important to have the bust dart or fullness in the correct position for a good fit. Measure from center of one shoulder to bust point (fig. 7).

Inside leg Measure from inside top of leg to length required (fig. 8).

Outside leg Measure from side of waist to length required. When measuring the leg for pants, you should wear shoes with heels the same height as those you will wear with the pants (fig. 9).

Depth of crotch The easiest way to take this measurement is to sit on a chair with your back straight and measure from the side of waist to the chair. Allow 1·3-2·5 cm ($\frac{1}{2}$-1 in) for ease of movement (fig. 10).

It is important to take your measurements correctly to help in choosing the proper pattern size.

Patterns and pattern sizes

If your measurements do not correspond with the body chart it is advisable to select the pattern according to your bust size and adjust the hips and waist as necessary.

Note: In this book the term "women's size" corresponds to "misses' size" in commercial pattern books.

How to use graph patterns

Graph patterns can seem somewhat complicated if you haven't used them before, but they are really very simple. Graphs are a way of giving readers full-sized garment patterns but scaled down so that they fit into a book or magazine page. They are designed in exactly the same way as the paper patterns which you buy. The only difference is that a graph is a plan from which you draw the pattern yourself. Graph patterns can be very useful, too, in that you can make minor adaptations to style or improve on body fit as you are drawing the pattern.

To make a paper pattern from a graph pattern, you will find it best to work on a flat surface; the floor will do. You will need this equipment:

Sheets of graph paper This is

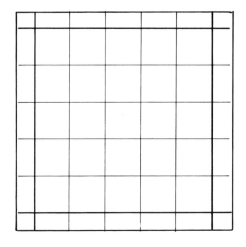

1. Pattern paper is divided into 5 cm (2 in) squares and 1 cm ($\frac{3}{8}$ in) squares.

called "dressmaker's pattern paper" and is usually obtainable from the notions department of stores. The sheets usually measure 90 cm by 62 cm (36 in by 24 in) and are sold in packages of three, usually enough for a dress pattern.

Yardstick or meter rule

Soft pencil

Drawing out the pattern Check the scale given with the pattern. Sometimes this will be marked on the graph itself; sometimes you will find it in the instructions. It will read

6   7   8   9   10

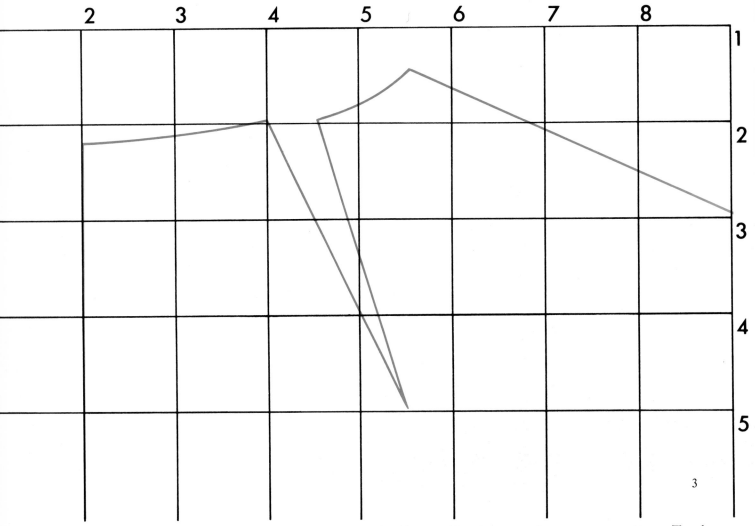

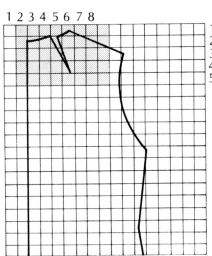

something like, "one square equals 5 cm (2 in)" but the scale will vary; sometimes one square will equal 2·5 cm (1 in). Your graph paper will be marked off into 5 cm (2 in) squares in thick lines and into 1 cm (⅜ in) squares in a lighter toned line. For the purpose of this exercise, use the heavy, 5 cm (2 in) square lines (fig. 1).

Number the graph pattern squares, first across the top and then down the side as shown in the diagram (fig. 2). Draw out the area of the graph pattern on your squared paper and number the 5 cm (2 in) squares in the same way, first across the top and then down the side (fig. 3).

You now have a perfect reproduction of the area you are going to work within, scaled up from the graph pattern.

To make it clear, we have tinted the area of the graph pattern we have enlarged.

Draw in any straight lines, such as the line indicating Fold.

Study the line in the square 2 across and 2 down. You will see that it starts just below a graph line, curving up slightly as it touches the square next to it. Reproduce as faithfully as you can the direction of the line on your graph paper. Don't worry if your line looks a little wobbly – you can always straighten it up later.

Compare your shoulder to waist, waist to hip and sleeve length with the graph you are copying. If you need to make any adjustments, do these before cutting out your pattern. To alter a bodice, follow a horizontal line 10 cm (4 in) above the waist and add or subtract the necessary length. To adjust a skirt pattern, follow a horizontal line just above the hipline of the pattern; on a sleeve follow horizontal lines above and below the elbow. Alter as described for the bodice. Adjust skirt and sleeve lengths slightly at the hem. (Also see Basic pattern alterations.)

Sometimes the graph pattern is multi-sized, in which case the outline for each size is marked with a different color or broken line. Simply follow the outline for the size you want.

Add all marks and words given on the graph pattern. You have now made your master pattern.

First steps before cutting out

If you are making a garment for the first time, pick a fabric that is easy to work with and not too expensive in case of catastrophe! A plain cotton or one with a small all-over print is ideal. Large patterns, checks or stretchy knits should not be used by beginners, nor should those such as velvet or lace that need special sewing techniques.

Some technical terms
Selvages The edges of the fabric, usually tightly woven and non-fraying.
Grain The straight threads running the length (warp) and width (weft) of woven fabrics. If the pattern piece has an arrow, this indicates that it should follow the direction of the grain.
Nap Any fabric with a piled surface, e.g. velvet. On such fabrics the pattern pieces must all run in the same direction, or a shaded effect will result.
One-way Designs that are printed or woven in one direction. Pattern pieces must be placed accordingly. Special pattern layouts are usually

1. To straighten fabric, pull a thread across the width and then use the line as a guide to cut the fabric evenly.

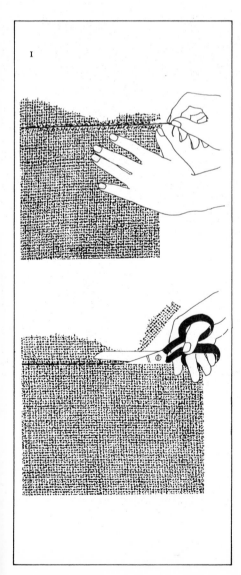

provided for "with nap" or "one way" fabrics.
Ease (or tolerance) Extra width included in patterns to allow for the movement of the body, so that the garment is comfortable to wear. Usually about 5 cm (2 in) on bust and hips and 2·5 cm (1 in) for the waist.
Notches or "balance marks" Small marks at side edges of pattern pieces to show which parts join which.

Preparing the fabric
Before laying out a pattern make sure that the fabric lies flat when both selvages are together, as the fabric often becomes slightly warped when wound onto the bolt, or can be stretched at the selvage on knitted fabrics such as jersey. If the cloth has a stripe or horizontal pattern, trim the cut edge until at a right angle to the selvage: with cotton or heavy linen it is usually possible to pull a thread across the width as a guide (fig. 1).
Place the two selvages together. Providing the weft is even, the material should lie flat; if it appears wrinkled pull on the bias at regular intervals down the complete length of the cloth. Then, with the material held lengthwise, gently pull on the selvage edge and on the fold line. Sometimes the fabric has been folded badly and it is necessary to press it.
If possible cut out patterns on a large table or on the floor, as the complete pattern should be placed on the fabric and cut at the same time. When a delicate fabric is being used it is advisable to place a heavy blanket underneath and pin the fabric to it at the edges. It is also necessary to use fine pins or fine needles on this type of fabric as ordinary pins will mark and leave unsightly holes.

All alterations such as shortening or lengthening pattern pieces should be made before placing them on the fabric.

Testing fabrics
To find out whether a washable fabric is colorfast wash a small square about 8 cm (3 in) square. Press while still damp onto some white fabric. The color will run onto the white fabric if it is not colorfast.
To test for shrinkage measure a similar square of fabric, or baste mark the outline of an 8 cm (3 in) square onto it in long stitches, before washing; measure again when dry and then compare the two measurements.
Fabrics in synthetic fibers do not shrink and many others are preshrunk by the manufacturer. If the test square shrinks you must preshrink the fabric before cutting. Wet a strip of sheeting the width and length of the fabric. Wring out any excess moisture. Place sheeting over fabric and roll up. Leave for several hours. Remove sheet and press fabric using a dry pressing cloth. Press along the straight grain of the fabric – not diagonally – until fabric is dry.

Laying out a pattern
Layout instructions and diagrams are usually provided with both commercial and graph patterns (fig. 2). Follow these carefully as they will show you the best and most economical way to arrange your pattern pieces on the fabric before cutting out. Alternative versions are usually given for different fabric widths or for fabrics with nap.

2. All patterns include layout diagrams to show you how to arrange the pieces in the most economical manner.

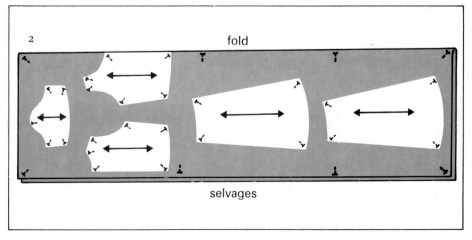

fold

selvages

Note whether seam and hem allowances have been provided on the pattern or whether you must allow extra space between the pattern pieces to provide for them. Also note if any pattern pieces have to be reversed or cut on the fold, and whether they are cut on a double or single layer. Sometimes, because of unusual widths of fabric, difficult stripes, or a big pattern repeat, it is necessary to place the paper pattern in a different way from the one suggested. Once you are more experienced you will be able to adapt layouts for yourself.

Always check that the straight grain mark on every pattern piece runs parallel to the selvages.

When pinning the pattern onto the fabric place the pins so that the points lie toward the center. Positioning of pins in this way holds the fabric firmly and there is less risk of scratching your hands when smoothing out pattern pieces. Pin fabric around edges to hold layers together on folded fabric.

Do not leave facings to be cut out later as those smaller pattern pieces can easily be mislaid.

Count all pattern pieces to make sure that none have been forgotten. Note whether any parts, such as pockets or collars, have to be cut twice.

Cutting out

Before starting to cut out the fabric make sure you have the necessary tools: a large pair of dressmaking shears for long, straight edges and a smaller sharply pointed pair for all the awkward corners and for cutting around notches.

The shears will have a pointed blade and a rounded blade. The pointed blade is placed downward when cutting out patterns to ensure that the two thicknesses of cloth are cut at the same time. The rounded blade is placed downward for such things as trimming large areas and grading (trimming seam allowances to different widths) so that there is no sharp point to cut the second layer of cloth.

Fabrics made from man-made fibers often blunt shears very quickly. A very light application of a silicone polish will help to prevent this. But allow it to dry thoroughly before using the shears.

Notches may be marked on patterns

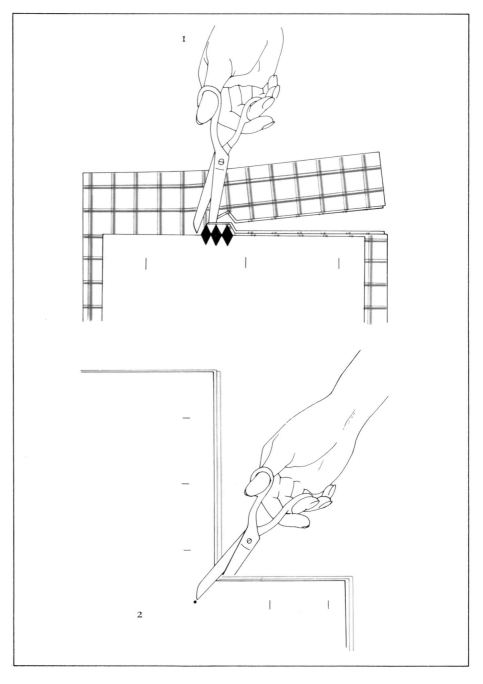

1. Cut notches carefully; they help to match pattern pieces. 2. Clip corners when you are ready to baste.

as diamonds or triangles and are often difficult to cut. Bypass these when using the big shears and go back to them using small pointed scissors. It is not practical to cut into each individual notch when there are two or three together, so cut straight across the top of them (fig. 1).

Often in a corner of a pattern piece there is a large dot and the word "clip" (fig. 2). Do not cut this until you are ready to baste to prevent fraying.

Using the large shears, with the pointed blade toward the table, make long clean cuts into the fabric. When using a patterned fabric check that both thicknesses of fabric are matching on all edges. It is sometimes advisable to cut each layer separately as some

types of cloth slip very easily. It is essential to cut fur fabric separately as only the backing must be cut.

Cutting bias strips These are required for making bindings or rouleau ties. To find the bias, fold the fabric so that the straightened edge is parallel to the selvage (fig. 1, right). The fold is on the bias grain.

Use a yardstick and tailor's chalk to mark out strips of the width required parallel to this fold (fig. 2). These may have to be stitched together later to make up the length required.

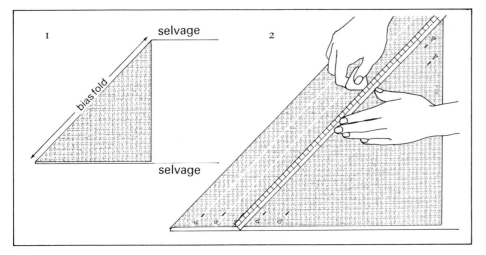

Marking, tacking and basting

It is essential to transfer all markings on the pattern to the fabric before removing pattern. Markings are made

Left. 1. To cut bias strips, fold over a corner of fabric and 2. mark the cutting lines with tailor's chalk.

Below: 1. Making tailor's tacks.
2. Marking darts with tailor's tacks.
3. Thread tacking along center back.
4. Trace tacking along center back and side seams.
5. Cutting through the tailor's tacks.

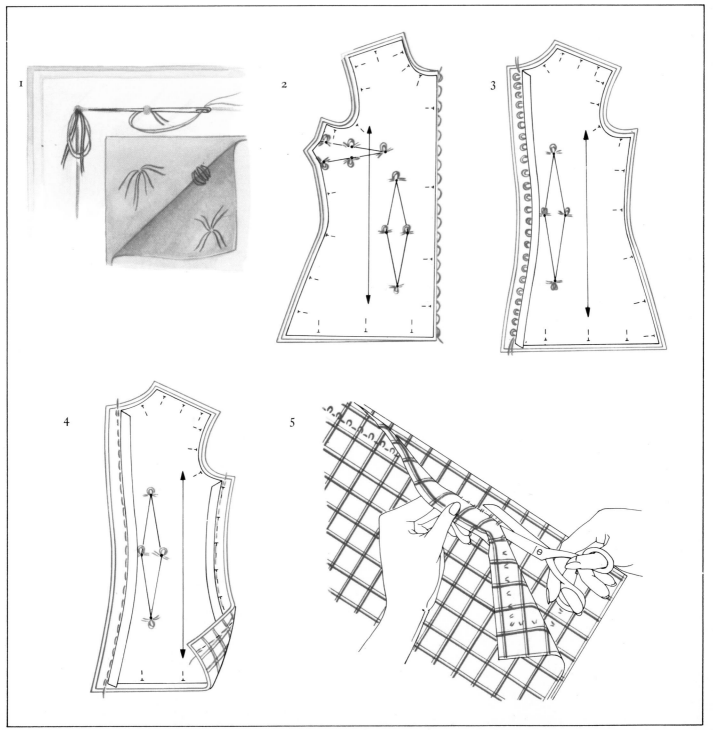

with tailor's tacks, large looped basting stitches for marking pattern details; thread tacks, for quick marking of grain or stitching lines; and trace tacks, for marking center front, center back or stitching lines.

Tailor's tacks Using double thread, without a knot, work a small stitch through the pattern and both thicknesses of the fabric, leaving about 2·5 cm (1 in) of thread free. Now work another stitch in the same place leaving a loop of thread of about 4 cm (1½ in); cut off the thread about 2·5 cm (1 in) from last stitch. To mark darts with tailor's tacks, take a large needle and make a hole in the pattern where the dots of the darts are marked. (With graph patterns make holes at the point of the dart, on the stitching line and halfway between the point and the stitching line.) Work the tailor's tacks as already described. Pocket positions, notches and balance marks are also marked with tailor's tacks. On cotton and heavy fabrics use basting thread, which grips the cloth better than most other threads and is less likely to slip out in the course of the work. With delicate fabrics use lightweight thread such as pure silk and a needle no larger than number 10, for otherwise permanent marks or holes may appear in the garment.

Thread tacking Fold pattern back at stitching line. Using double thread, without a knot, work a continuous line of small basting stitches through the two thicknesses of fabric, leaving a loop of thread about 4 cm (1½ in) between each stitch (fig. 3, p.13).

Trace tacking Fold back pattern at stitching line. Using single thread, without a knot, work a row of small basting stitches through single fabric (fig. 4, p.13). Place pins on this line of tacking through both thicknesses of cloth. Turn fabric over and work another row of trace tacking between the pins.

It is essential when marking stitching lines to continue right to the end so that the lines of tacking cross at the corners. It is advisable when working thread tacking for stitching lines to use a different colored thread from that used for the notches to avoid confusion.

The simple unbroken lines of this smock are good for stripes and checks.

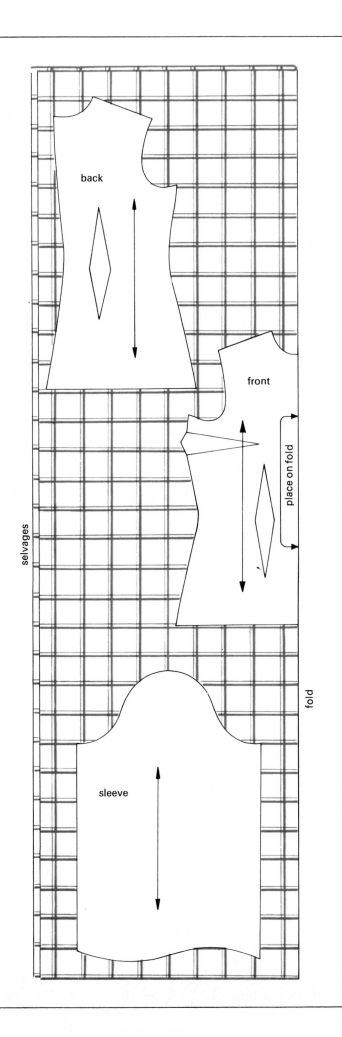

Labels in figure: back, front, place on fold, selvages, fold, sleeve

I

Do not use a very dark thread on a light colored fabric as it could leave marks.

Center front or **center back** Place on a fold of the cloth, and mark out with trace tacking stitches through the single fabric on fold, Start and finish with backstitches.

Fold lines Use for such things as pleats, marked with thread tacking or trace tacking.

A very simple pattern can usually be transferred onto the fabric by working tailor's tacks on each corner where the stitching lines cross each other and at about 10 cm (4 in) intervals on the stitching lines.

Tailor's chalk Use to save time in marking out a pattern but remember that it contains a certain amount of grease and can sometimes leave a permanent mark.

When all markings have been transferred to the fabric remove pattern and cut through tailor's tacks and thread tacking (fig. 5 p. 13). Do this by gently pulling the two pieces of fabric apart and, with small scissors, cutting through the center of the stitch. Sometimes a pattern will have a great many pieces. To avoid confusion it often helps to pin a small piece of paper at the bottom edge, and write on it the name of the pattern piece after you have cut it out.

Special cutting directions

Patterned fabrics or those with a pile need more attention at the cutting out stage. Designs with simple unbroken lines are best for all these fabrics.

Stripes, plaids and checks Designs such as these must be in line on each piece of the garment, including the sleeves. It is often easiest to place the center back body piece onto the fabric, then, matching the bottom edge of the other pieces, work around to the center front. The sleeves must match at the underarm point so that the pattern runs in a continuous line around the arm (fig. 1). When a side bust dart is used it is not always possible to match the pattern at the underarm, but this usually affects only 5-8 cm (2-3 in). It is not always

1. On patterned fabrics it is important that the design of the fabric matches when cutting out.

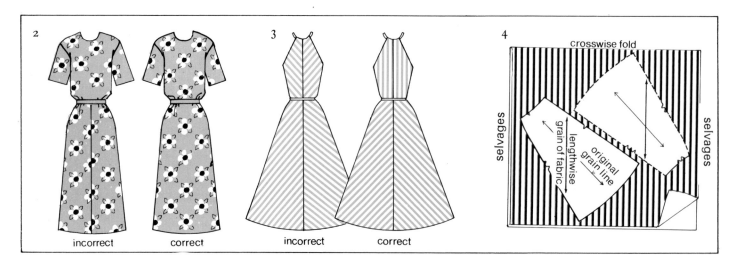

2. Large motifs should not lie over obvious figure features. 3. Diagonal stripes are best on center back or front openings and 4. A new grain line should be placed parallel to selvages.

possible to match vertical and horizontal stripes on the shoulder line as there is usually about 1·3 cm (½ in) of ease on the back. Match instead at armhole edge, as often the neck edge is covered by a collar.

Pockets, tabs and flaps must also line up in the pattern unless intended otherwise. Sometimes these are cut on the bias of a checked fabric as a design feature, or cut with the vertical stripes or ribs of the fabric running horizontally.

Avoid using designs with too many pieces to be matched, or widely flaring skirts. Uneven plaid designs are particularly difficult to work with.

Flower prints and unusual patterns

If these have a one-way motif, make sure, when laying out the pattern, that the design runs in the right direction on all the pieces. As with plaids, avoid patterns with many pieces. You may find problems, too, with prints that have really large motifs. The least complicated way to use these is for large flowing designs such as caftans or full-length skirts. On other garments try to arrange the pattern pieces so that motifs are in the same position on back and front and on the sleeves. Make sure that really large motifs do not lie directly over the bust or seat (fig. 2).

Pile fabrics

Velvet, corduroy and fake fur come into this category. In all cases the pile

of the fabric must lie in the same way on each piece. Test by smoothing the surface in one direction with your hand. Always use a "with nap" layout.

Using diagonal stripes If you want to do this choose a pattern with a center seam or front or back opening (fig. 3). Mark a new grain line on the pattern pieces at 45° to the straight grain line. To cut out, fold the full width of the fabric crosswise, with right sides together. Lay the pattern pieces on the fabric with the new line parallel to selvages (fig. 4). Notches to be joined must be on the same stripe. Stripes must also match at

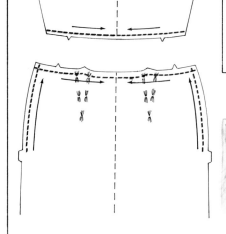

center and side seams *on the seamline*, not the seam edge. For accurate stitching use slip basting to hold the pieces together (see Preparing for fitting). If the stripes are uneven, lay the pattern pieces on the fabric in one direction.

Preparing for fitting

The garment is now ready to be put together. Here are some useful preliminaries.

Stay stitching Use to keep the shape of necklines or waistlines to prevent their stretching during assembly. A line of machine stitching is made in the seam allowance 1·3 cm (½ in) from the raw edge. Work with thread to match the fabric. Stitch in the directions shown (fig. 1 below).

Basting stitches Temporary stitches which are used to hold the garment sections together. Make even stitches by hand, about 6 mm (¼ in) long (fig. 2 below). Work on a flat surface such as a table. Before you begin basting

1. Work stay stitching in the direction shown. 2. This diagram shows how to do stay stitching.

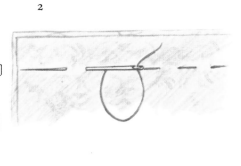

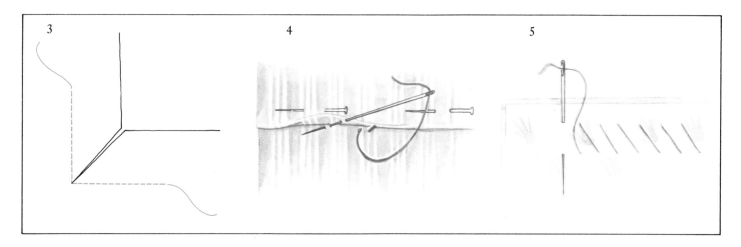

3

place the seam edges together, pin at each end and in the center and match any notches. Place pins at right angles to the seamline. Once you are more experienced you can pin, then stitch simple garments together without basting.

Baste all darts and main seamlines, center front, sides and shoulders. Use single thread without a knot. Start and finish each line with three back-stitches, as knots can cause permanent holes or damage when pulled while trying on the garment. It is important that the garment be basted well to achieve a good fitting. Any alteration is made during the fitting. The garment is then re-basted to the correct line, tried on again, and if it is then satisfactory it is ready to be stitched. All tailor's tacks are removed at this stage to avoid stitching over them.

Reinforcing   This is often necessary to strengthen seams on a corner. It is done before the seam is stitched. Stitch about 2·5 cm (1 in) to either side of the point. Inward corners are clipped as shown (fig. 3).

Slip basting   This is used for matching stripes, plaids or patterns accurately, also for attaching curved pattern sections or to secure fitting adjustments that have been made on the right side. Working on the right side, turn under the seam allowance. Position on corresponding section and pin carefully. Using single thread, slip needle through upper fold, then lower section, taking small stitches. When finished the seam will be basted on the wrong side (fig. 4).

Diagonal basting   This is used to keep separate layers together, e.g.

3. Reinforcing is used to strengthen corner seams. 4. Working slip basting. 5. Working diagonal basting.

to secure interfacings firmly against fabric during assembly or to hold facing edges in place ready for pressing. Make slanting stitches about 6 mm ($\frac{1}{4}$ in) long and the same distance apart working at right angles to the edge of the fabric through all layers (fig. 5).

All about seams
Basic seams
There are many types of seam, all of which serve the same purpose but each of which has individual advantages. The seam must be chosen to suit the fabric and the design of the garment, which means considering whether or not the fabric will fray and if the seam is to show. Always remember to press seams well after stitching and before finishing.

Plain seam   This is the most commonly used seam in dressmaking as it is suitable for most fabrics.

Placing right sides together and matching notches, baste and stitch on the seamline. To join a bias edge to a straight edge pin, baste and stitch with

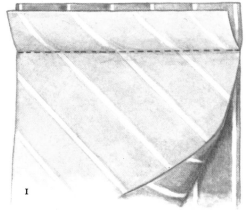

1

the bias side upward (fig. 1). If joining two bias edges stretch fabric slightly as you stitch over tissue paper.

Seam finishes   Your dressmaking will be neater, stronger and more professional-looking if you finish off each line of stitching firmly. Start and finish each seam with a backstitch, either by hand or by running your machine backward for 6 mm ($\frac{1}{4}$ in). Thread ends should be knotted and the ends cut off. If the stitching line ends before the edge of the fabric, pull one of the thread ends through to the other side. Tie both thread ends together and cut off surplus.

Useful hand stitches
Backstitch   This stitch is used for starting and finishing most hand stitching and is useful for repairing broken machine lines (fig. 1 p. 18). Using single thread, and placing right sides of work together, insert needle into fabric and make a small stitch on the wrong side. Put needle back into the hole where the thread first entered the fabric. Make another stitch through the fabric twice the length of the first. Insert the needle back in the hole where it came out for the previous stitch. Continue in this way until the line of stitches is complete.

Blanket stitch   Useful as a decorative finish on a raw edge. The thread loops underneath the needle, which lies vertically in the fabric. Make a loop or bar for a hook by working blanket stitches close together over a group of threads (fig. 2 p. 18).

Hemming   Used to hold all types of

1. A plain seam.

hems in place. Take a tiny stitch in the garment, then bring the needle diagonally up through hem edge. Make stitches 6 mm ($\frac{1}{4}$ in) apart (fig. 3).

Herringbone stitch Useful for holding two layers of fabric together, e.g. attaching raw edges of facings or making hems on stretch fabrics.
Work from left to right taking a small stitch in hem, then one in the fabric (fig. 4). (Catch stitch is similar, but only one thread is picked up.)

Overcasting Used to prevent raw edges from fraying. Make diagonal, evenly-spaced stitches over the edge of the fabric (fig. 5).

Prick stitch A version of back-stitch, worked over a single thread of fabric, forming a tiny surface stitch (fig. 6).

Running stitch Used for easing, i.e. gathering, a slightly longer piece onto a smaller one such as for putting in a sleeve. For making gathers and –

worked in even rows – for shirring. Weave needle in and out of fabric before pulling through. Make stitches an even size, 2-6 mm ($\frac{1}{16}$-$\frac{1}{4}$ in) long. Several stitches can be made on the needle at same time. Draw up stitches if gathers are required (fig. 7).

Slip-stitch Used to attach one piece of fabric to another when one edge is turned under – as in hemming, inserting linings ane attaching bias binding and trimmings. Slide the needle through the folded edge of the fabric, then – directly opposite and barely outside the fold – pick up a thread of the under fabric. Continue in the same way, spacing evenly, from 3 to 6 mm ($\frac{1}{8}$ to $\frac{1}{4}$ in) apart (fig. 8).

Finishing seams

When each seam is finished remove the basting, fasten the thread ends and press the seam. The method of finishing depends on the type of fabric used.

Overcasting This can be done separately on each pressed-open seam

allowance or alternatively, both seam allowances can be pressed together and overcast as one, e.g. on waists or armhole seams (fig. 1 p. 19).

Zigzag stitch This is a useful machine finish for many types of fabric with a tendency to fray. Use a small stitch on a fine fabric, a large zigzag stitch on a heavier fabric (fig. 2 p. 19).

Turned under Thin fabrics can be turned under for 3 mm ($\frac{1}{8}$ in) and machine stitched close to the fold (fig. 3 p. 19).

Bound Thick fabrics that fray can have seam edges bound with bias or seam binding. Fold the binding around

These hand stitches are useful for finishing raw edges, and their use will add a couture finish to any garment. Shown below are: 1. back stitch, 2. blanket stitch, 5. overcasting or oversewing, 6. prick stitch, running stitch and 8. slip-stitch.

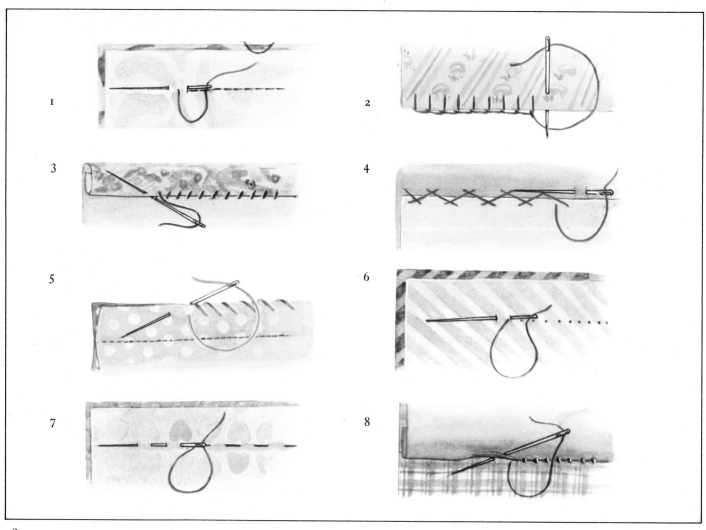

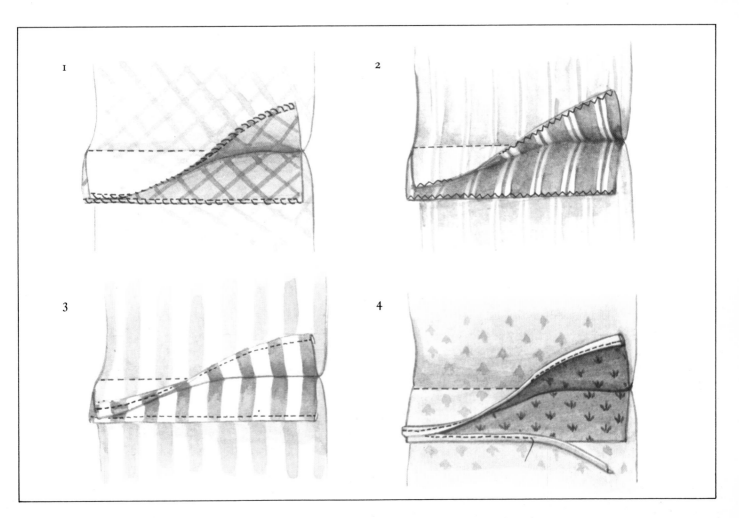

Figure 1, 2, 3, 4 illustrations

Seams can be finished using one of these methods: 1. overcasting, 2. zigzag stitch, 3. edge turned under, 4. edge bound.

the edge of the fabric and stitch close to the edge (fig. 4 above).

Useful seams and processes

Channel seam A decorative seam to use on dresses and blouses. Turn under 1·5 cm ($\frac{5}{8}$ in) on both seamlines. Baste. Place both folds with edges touching, on a separate strip of the same fabric the same length as the seam and cut on the same grain. Baste and stitch the distance of the presser foot from the fold line on either side. Remove the basting, and turn to the wrong side. Finish the inside edges (fig. 1 below).

Double topstitched seam This is an ordinary open seam with the seam allowances topstitched down. It is flat and decorative and can be used on dresses, skirts, jackets and coats. Placing right sides together and match-ing notches, baste and stitch on the seamline. Press open on the wrong side. If the fabric frays, finish the seams before topstitching. Working on the right side, machine stitch the required distance along each side of the seam (fig. 2 below).

Flat fell seam This seam can be worked on the inside or outside of a garment on thick or thin fabrics.

1. Channel seam.
2. Double topstitched seam.

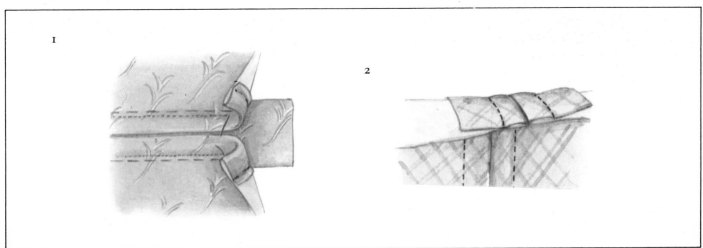

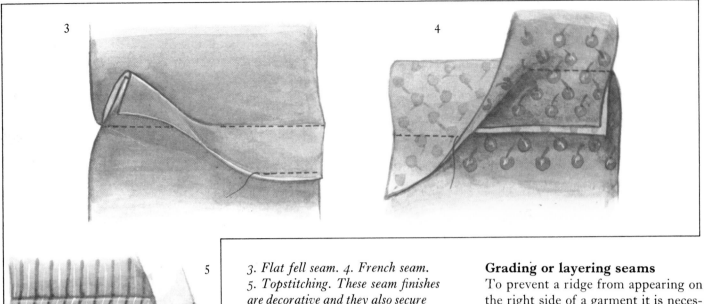

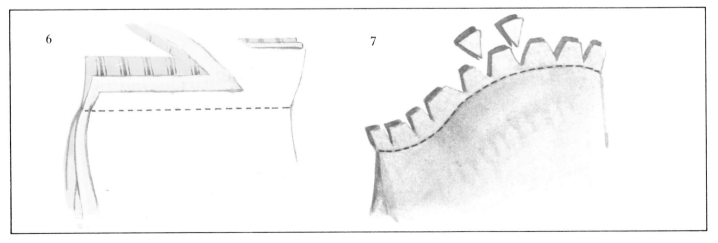

Stitch a plain seam and press it toward one side. Trim the lower seam allowance to 6 mm ($\frac{1}{4}$ in). Turn under the edge of the other seam allowance 6 mm ($\frac{1}{4}$ in) and place it over the trimmed seam allowance. Stitch close to the folded edge (fig. 3).

French seam This is used on sheer fabrics, baby clothes and underwear. It looks like a plain seam on the right side but the raw edges inside are neatly enclosed.
Placing wrong sides together and matching notches baste on the seam-line 1·5 cm ($\frac{5}{8}$ in) in. Stitch at 6 mm

3. Flat fell seam. 4. French seam.
5. Topstitching. These seam finishes
are decorative and they also secure
seam allowances.

($\frac{1}{4}$ in) outside the actual seamline. Remove the basting and trim the seam to just under 6 mm ($\frac{1}{4}$ in). Press the seam allowances together to one side. Turn so that the right sides are together. Baste and stitch on the seam-line, enclosing the raw edges (fig. 4). Press all French seams toward the back of the garment.

Topstitching This is used to emphasize design details or to keep seam edges flat (fig. 5). Stitch a plain seam, then press it to one side. Add another row of stitching, called topstitching, on the right side of the fabric, keeping a constant distance from the seam (the presser foot is a useful guide). Use buttonhole twist in the machine. When you reach a corner, stop before the edge, lowering needle into the fabric. Raise the presser foot and turn the fabric at a right angle so the stitching line continues the same distance away from the edge.

Grading or layering seams
To prevent a ridge from appearing on the right side of a garment it is necessary, especially where an interfacing has been used, to trim the seam allowances to different widths. These are usually: interfacing 2 mm ($\frac{1}{16}$ in); next layer 3 mm ($\frac{1}{8}$ in); next layer 6 mm ($\frac{1}{4}$ in) (fig. 6).

Slash, cut, clip or notch
It is necessary on an inward curved seam, such as a neckline, armhole or shaped stitching line, to cut (slash or clip) almost to the machine line to enable the seam allowances to spread out and press flat (fig. 1). On an outward curve, such as on a round pillow, it is necessary to cut V-shaped notches to reduce the bulk of the seam allowance (fig. 7).

Understitching
This is a line of machine stitching used to prevent neck facings from rolling outward. It is done after the facing is

So that seams lie correctly, either:
6. Layer or grade seams, 7. slash,
clip or notch curves.

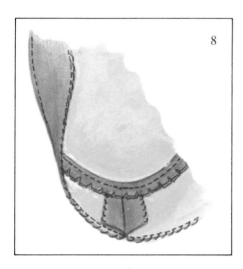

8. *Facings should be understitched.*

stitched in place and the seam allowances have been graded. Turn facing and seam allowances away from the garment. Stitch on the right side, through facings and seam allowances, close to the seamline (fig. 8).

The art of pressing

Pressing is a very important part of dressmaking. It improves the appearance of the garment and also helps you to work neatly and accurately. It is essential to press each seam after it has been stitched. It is easier to press on an ironing board, but a table well-padded with a blanket and covered with a cloth is quite adequate for flat seams. A thickly padded glove is useful for pressing small areas.

Basic pressing rules

A. Always check that the base of the iron is clean. If not, clean with a specially-made cleaning agent. Always polish the base after cleaning by rubbing with a clean soft cloth. Check that vents or holes are not blocked.

B. If using a steam iron it is essential to use distilled water, unless you are in a soft-water area, as tap water leaves a deposit in the iron. Distilled water can be bought from a drugstore.

Do not over-fill the iron as the water can splash and mark the fabric.

C. Always test on a piece of fabric from which you are making the garment. Test fabric's reaction to temperature, steam and moisture.

D. When using a damp cloth, use a piece of linen if possible. The highest setting on the iron is for linen and this therefore prevents scorching.

E. Set the iron to the correct setting.

F. Remove all basting or pins in the seams before pressing.

G. Press on the wrong side of the garment.

H. Pressing is not ironing. In pressing the iron is placed gently down onto the garment, lifted and placed down again. The iron is not moved backward and forward as in ironing. Press with the grain of the fabric, being careful not to stretch edges or curves by pulling fabric. Delicate fabrics which do not require steam pressing should be pressed with a piece of cheesecloth between iron and fabric.

I. Do not over-press by holding the iron on one part of the garment too long. This can leave an imprint of the iron permanently showing on the right side.

J. Do not press plastic coated fabric with an iron. If open seams are required, they must be glued down.

Pressing for a perfect finish

Seams Press either open or toward the center back or center front if edges are to be finished together. Always press a seam before it is finished; this prevents ridges forming on the right side of the garment.

Darts Darts are always pressed toward the center of the body: front toward the center front; back toward the center back; side bust darts toward the waist; and sleeve elbow darts down. On thick fabric the dart may have to be cut and pressed open. Be careful not to stretch this type of dart and do not cut right to the point.

Facings Have the garment flat on the ironing board or table and, where the facings have been attached, press lightly on the very edge. Remove the basting stitches and press again to remove any stitch marks. It is advisable to insert a cloth or piece of paper between the facing and the garment when pressing the edge (fig. 1). This prevents ridges on the right side. This is sometimes also advisable for seams and hems.

Pleats When pressing pleats, it is essential to have the edge of the pleat fold on the wrong side parallel with the edge of the ironing board. Press on the folds, remove basting stitches and press again to remove stitch marks (fig. 2). After pressing in pleats with a damp cloth, hang up the garment right away to let the pleats dry completely before doing any more work on the garment.

Pressing a shoulder seam Using a pressing glove, turn your hand upward and place it under the shoulder join, with the glove extended about 1·3 cm (½ in) beyond the join into the sleeve (fig. 3). Place the tip of the iron gently onto the seamline with the seam allowances toward the sleeve and at the same time slightly lift the tips of the fingers in the mitt. This will round the top of the sleeve in the armhole and

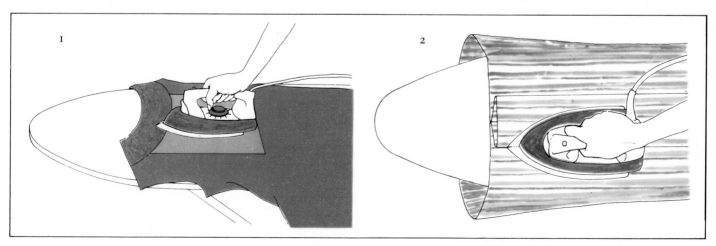

help to remove any wrinkles. Continue in this way until the top of the sleeve has become smooth and molded. Do not over-press by holding the hot iron and damp cloth on one spot for too long. You can also use a tailor's ham for this purpose.

Pressing a hem Place the garment on the ironing board and gently press. Lift the iron and press again. The nose of the iron should be pointed toward the waistline of the garment (fig. 4). Do not move the iron backward and forward, or from side to side as this will stretch the fabric. Also avoid pressing along seam edge of hem.

Shrinking When there is excess fullness on a garment, such as at the hemline on a flared skirt, or on a tight fitting sleeve without elbow darts, a natural fabric can be shrunk to prevent pleats or creases on the right side. Add a gathering thread on the stitching line, pull up to the required length and press with a damp cloth a little at a time. After each press, gently pat the fabric; this helps to flatten any bulges. Continue in this way until all the fullness has been eliminated. Remove the gathering thread.

Collars With under-collar facing upward press on the very edge. Remove basting stitches and press again (fig. 5).

Pressing gathers Gathers should never be pressed flat. Place the garment on the ironing board and, with wrong side of fabric upward, press from the lowest edge, on the straight grain, up toward the gathers. Nose the tip of the iron into the gathers, then move the garment around the board and press the next section in the same way (fig. 6). On finishing, hang up the garment immediately.

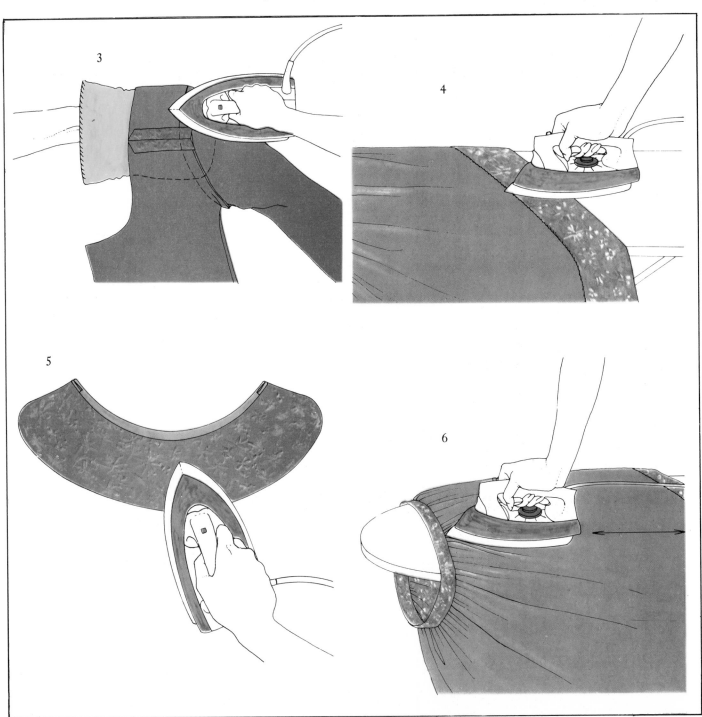

Dressmaking

Sundress

More basic know-how

Included in this section are hems, facings, gathering and all kinds of fastenings. Some of the information is given in more detail than is needed for the first dressmaking projects in this book, but is grouped together for convenient reference later.

Buttons and buttonholes

Hand-worked buttonholes Buttonholes in soft or delicate fabrics should always be made by hand. Button and buttonhole positions are usually marked on the pattern and these markings should be transferred to your fabric before the pattern is removed. If you have had to alter the pattern by lengthening or shortening, alter the buttonhole positions accordingly. Do not cut the buttonholes themselves until you are ready to sew them.

The buttonhole stitch that is used is often confused with blanket stitch, but the thread is placed at the back of the needle for buttonhole stitch (fig. 1). This forms a knot on the very edge of the buttonhole which gives strength and longer wear. Horizontal buttonholes have one rounded end and one square end. Vertical buttonholes (used where there is less "pull") have two rounded ends.

Always make a test buttonhole on a piece of double fabric first.

To establish the buttonhole size, measure the length of the button by placing it on the fabric. Place a pin at either side. The thickness of the button must also be considered, as a thick button needs a larger sized buttonhole. An extra 6 mm ($\frac{1}{4}$ in) is sometimes allowed to take this into account.

Work a row of stitching around the edge of the cut and overcast before buttonholing to prevent fraying (fig. 2). For closely woven fabrics use ordinary sewing thread; for heavier or fraying fabrics use buttonhole twist. When stitching buttonholes the general rule is that nine stitches are worked at the rounded end and nine stitches at the square end (fig. 3a, b). Have about 68 cm (27 in) of thread in the needle so that it will be sufficient to complete the whole buttonhole.

Machine-made buttonholes These can be made with a machine that can produce a close zigzag stitch or has an automatic buttonhole-making device (full instructions will be found in the instruction manual that accompanies your machine).

Buttons These should be selected with care, as they can add an individual look to a very simple garment. The size and the thickness of the buttons must be suitable for the garment. For example, heavy rough-faced ones should not be attached to a fine fabric as they will tear the threads. When purchasing buttons it is advisable to ask whether or not it is safe to use an iron near them, as they may have a synthetic content like nylon. Most large stores have various types and sizes of button molds, to which you can attach your own fabrics. Some stores have a button covering service. It is advisable to buy one or two extra buttons in case of loss or breakage. When sewing on the buttons, use a suitable thread for the fabric and work at least four stitches through the same place on the fabric. If using a button without a shank, insert a pin or matchstick between the button and the fabric and work the stitches over it. Then wind the thread several times around the stitches between the button and fabric. Take the thread to the wrong side and fasten off with three very small backstitches.

Some other fastenings

Metal snap fasteners Usually silver or black, in various sizes, these are used at the top of an opening. The snaps are in two parts, convex and concave. The convex part is always attached to the top part of the opening on the wrong side, as near to the edge as possible and invisible from the right side (fig. 1). The snap is sewn on with about four stitches to each hole, and the thread taken just beneath the

1. The thread is kept behind the needle to work buttonhole stitch, 2. Overcast the cut to stop fraying, 3a-3b. Make nine stitches at each end of buttonhole.

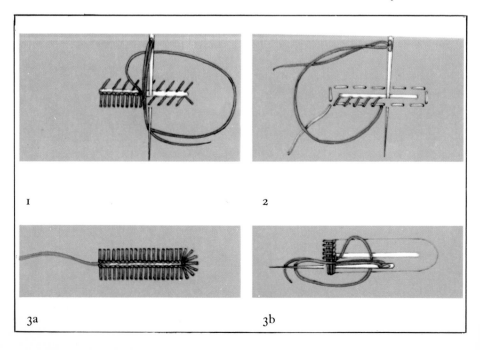

1

2

3a

3b

fabric into the next hole. The stitches must not show on the right side. Fasten off with three backstitches. The convex part is attached first, then the concave part of the snap placed in the correct position by either of two methods: (a) by pushing a pin through both parts of the snap to obtain the correct position on the other edge of the garment, then marking, (b) by pressing the two parts of the snap together and rubbing the concave half with tailor's chalk and pressing onto the garment in the correct position. Sew on in the same way as for convex part, this time letting the stitches go through the fabric; fasten off on the wrong side with three backstitches.

Nylon snap fasteners These are in one size only and are used for baby clothes or fine fabrics. They are attached in the same way as the metal variety.

Hooks and eyes These are in silver and black. They are usually sewn a short distance from the opening itself and are mostly used for extra strength on waistbands. They are sewn on with the hook pointing toward the opening with the flat side to the fabric. After sewing through the holes, slip the needle just beneath the fabric and work three backstitches under the tip of the hook (fig. 2).
The eye should also be facing the opening. After sewing through the holes, work three backstitches just above the hole on each side to help keep the eye flat.

Straight eyes Used with hooks, these are attached very near the edge of the fabric. Sometimes the eye can be replaced by a buttonhole-stitched loop made in a thread which matches the fabric, so it is almost invisible (fig. 3).

Touch and close fastener This is made of two layers of fabric tape, and comes in several different widths and is usually in black or white. One layer is faced with a strip of small nylon loops and the other with a strip of soft piled nylon. The looped side is

1. Position for snap fasteners.
2. Stitching hooks and eyes.
3. Hooks, straight eyes and thread loops. 4. Touch and close fastening.

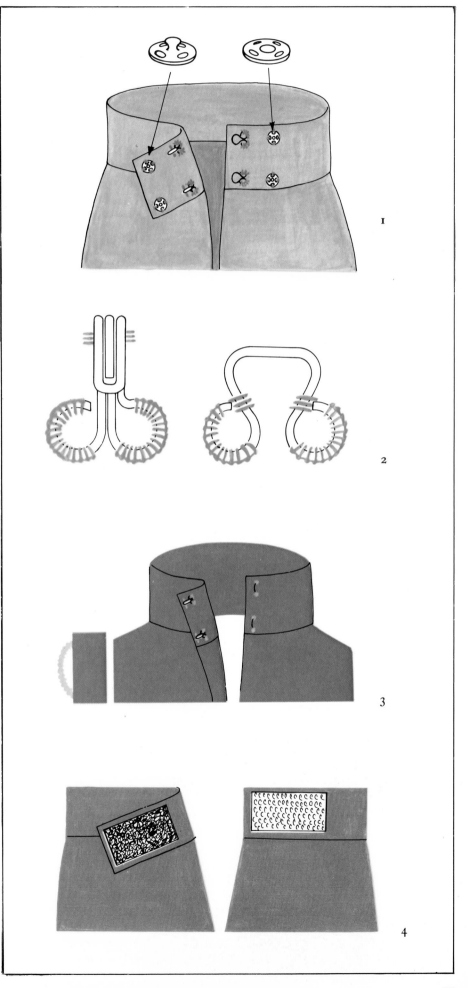

1

2

3

4

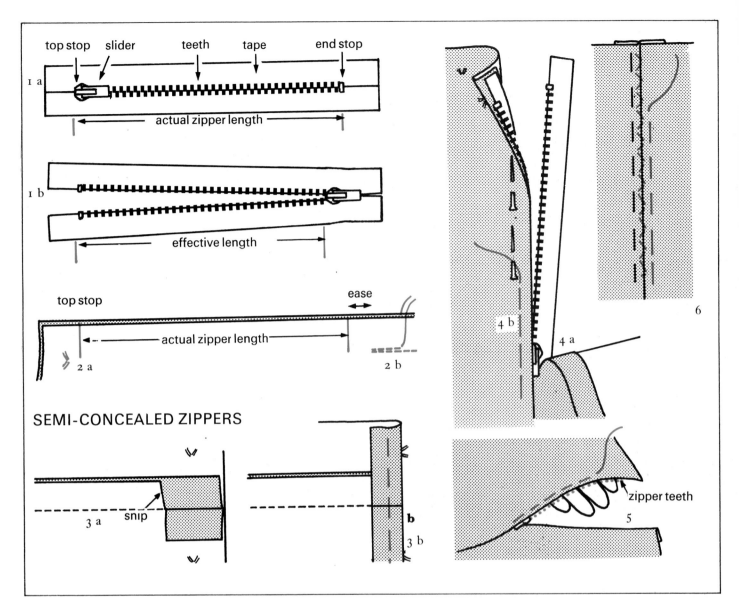

1a, 1b, *The parts of a zipper.*
2a. *Determining zipper length.*
3 to 9. *Putting in centered seam zip.*

always placed on the underwrap with the hooks facing outward. The piled side is placed on the overlap with the pile facing inward (fig. 4). Cut off about 5 cm (2 in) from strip, separate the layers and machine stitch in place around the edges of each half.

Zippers

*Technique included: working half-backstitch.

A zipper consists of two rows of interlocking teeth secured to two strips of tape, which are sewn to the garment fabric. The two strips of tape are secured with an end stop and the teeth are opened or closed by the slider. The slider and end stop take up about 1·3 cm (½ in) of the effective zipper length (fig. 1a and 1b).

There are zippers designed to suit every dressmaking and tailoring need. They are available with metal and with nylon teeth. Nylon zippers are less conspicuous, but are not so strong as metal zippers, which are usually preferable for outdoor wear.

Fabric and suitable zipper type
Sheers, silks, poplin, fine crêpe: featherweight metal or nylon teeth with cotton tape.
Medium-weight wools, linen: light-weight metal or nylon teeth with cotton tape.
Heavier tweeds; where strength is required: skirt-weight metal teeth.
Man-made fibers, fine to medium-weight: nylon teeth with nylon tape.
Parkas or jackets – any fabric: open ended with metal or nylon teeth.
All fabrics (except loosely woven tweeds): "invisible" with metal teeth or nylon teeth.

Length of zipper required Before purchasing the zipper for a particular garment, consult the pattern for the suggested length and always purchase this length unless the pattern is to be shortened or lengthened. If in doubt, leave the purchase of the zipper until the garment is fitted.

Do not purchase too short a zipper, as this causes strain and the zipper might break, which will necessitate a complete replacement with a new zipper.

The opening left in a garment for inserting a zipper should always be a little longer than the actual zipper teeth to allow the fabric to be eased to the tape. Allow 1 mm ($\frac{1}{16}$ in) extra opening per 2·5 cm (1 in) of zip. For zippers longer then 40 cm (16 in) allow a total of 2·5 cm (1 in) extra.

Also, the zipper teeth should never go right up to the neck finish or waistband, so allow an extra 6 mm (¼ in) here (fig. 2a).

Zipper seams When sewing a zipper seam, finish the end off very securely. This prevents strain on the zipper (fig. 2b).

Snip through the waist seam allowance if any, 3·2 cm (1¼ in), from the edge of the opening and press open (fig. 3a). Baste and press the zipper opening back on the seamline (fig. 3b).

Methods of sewing zippers
Note When setting in a zipper always work on the right side of the garment so that the sewing lines can be kept straight.

Centered seam zipper This method is used on dresses with collars, either at the front or the back, medium to heavy-weight tweed skirts, trousers and open ended zippers.
Baste and press zipper opening back

on the seamline. Open the zipper and place it behind the folded edges of the opening with the end stop to the end of the machine stitching (fig. 4a).
Pin and baste one side of the zipper in place, with the teeth just behind the fold and basting 6 mm (¼ in) from the fold (fig. 4b). The extra length allowed for the opening is eased along the zipper length by holding the zipper and fabric as shown (fig. 5).
Bring up the other side of the zipper and catch the two fold edges together (fig. 6), so that the two sides be matched in length and pattern.
Baste the second side 6 mm (¼ in) away from the fold.
For a couture finish, sew in the zipper by hand using a tiny half-backstitch (fig. 16 p. 24). Work each side from the bottom up, angling the bottom end to the seamline (fig. 7). If you wish to

machine stitch the zipper in place, use a zipper foot to allow the stitching to be closer to the zipper.
Stitch to within 5 cm (2 in) of the top of the zipper, leave the needle in the work and lift the foot (fig. 8a).
Unpick 8 cm (3 in) of the catch stitches and ease the slider down past the foot (fig. 8b). Complete the stitching. This method prevents the stitching line from widening at the slider. Finally, finish the back by stitching the zipper to the seam allowance (fig. 9).

Decorative zippers These are mostly used in jumpers and pockets. Baste the zipper in place as shown for the centered zipper. Sew the facings

10. A center front decorative zipper.
11. Open ended zipper on jacket.

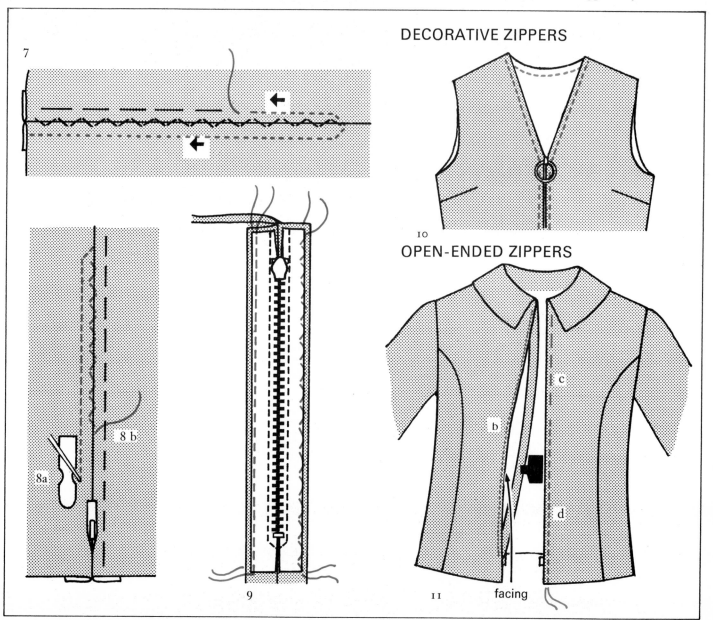

DECORATIVE ZIPPERS

OPEN-ENDED ZIPPERS

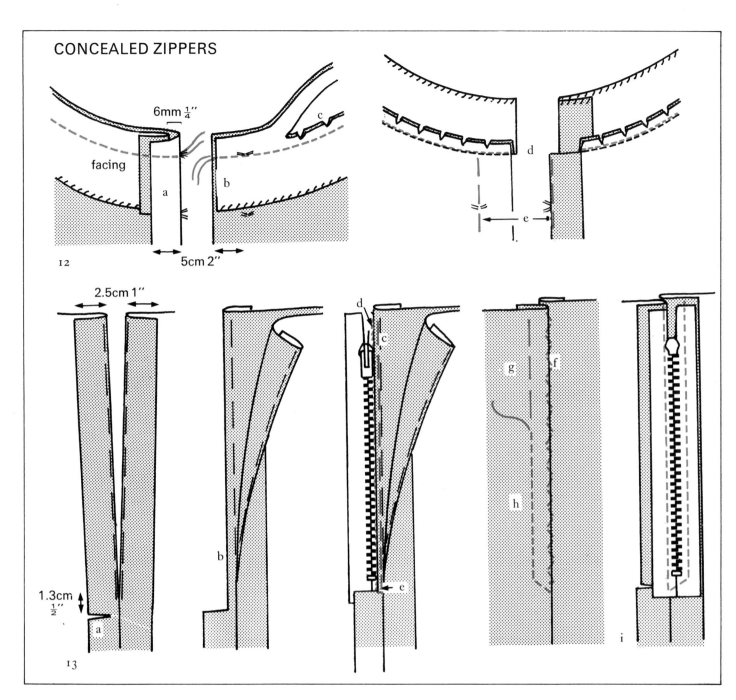

CONCEALED ZIPPERS

6mm ¼″

facing

a

5cm 2″

12

2.5cm 1″

b

1.3cm ½″

a

13

12, 13. Inserting a concealed zipper.

in place and complete the hem.

For a jumper, topstitch around the neck and down to the hem, 6 mm (¼ in) away from all edges (fig. 10).

For pockets, topstitch evenly all around the zipper before applying the pocket to the garment.

Open ended zippers Assemble the garment, leaving the zipper opening between the facings and the fronts. Press the seam allowances back (fig. 11a). Separate the zipper and slip the two sections in the openings, and place so that the teeth are just hidden behind the fold between garment and facing (fig. 11b). Pin and baste through

the front, the zipper tape and the facing (fig. 11c). Topstitch; use strong thread or buttonhole twist threaded on top of the machine (fig. 11d).

Concealed zippers Use for dresses without collars, lightweight skirts.

Note The zipper seam should be cut with a 2·5 cm (1 in) allowance.

Preparation of dress facing Place the right side of the neck facing on the right side of the dress, matching shoulder seams and center front. On the left hand side, turn back the facing 6 mm (¼ in) from the dress sewing line. Turn the dress seam allowance back to the sewing line (fig. 12a). On the right hand side, take the facing

straight to the edge (fig. 12b).

Machine stitch the facing in place; trim seam to 6 mm (¼ in). Snip at 1·3 cm (½ in) intervals (fig. 12c).

Turn the seam allowance of the left hand side of the dress toward the facing and press flat (fig. 12d).

For all openings using the concealed zipper method, work a line of basting along the sewing lines of the opening (fig. 12e).

For side skirt or pants zipper, read "back" for "right hand side" and "front" for "left hand side."

Snip the right hand side seam allowance to within 3 mm (⅛ in) of the seam, 1·3 cm (½ in) below the end of the opening (fig. 13a).

Fold the seam allowance along this

new line so that it projects beyond the seamline by 3 mm ($\frac{1}{8}$ in) (fig. 13b).

Place the zipper right side uppermost behind this line, with the end stop just above the end of the opening. Pin and baste in place, with the fold just missing the zipper teeth (fig. 13c). Hem firmly right down to the end of the 3 mm ($\frac{1}{8}$ in) extension (fig. 13d). Snip the remaining 3 mm ($\frac{1}{8}$ in) seam allowance (fig. 13e).

Bring the left hand side over so that the fold lies along the original sewing line on the right hand side. Temporarily baste in place (fig. 13f). Baste 1·3 cm ($\frac{1}{2}$ in) away from the fold on the left hand side (fig. 13g).

Using a half-backstitch (see fig. 16), sew up from the seamline at an angle and up the 1·3 cm ($\frac{1}{2}$ in) line, or machine stitch, making sure to stitch a straight line (fig. 13h).

Fig. 13i illustrates the wrong side of the garment and zipper, showing how it should lie in position. Slip-stitch ends of facing in place.

Zipper guards These are used to protect underwear and sensitive skins from being rubbed by the zipper teeth, and they give a very professional finish to the garment.

Measure the zipper opening and add 3·8 cm (1$\frac{1}{2}$ in). Cut one piece of lining and one piece of fabric as shown (fig. 14a). Place right sides together and stitch the curved side (fig. 14b). Turn right side out and baste around the stitched edge. Press flat (fig. 14c). Place the long raw edge on the right hand side zipper tape, making sure that the fabric side of the guard is toward the zipper (fig. 14d). Stitch through the guard, zipper tape and seam allowance (fig. 14e). If the garment is unlined, finish the raw edge (fig. 14f).

Include the top of the guard into an extended zipper guard or neck facing.

Invisible zippers These give an opening which looks like a seam, and

14-16. Zipper finishes: half-backstitch.

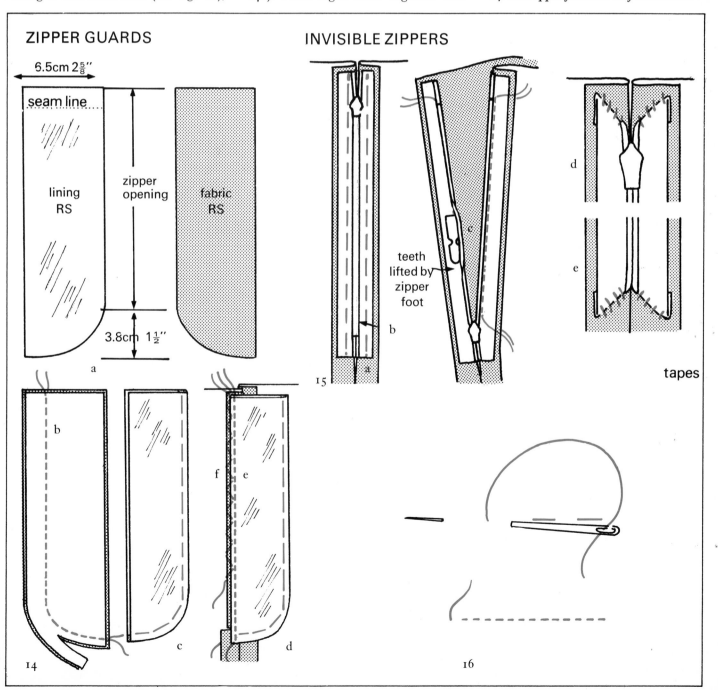

ZIPPER GUARDS

6.5cm 2$\frac{5}{8}$″

seam line

lining RS

zipper opening

fabric RS

3.8cm 1$\frac{1}{2}$″

a

b

c

d

14

INVISIBLE ZIPPERS

teeth lifted by zipper foot

a

b

15

d

e

tapes

16

are good for all fabrics except loose, bulky tweeds on which the fibers might be caught by the slider.

After fitting the garment, sew the zipper seam, leaving an opening 2·5 cm (1 in) longer than the zipper teeth. Baste opening and press.

On the wrong side center the closed zipper over the seam with the zipper teeth uppermost (fig. 15a p. 29).

Pin and baste through the zipper tape and seam allowance only (fig. 15b).

Remove the seam basting and open the zipper carefully. Keeping the teeth uppermost, stitch through the tape and seam allowance only, stopping when the zipper foot meets the slider. Stitch the other side of the zipper (fig. 15c).

Close zipper. Lift zipper and seam allowance up and complete the seam, still using the zipper foot.

Secure the zipper tapes to the top by folding the ends outward and sew to the seam allowances (fig. 15d).

The tapes at the bottom edge are also sewn to the seam allowances (fig. 15e).

*Half-backstitch Bring the thread up after fastening firmly on the wrong side. Take a tiny 1·5 mm ($\frac{1}{16}$ in) stitch back and come up 4·5 mm ($\frac{3}{16}$ in) forward (fig. 16).

Facings and interfacings

Facings are used to finish a raw edge neatly. They can be cut to the same shape as the edge of a garment, stitched around the edge and then turned to the inside – e.g. to finish a neck or armhole. A facing can also be

1. Cutting new facing.

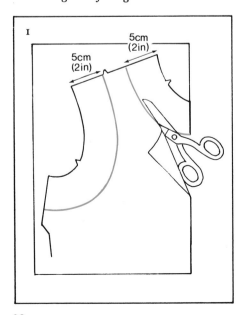

a turned-back extension of the garment – e.g. down a front or back opening. On a part of a garment consisting of two layers – e.g. a wide shoulder strap or belt, the under layer can also be referred to as a facing.

To cut a facing (if this is not already part of the pattern). Take the front bodice pattern piece and place on a large sheet of paper. Draw around the outline of shoulder and area to be faced – e.g. neck and/or armhole. Working from the outside edge, measure 5 cm (2 in) and draw a curve parallel to neck or armhole curve. Cut off facing pattern along drawn line. Repeat for back of bodice pattern.

Interfacing is used to add firmness to areas of a garment like collars, waistbands, cuffs or facings. Either a woven or non-woven interfacing fabric can be used.

The interfacing is cut to the same shape as the facing and either trimmed and catch-stitched to the facing seamline before it is attached or basted to the facing and joined to the garment as it is sewn.

Hems

*Technique included: invisible hemming (or blind stitch).

Beautifully finished hems are most important, as they add a professional finish to a carefully made garment. The length is dictated by fashion to a certain extent, but it must be right both for the garment and for the particular figure.

To gauge the effect of the garment always wear the appropriate shoes for the outfit and add a belt if the design has one. Check the length of the garment by standing in front of a mirror, and always wear the jacket when looking at a suit to see that the proportion of jacket to skirt is correct.

Hem length There are various ways to obtain the right hem length:

From the back neck, measure the length of the pattern and adjust if necessary (fig. 1a).

After cutting out, make tailor's tacks along the hemline and pin the hem up to the line when fitting (fig. 1b).

Place a dress of the right length on a hanger with the new dress over it. Pin up the new hem to match (fig. 2).

Ask a friend to measure up from the ground and mark the line with pins (fig. 3).

Use a skirt marker. If the marker is the kind requiring chalk marks, measure 1·3 cm ($\frac{1}{2}$ in) longer than needed to avoid the possibility of the chalk marking the fabric permanently. Turn up 1·3 cm ($\frac{1}{2}$ in) above the chalk line (fig. 4).

Preparation before finishing Run a line of basting along the hem fold (fig. 5).

Most hems are 5 to 6·5 cm (2 to 2$\frac{1}{2}$ in) deep, so trim evenly to the required depth (fig. 6). Exceptions are for blouses, 2·5 cm (1 in); faced hems, 1·3 cm ($\frac{1}{2}$ in); long skirts of fine fabric, 1·3 cm ($\frac{1}{2}$ in).

Trim all seam allowances to 6 mm ($\frac{1}{4}$ in) between the hemline and the hem edge (fig. 7).

Hem finishes For non-fraying fabrics overcast or zigzag along the cut edge.

For fraying fabrics use one of the following methods:

Zigzag 6 mm ($\frac{1}{4}$ in) away from the cut edge and trim to the machine stitching (fig. 8a).

For straight headlines, edge with straight binding (fig. 8b).

For curved or bias edges, ease the hem and edge with bias binding (fig. 8c).

For fine cottons (mainly children's clothes and summer dresses), fold under the raw edge for 1·3 cm ($\frac{1}{2}$ in). For pleats which are seamed, the seam allowances are snipped the hem depth above the hemline and pressed open below the snip. Above the snip, the seam allowances are finished and pressed together (fig. 9).

After finishing the raw edge, press it, making sure it is away from the body of the garment.

Fold the hem up on the basted line, slip a piece of stiff paper inside the fold and press well. Use a damp cloth rather than a steam iron as it is easier to control the amount of steam this way. Baste through the folded edge to keep it firmly in place.

Types of hem

Plain This is used for absolutely straight hems, i.e. skirts and pants. Baste the hem 1·3 cm ($\frac{1}{2}$ in) below the

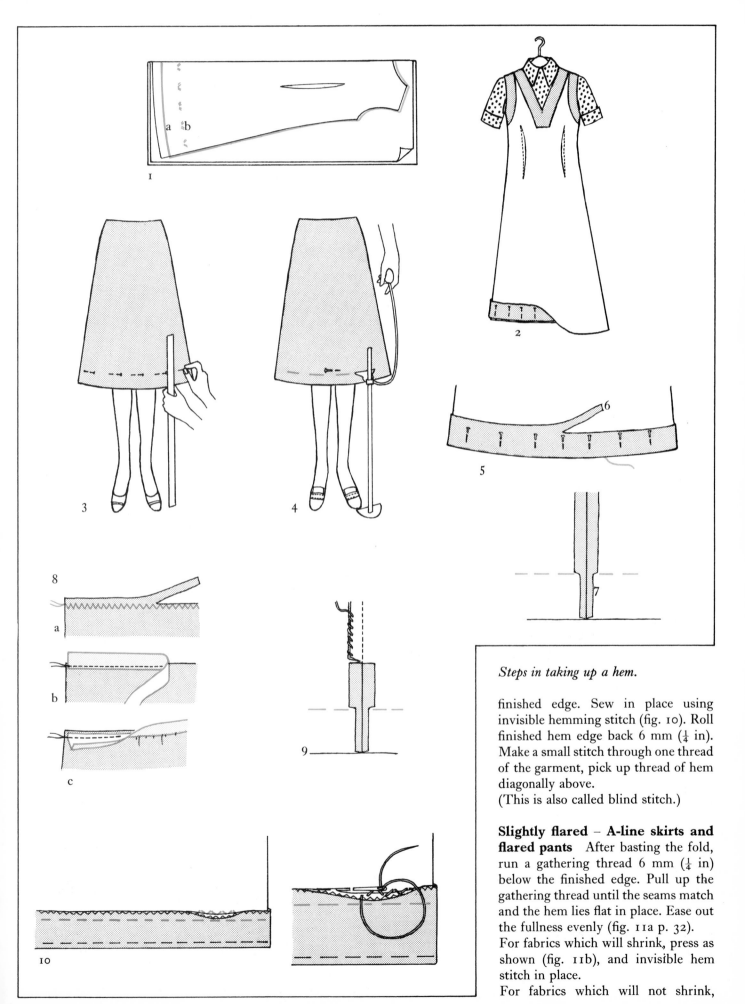

Steps in taking up a hem.

finished edge. Sew in place using invisible hemming stitch (fig. 10). Roll finished hem edge back 6 mm ($\frac{1}{4}$ in). Make a small stitch through one thread of the garment, pick up thread of hem diagonally above.

(This is also called blind stitch.)

Slightly flared – A-line skirts and flared pants After basting the fold, run a gathering thread 6 mm ($\frac{1}{4}$ in) below the finished edge. Pull up the gathering thread until the seams match and the hem lies flat in place. Ease out the fullness evenly (fig. 11a p. 32).

For fabrics which will shrink, press as shown (fig. 11b), and invisible hem stitch in place.

For fabrics which will not shrink,

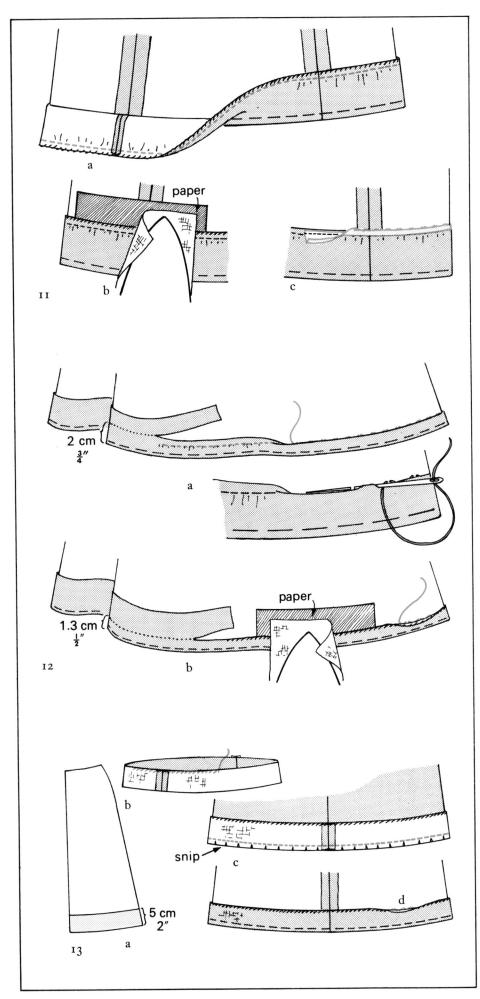

attach bias binding, stretching it slightly. Fold the binding over the raw edge and slip-stitch in place (fig. 11c).

Very flared skirts It is not easy to make a deep hem for these, so they are usually finished either with a narrow or a faced hem.

Narrow hem for lightweight fabrics Cut the hem depth to 2 cm (¾ in). Do not finish the edge. Run a gathering thread 6 mm (¼ in) from the cut edge. Turn under 6 mm (¼ in) and pull the gathering thread so it lies easily against the skirt. Slip-stitch the hem through the fold (fig. 12a).

Narrow hem for heavier fabrics Cut the hem depth to 1·3 cm (½ in) and finish the edge with overcasting or zigzag stitch. Press the hem up over the paper and stitch with invisible hemming stitch (fig. 12b).

Faced hem for all fabrics If extra bulk is not desirable, then lining or net can be used for the facing fabric. Cut a 5 cm (2 in) facing from the skirt pattern (fig. 13a).
Sew the facing seams together and finish the shorter edge (fig. 13b).
Place the facing on the right side of the skirt hem and stitch (fig. 13c).
Snip if necessary, turn to inside and press. Sew the facing to the skirt with invisible hemming stitch (fig. 13d).

Rolled hem for sheer fabrics Trim the hem to 6 mm (¼ in). Turn under 3 mm (⅛ in) (fig. 14a) and either slip-stitch hem (fig. 14b) or machine stitch (fig. 14c).

Tailored hem for jackets, coats and sleeves A strip of canvas is used to support the weight of a coat or jacket hem and to give a good line.

Cut 5 cm (2 in) strips of canvas on the true bias of the fabric (fig. 15a). Lay the canvas above the hemline and catch stitch to the garment (fig. 15b). Turn up the hem and sew it to the canvas with invisible hemming stitch (fig. 15c).

Lining hem finish for jackets and

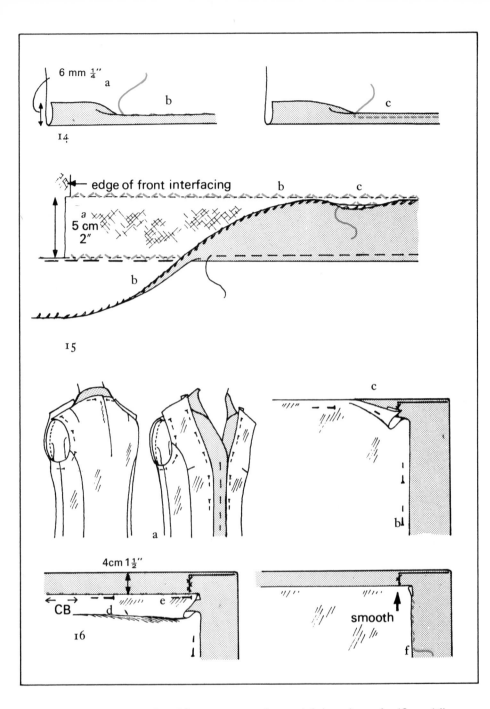

14

edge of front interfacing

5 cm
2"

15

4cm 1½"

CB

16

---

14. Rolled hem. 15. Tailored hem.
16. Lining hem finish.

coats Finish the coat or jacket and press it well. Make the lining and press this too. (A lining pattern has extra width included in the center back and also in the length. This is to allow for ease in wear and to prevent the lining pulling the outer fabric.)
Pin the lining to the jacket, matching seamlines, armholes and style lines (fig. 16a).
Fold under and pin the front edges (fig. 16b).
Fold and pin the hem allowance to the exact length of the jacket or coat (fig. 16c).
Lift up the folded edge 2·5 to 4 cm

(1 to 1½ in) and re-pin (fig. 16d).
Slip-stitch the hem along the fold (fig. 16e).
Fold down the pleat at front edges and finish slip-stitching (fig. 16f).

Gathering and shirring
Gathering This produces soft folds in light fabrics. Gathering enables a larger piece to join onto a smaller one, e.g. a gathered skirt joined to a plain top. Gathers also add fullness on shoulders and sleeves, and are used to make ruffles.

Shirring This is a form of elasticized gathering, usually done by machine in which several rows of equally spaced stitches produce a decorative effect.

Gathering by hand Use single thread on lightweight fabrics and double thread on heavy-weight fabrics. Start with three backstitches and work small straight running stitches. Do not fasten off at the end of the row but leave the thread hanging. With right sides together, pin center of gathering to center of part of garment to which it is to be attached, and pin together at each end. Pull up gathering thread to fit. Wind thread around a pin in a figure eight. Put in more pins before basting. Pins should be placed vertically to enable basting to be done on the gathering line without pins scratching fingers.

By machine Loosen top tension on machine slightly, and turn stitch length selector to the longest stitch. Working on the right side of the fabric, stitch along the stitching line. Pull up gathering from both ends. Wind thread around pins in figure eights.
Tighten top tension when you have finished gathering.

Ease This is extra fullness in one pattern piece, e.g. on the cap of a sleeve. One section is slightly larger than the other and the surplus is reduced by gathering for a short distance (marked on the pattern) until the two pieces fit exactly.

Joining gathered skirt to bodice Gather skirt with two rows of gathering stitches for extra strength and pull

When gathering, the threads must be pulled evenly and fullness eased.

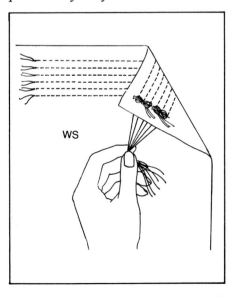

WS

Top right. These two diagrams show how to join a gathered skirt to a bodice.

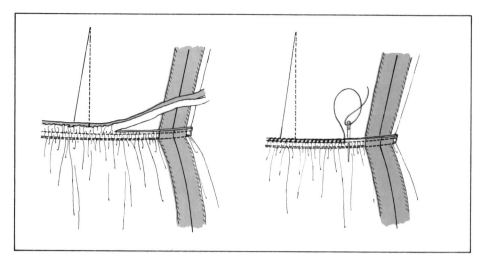

up gathers until skirt fits bodice (use synthetic thread for gathers to prevent thread from breaking). With right sides together, pin the bodice to the skirt, matching center front and back and side seams. Baste and stitch with gathered side upward. Make a second row of stitching 6 mm ($\frac{1}{4}$ in) from the first in the seam allowance. Press the seam upward, being careful not to flatten gathers. Finish·by overcasting seam allowances together.

Girl's sundress

This sundress can also be teamed with T-shirts and blouses to be worn as a jumper on cool days. Stripes used vertically give no matching problems, but the design looks just as good made in a plain fabric. The pattern is cut from a simple diagram.
*Technique included: patch pockets.

Measurements

The pattern and instructions are given to fit a child 6, 8, 10 or 12 years of age. Chest sizes 63·5 cm (25 in), 69 cm (27 in), 72·5 cm (28$\frac{1}{2}$ in) and 76 cm (30 in).

Making the pattern

The measurements given for the pattern pieces are for a size 6. For the larger sizes the measurements given in the chart must be added to the basic size 6 measurements when cutting the pattern.

Suggested fabrics

Cotton, denim, corduroy, lightweight wool.

You will need:

115 cm (45 in) wide fabric with or without nap, all sizes, 1·60 m (1$\frac{3}{4}$ yd). 90 cm (36 in) wide interfacing, all sizes, 30 cm ($\frac{1}{4}$ yd).
Sewing thread to match fabric.
Two 1·3 cm ($\frac{1}{2}$ in) buttons.
15 cm (6 in) zipper.
Hook and eye.
Graph or plain paper for pattern.

Cutting out

A 1·5 cm ($\frac{5}{8}$ in) seam allowance has been allowed on all edges except the dress center front and the front and

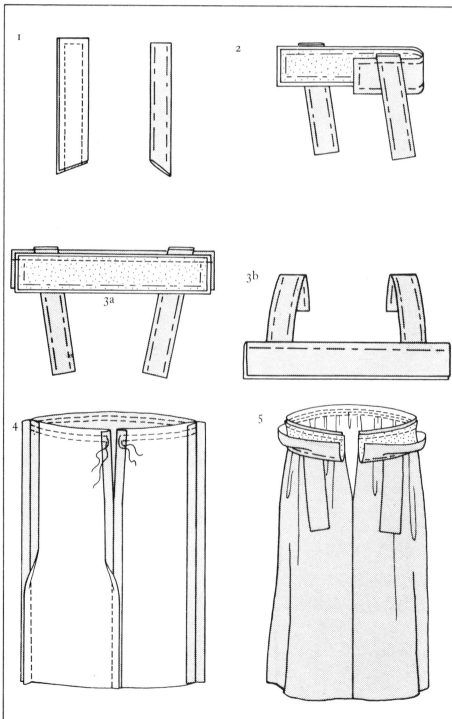

back band center front. 6.5 cm (2⅝ in) hem allowance has been included on the lower hem edges. The positions for the back shoulder straps move toward the center back by the same amount that is graded up for the larger sizes and the side on the front and back band by half this amount.

To make the dress

Shoulder straps 1. With right sides together, baste and stitch the shoulder strap facings to the shoulder straps around the outer edges, leaving the slanted edge open. Trim seams and cut across corners. Turn straps right side out. Baste close to stitched edges and press flat.

Band 2. Baste interfacing to the wrong side of the front and back band. With right sides together, matching raw edges, baste the shoulder straps to either side of the center back in positions marked.

3. With right sides together, baste and stitch the band facing to the band along the top edge, securing the straps when doing so. Trim interfacing close to stitching and grade the seam. Press seam toward band. Turn facing to the inside and baste close to the stitched edge. Press flat.

Center back and side seams 4. With right sides together, baste and stitch the center back of the dress to within 12 cm (4½ in) of the top edge. With right sides together, baste and stitch the side seams. Press seams open. Add two rows of gathering stitches around the top edge of the dress.

Joining the dress to band 5. With right sides together, matching center fronts, sides and center backs, pin the dress to the band, pulling up the gathers to fit. Baste, spreading the gathers evenly. Stitch entire seam, having the band facing free. Trim interfacing close to stitching and grade seam. Press seam toward band. Insert the zipper into the center back opening.

6. On the inside, turn under the seam

This cool and comfortable sundress for a young girl makes use of the more basic sewing skills and is, therefore, a good dress for beginners. For it you make buttonholes, attach a gathered skirt, and make a plain hem. You will also learn how to make patch pockets.

allowance of the band facing and slip-stitch to the stitching line and to the zipper line.

*Patch pockets 7. Baste the inter-facing to the wrong side of the pocket band. Catch stitch to the fold line. Turn under the seam allowance of the other edge and baste. With right sides together, baste and stitch the pocket band to the pocket. Trim interfacing close to the stitching. Press seam toward band.

8. With right sides together, fold band along fold line and stitch the side edges as shown. Trim interfacing close to stitching and cut across corners. Turn band right side out. On the inside, slip-stitch the band facing to the stitching line. Turn in seam allowance around outer edge of pocket and baste. On the outside, topstitch band 6 mm ($\frac{1}{4}$ in) away from seamline.

Repeat steps 7 and 8 for second pocket.

9. Baste the pockets to the dress front in positions marked on the pattern. Topstitch 6 mm ($\frac{1}{4}$ in) in from outer edge of pockets. Press flat.

Hem 10. Try dress on child and mark the hem. Turn up the hem and baste close to the folded edge. Trim hem to an even width. Finish the raw edge with hand overcasting or machine zigzag. Sew the hem to the dress using invisible hemming stitch.

To finish 11. Check length of shoulder straps and make hand-worked or machine stitched buttonholes on the front band in positions marked. Sew buttons to the shoulder straps in positions marked. At the center back, sew a hook and eye to the top edge of the band.

Follow the diagram below when laying the pattern pieces on the fabric.

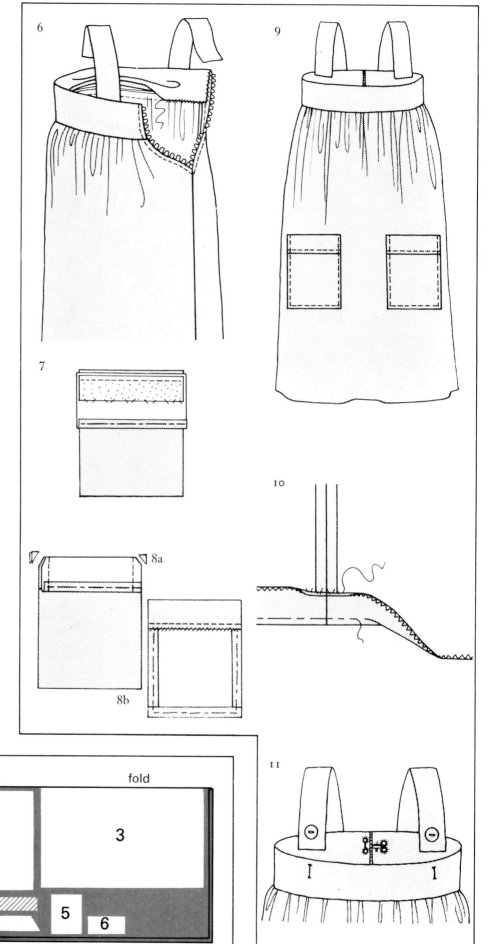

<table>
<tr><td colspan="5">

Additional measurement chart in centimeters
(inches given in brackets)
</td></tr>
</table>

Size		8	10	12
Front and back band (length)		2·5 (1)	4·5 (1¾)	6·5 (2½)
Shoulder straps (length)		1·3 (½)	2·5 (1)	3·8 (1½)
Side seams front				
and back		1·3 (½)	2·5 (1)	3·8 (1½)
Hemline		5 (2)	10 (4)	15 (6)

Measurement chart for dress

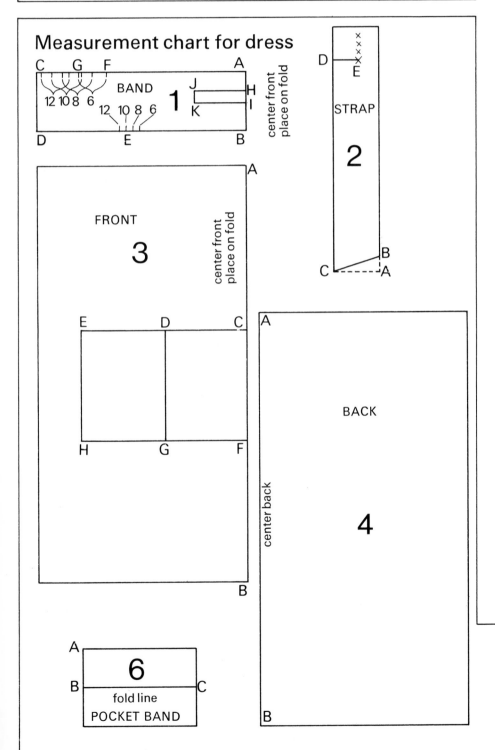

Measurement instructions for drafting the pattern

Front and back band (diagram 1)
Draw a rectangle measuring 35 cm by 8 cm (13¾ in by 3¼ in).
A to B = center front
C to D = center back
B to E = 15·3 cm (6⅛ in) – match to side seams.
A to F = 19 cm (7½ in)
F to G = 4·7 cm (1⅞ in)
F to G = back shoulder strap position
A to H = 3·2 cm (1¼ in)
A to I = 5 cm (2 in)
H to J and I to K = 8 cm (3¼ in)
J to K = buttonhole position

Shoulder straps (diagram 2)
Draw a rectangle measuring 7·5 cm by 36·5 cm (3 in by 14⅜ in)
A to B = 2·2 cm (⅞ in)
C to D = 31 cm (12¼ in)
D to E = 3·8 cm (1½ in)
E = button position

Dress front (diagram 3)
Draw a rectangle measuring 31·8 cm by 63 cm (12½ in by 24¾ in)
A to B = center front
A to C = 26·8 cm (10½ in)
C to D = 11·5 cm (4⅝ in)
D to E = 15 cm (6 in)
A to F = 44·3 cm (17½ in)
F to G = 11·5 cm (4⅝ in)
G to H = 15 cm (6 in)
E to H and G to D = pocket position

Dress back (diagram 4)
Draw a rectangle measuring 33·3 cm by 63 cm (13⅛ in by 24¾ in)
A to B = center back

Pocket (diagram 5)
Draw a rectangle measuring 18·5 cm by 16·3 cm (7¼ in by 6½ in)

Pocket band (diagram 6)
Draw a rectangle measuring 18·5 cm by 12 cm (7¼ in by 4¾ in)
A to B = 6 cm (2⅜ in)
B to C = fold line - this line being horizontal

Mother and Daughter Aprons

More basic know-how
Ruffles

Ruffles can give a pretty finish to many garments and they are not difficult to apply. They can be straight or bias-cut. To produce the fullness needed for a ruffle, cut the fabric two to three times longer than the finished length then gather up to required size. Deep ruffles need more fullness than narrow ones. A long length of ruffle may have to be pieced before it is applied. Any seams should be pressed open before gathering the ruffle. Finish outer edge of ruffle with a narrow seam.

Ruffle on a straight edge With right sides together, pin the gathered ruffle to the edge, leaving 1·3 cm (½ in) of the hem edge extending. Stitch with ruffle side up (fig. 1). Trim the seam allowance on the ruffle to 3 mm (⅛ in). Fold the hem edge under for 3 mm (⅛ in) then fold it over the trimmed seam and stitch in place (fig. 2). Press seam toward garment.

Ruffle in a seam Prepare ruffle and pin and stitch to one seam edge of garment as described for ruffle on a straight edge. With right sides together place section with ruffle attached onto second section. Pin and baste. Make a second line of stitching to enclose ruffle. Turn right sides out and press.

Ruffles on collars and cuffs Prepare narrow ruffle as previously described. With right sides together, pin ruffle to outer edge of top collar or cuff. When corner is reached ease gathers around, pushing them closer together at this point to give extra fullness. Stitch with ruffle side up (fig. 3) leaving finished outer edges free. Press carefully. With right sides together, pin, baste and stitch under collar or cuff onto outer section enclosing ruffle. Trim seam allowances to 6 mm (¼ in). Turn right side out and press carefully.

Ruffle with heading Finish both long edges of ruffle and make line of gathering below the top edge to depth

Matching aprons for mother and daughter have a ruffle-trimmed yoke.

1, 2. Ruffle on a straight edge.
3. Ruffle on collar or cuff. 4. Ruffle with a heading and ruffle in a seam.

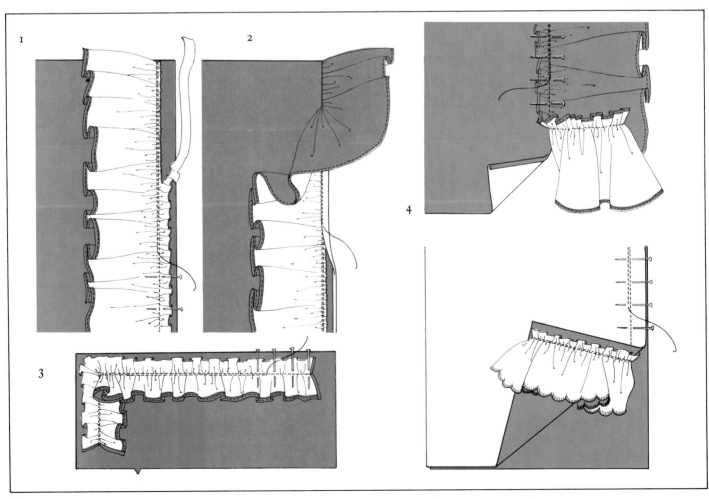

required for heading (fig. 4). Press a 3 mm ($\frac{1}{8}$ in) double fold on edge of garment. Pin ruffle on right side with gathering line close to folded edge. Stitch along this line to attach ruffle to garment. This technique can be used to add a flounce to the hem of a skirt.

Mother and daughter aprons

These frilly aprons are both practical and feminine.
*Techniques included: applying ruffles to yoke, bias binding.

Measurements

The mother's apron is given in sizes 8/10/12/14 and the daughter's apron is given to fit chest sizes 61 cm (24 in), 66 cm (26 in), 71 cm (28 in) and 76 cm (30 in). Each size is indicated on the graph pattern by a cutting line of a different color.

Making the pattern

Draw up the pattern to scale from the graph pattern given here. One square represents 2·5 cm (1 in) square.

Suggested fabrics

Mix and match cottons, eyelet embroidery (broderie anglaise).

You will need:

To make the mother's apron:
90 cm (36 in) wide fabric without nap in main color, 2·75 m (3 yd) all sizes.
90 cm (36 in) wide fabric without nap in contrast color, 1·20 m (1$\frac{1}{4}$ yd), all sizes.
Two 1·5 cm ($\frac{5}{8}$ in) buttons.
T9 make the daughter's apron:
90 cm (36 in) wide fabric without nap in main color, 1·80 m (1$\frac{3}{4}$ yd), all sizes.
90 cm (36 in) wide fabric without nap in contrast color, 1·10 m (1$\frac{1}{8}$ yd), all sizes.
One 1·5 cm ($\frac{5}{8}$ in) button.
For both aprons you will need:
Sewing thread to match fabric.
Graph paper for pattern.

Cutting out

There are no seam allowances included on the pattern. When cutting out, allow at least a 1.5cm ($\frac{5}{8}$in) seam allowance on all garment edges.
Note No pattern pieces are given for the apron ties or the underarm bias strips, so cut the following pieces from the main color fabric as indicated on the cutting layouts.

Mother's apron

For ties cut two pieces measuring 91·5 cm by 8·5 cm (36 in by 3$\frac{1}{4}$ in) and for the armhole bias strips cut two pieces measuring 30·5 cm by 2·5 cm (12 in by 1 in).

Daughter's apron

For ties cut two pieces measuring 66 cm by 6·5 cm (26 in by 2$\frac{1}{2}$ in), and for the armhole bias strips cut two pieces measuring 23 cm by 2·5 cm (9 in by 1 in).
Note All the above measurements for ties and bias strips include seam allowance.

To make both aprons

Ruffles 1. With right sides together, notches matching, join the front ruffle between back ruffle pieces.

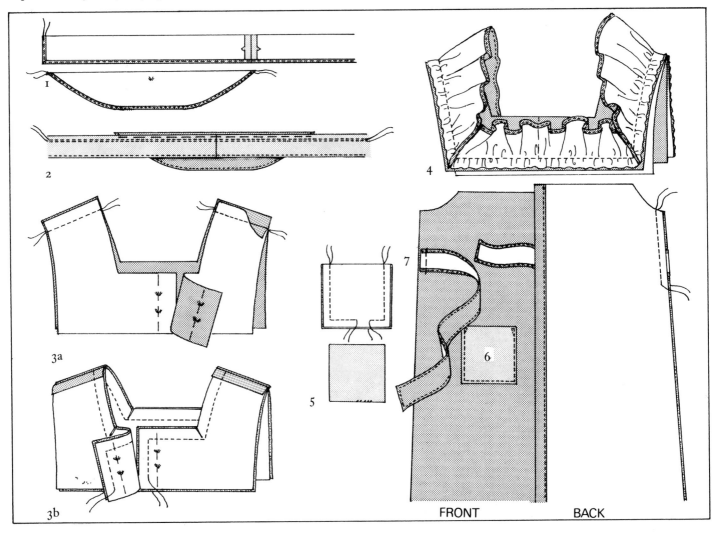

FRONT   BACK

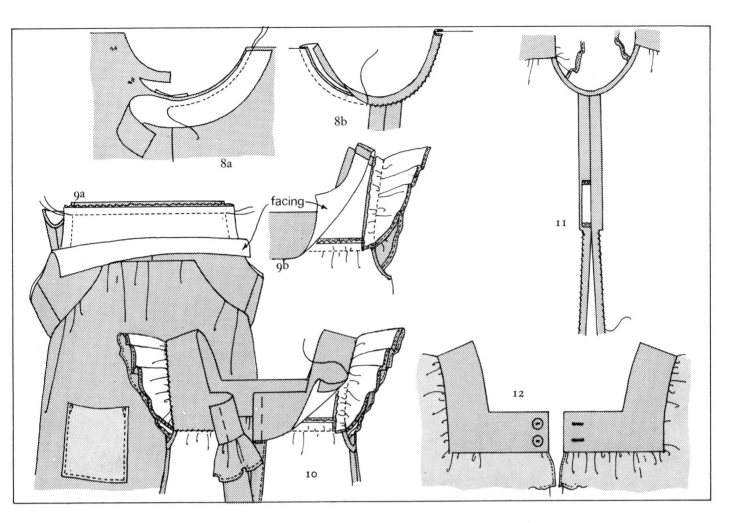

Press the seams open.

To finish the outer ruffle edges turn under 3 mm ($\frac{1}{8}$ in) and press flat. Turn under another 6 mm ($\frac{1}{4}$ in) and machine stitch.

Finish the curved edge of the under ruffle in the same way. Press flat.

2. With the right side of both ruffles facing upward, place the under ruffle beneath the main ruffle, matching the dot to the shoulder seam, and baste in place. Work two rows of gathering stitches the length of the main ruffle.

Yoke 3. With right sides together, stitch the back yokes to the front yoke at the shoulder seams. Press the seams open.

Repeat for the yoke facing.

With right sides together, stitch the yoke facing to the yoke at the neck edge, and down the center back as shown. Clip the corners and turn the yoke right side out. Baste around the stitched edges and press flat.

*Applying ruffles to yoke 4. With right sides together, pin the prepared ruffle to the yoke edge, matching the entire front and the shoulder seams. Pull up the gathering threads, distribute the gathers evenly, and stitch.

Pockets 5. With right sides together, fold the pocket in half and stitch around three sides leaving a small opening for turning the pocket right side out.

Grade the seams and turn the pocket right side out. Baste around all edges and press flat. Slip-stitch the opening to close. Repeat for second pocket.

6. Place the pockets in the positions indicated on the front skirt. Baste and topstitch in place.

Skirt and ties Finish the center back skirt edges and three edges of the ties (leaving one short edge raw), as instructed in step 1.

7. With right sides together, baste the ties to the front skirt as indicated.

With right sides together baste and stitch the skirt backs to the skirt front at the side seams, from the armhole to 1·3 cm ($\frac{1}{2}$ in) below the tie. Press the seams open.

8. Trim the armhole seam allowance to 6 mm ($\frac{1}{4}$ in). *With right sides together, stitch the bias strip to the armhole. Press the bias strip away from the armhole and then turn under 6 mm ($\frac{1}{4}$ in) and press flat. Hem the fold edge of the binding to the line of

stitching around the armhole. Press flat. Ready-made bias binding is applied in the same way (seam allowances on this type of binding are ready-pressed).

Joining skirt to yoke 9. Add two rows of gathering stitches across the top of skirt and back. With right sides together, pin the front skirt to the front yoke and the back skirts to the back yokes. Pull up the gathers and distribute them evenly.

Stitch, being careful not to catch yoke ruffle edge in seam. Press toward yoke.

10. Turn under the seam allowance of the yoke facing and hem to the line of stitching as shown. Press flat.

Side and hem edges 11. Turn under 6 mm ($\frac{1}{4}$ in) on the side seam and hem edges and press flat. Turn under the rest of the seam allowance and stitch by hand. Clip the seam allowance 1·3 cm ($\frac{1}{2}$ in) above the end of the side seam to allow the seam to lie flat. Press side and hem edges flat.

Buttons and buttonholes 12. Work one buttonhole on the child's apron and two on the mother's apron on the back yoke as shown. Stitch on buttons to correspond.

Graph pattern for mother's apron

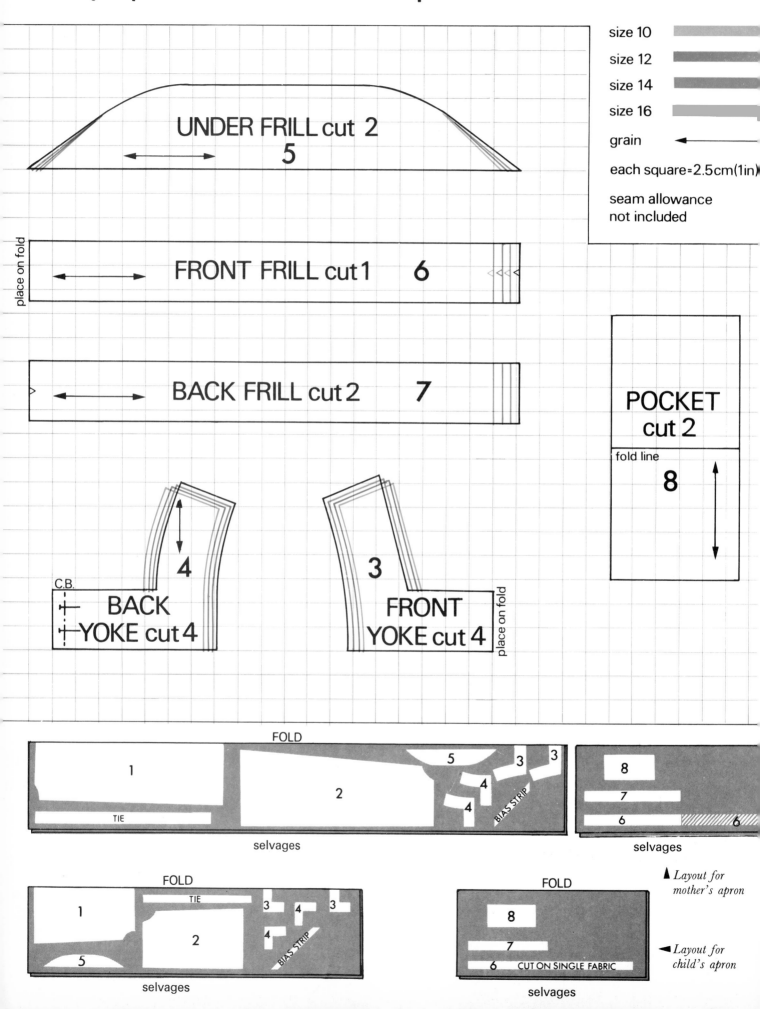

UNDER FRILL cut 2
5

FRONT FRILL cut 1 **6**

place on fold

BACK FRILL cut 2 **7**

POCKET
cut 2

fold line
8

C.B.

BACK
YOKE cut 4
4

FRONT
YOKE cut 4
3

place on fold

size 10
size 12
size 14
size 16
grain
each square=2.5cm(1in)
seam allowance
not included

FOLD
1
TIE
2
5
3 3
4
4
BIAS STRIP
selvages

8
7
6   6
selvages

FOLD
TIE
1
2
3 4 3
4
BIAS STRIP
5
selvages

FOLD
8
7
6   CUT ON SINGLE FABRIC
selvages

▲ *Layout for
mother's apron*

◀ *Layout for
child's apron*

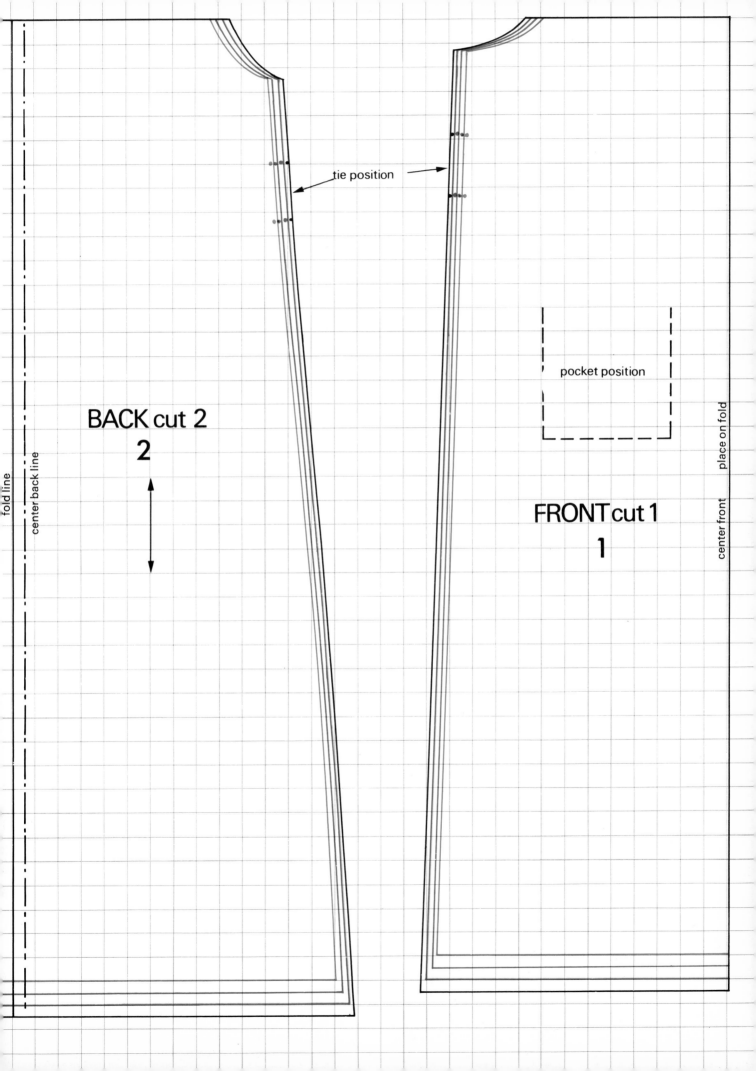

tie position

BACK cut 2
2

pocket position

FRONT cut 1
1

fold line

center back line

place on fold

center front

Graph pattern for daughter's apron

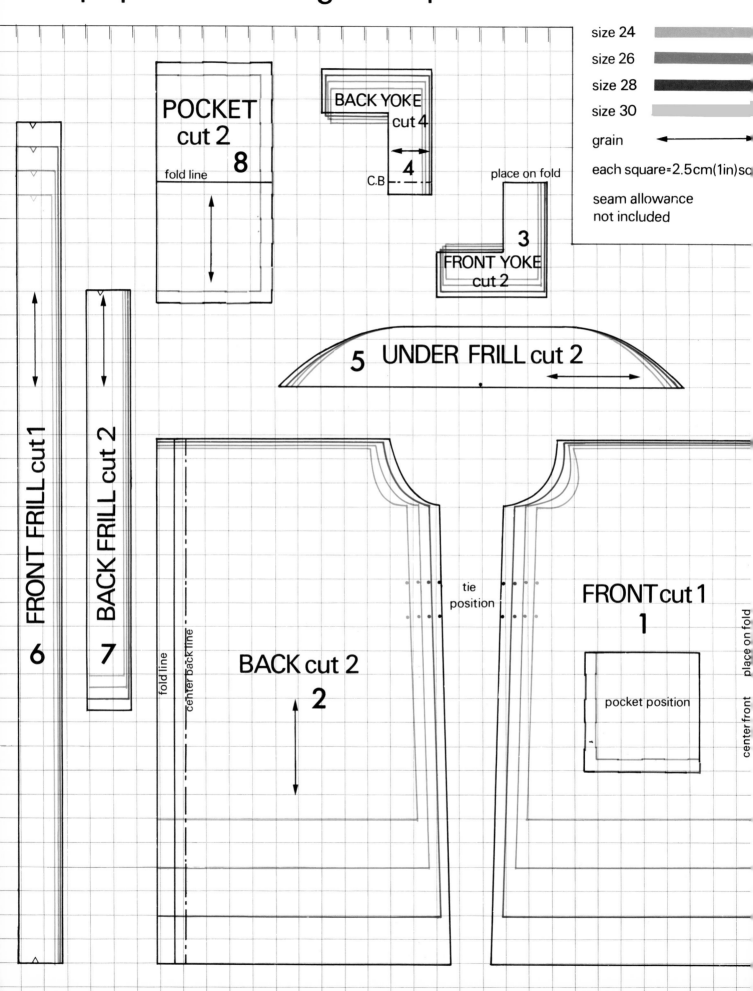

size 24
size 26
size 28
size 30

grain

each square=2.5cm(1in)sq

seam allowance
not included

POCKET
cut 2
8
fold line

BACK YOKE
cut 4
4
C.B

place on fold

3
FRONT YOKE
cut 2

5 UNDER FRILL cut 2

FRONT FRILL cut 1
6

BACK FRILL cut 2
7

fold line

center back line

BACK cut 2
2

tie
position

FRONT cut 1
1

pocket position

center front

place on fold

Toddler's Dress

A simply charming dress to make for a toddler. It takes very little fabric and could be made from very small remnants, with yoke, main dress and collar and cuffs in different fabrics, chosen to mix and match. The yoke edge could be trimmed with lace for a party dress. The design could also be adapted without the yoke insertion as a jumper.
*Techniques included: attaching collar and neck facing, faced sleeve opening, setting in sleeves.

Measurements
The pattern and instructions given here are to fit a child of 1, 2 or 3 years of age. Chest sizes 51 cm (20 in), 53 cm (21 in) and 58·5 cm (23 in). Each size is indicated on the graph pattern by a cutting line of a different color.

Making the pattern
Draw up the pattern to scale from the graph pattern given here. One square represents 2·5 cm (1 in) square.

Suggested fabrics
Cottons, cotton blends, lightweight woolens and woolen blends.

You will need:
90 cm (36 in) wide fabric, without nap, all sizes 1·20 m (1¼ yd) main fabric.
90 cm (36 in) wide fabric, without nap, all sizes 30 cm (¼ yd) contrast fabric.
90 cm (36 in) wide non-woven or iron-on interfacing, all sizes 30 cm (¼ yd).
15 cm (6 in) zipper.
Five 1 cm (⅜ in) buttons.
Sewing thread to match fabrics.
Graph paper for pattern.

Cutting out
A seam allowance of 1·5 cm (⅝ in) has been included on all seam edges and a hem allowance of 4 cm (1½ in).

To make the dress
Yoke 1. With right sides together and notches matching, ease and pin

the dress to the yoke. Baste and stitch. Finish the raw edges together by overcasting and press seam toward yoke. On the right side work a row of top-stitching in contrasting thread 6 mm (¼ in) from yoke seam on the yoke, through all thicknesses of fabric.

Center back, side and shoulder seams 2. With right sides together, and notches matching, baste and stitch center back seam to end of zipper opening. Finish raw edges by overcasting. Press the seam open. Insert the zipper in the center back opening. With right sides together, and notches matching, baste and stitch the front to the back at the side and shoulder seams. Press the seams open and finish the raw edges by overcasting.

Collar 3. Apply the interfacing to the wrong side of two collar pieces. With right sides together and notches matching, baste and stitch the collar facings to the collar sections. Trim and notch the seam allowance. Turn right side out and baste close to stitched edges. Press flat.

*Attaching collar and neck facing to dress 4. Matching notches and the dot to the shoulder seam, pin the two collar sections to the neck edge of the dress, so that the front edges meet. Baste.

5. With right sides together, baste and stitch the front and back neck facings together at the shoulder seams. Press seams open.
With right sides together and notches

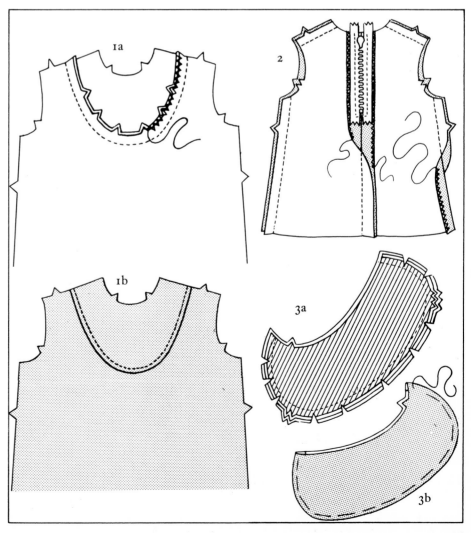

45

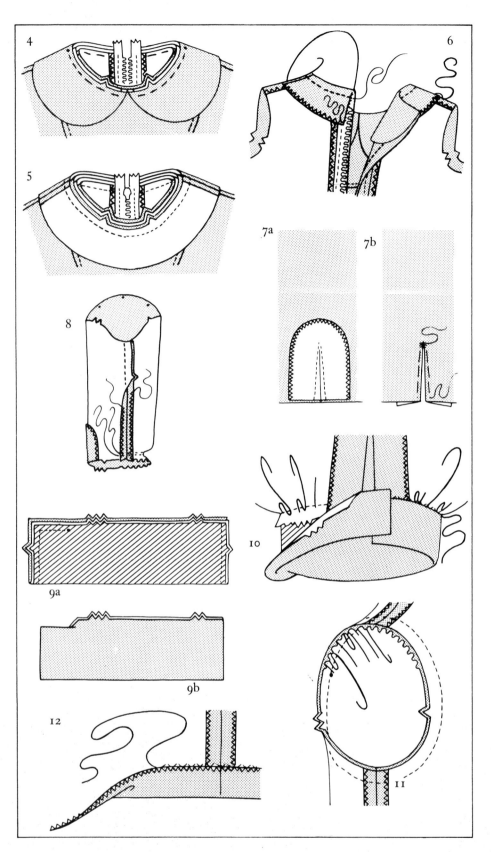

facing to the lower sleeve edge as indicated on the pattern. Stitch, taking 6 mm ($\frac{1}{4}$ in) seam, tapering to dot. Slash opening almost to the point. Turn facing to inside and baste close to stitched edge. Press flat. Catch stitch facing to sleeve.

8. With right sides together and notches matching, baste and stitch the underarm seam of sleeve. Press seam open and finish raw edges by overcasting. Work two rows of gathering stitches around lower edge of sleeve.

Repeat steps 7 and 8 for second sleeve.

Attached cuffs 9. Apply interfacing to the wrong side of the cuff piece with one edge on the fold line.

With right sides together, fold the cuff on the fold line. Baste and stitch across the ends and to dot as shown. Trim the seam allowances and clip to the dot. Turn cuff right side out. Baste close to stitched edges and press flat.

10. With right sides together, and notches matching, pin the interfaced half of the cuff to the lower sleeve edge, pulling up the gathers to fit evenly. Stitch. Trim seams and press cuff. Turn under the seam allowance on the remaining edge of the cuff and sew to the stitching line. Press flat.

Repeat steps 9 and 10 for second cuff.

*Setting in sleeves 1. Work two rows of gathering stitches between the dots at the top of the sleeve. With right sides together and notches and under-arm seams matching, pin the sleeve into the armhole, pulling up gathers to fit evenly. Stitch the seam with the sleeve uppermost. Press the seam toward the sleeve and finish the raw edges together by overcasting.

Repeat for second sleeve.

Hem 12. Try the dress on the child and mark the hemline. Turn up the hem and baste close to the fold line. Trim the hem to an even width and finish the raw edge by overcasting. Sew the hem to the dress using invisible hemming stitch. Press flat.

To finish Work a hand or machine buttonhole on each cuff as indicated on pattern. Sew buttons to underwrap of cuff directly under buttonholes. On the center front of the yoke, sew three buttons 2.5 cm (1 in) apart, with the top button 2.5 cm (1 in) below neck edge.

Make this sweet little dress and learn how to set in sleeves and use facings.

and shoulder seams matching, baste and stitch the neck facing to the neck edge over the collar. Trim seams and clip curves where necessary.

6. Finish the raw edge of the facing by overcasting. Turn the facing to the inside and baste close to the stitched edge. Catch stitch the facing to the shoulder seams. Turn under the ends at the center back and slip-stitch to the zipper tape.

On the right side add a row of top-stitching close to the collar and facing neck edge through all thicknesses.

*Faced sleeve opening 7. Finish the outside edge of the sleeve opening facing by overcasting.

With right sides together, baste the

Graph pattern for dress

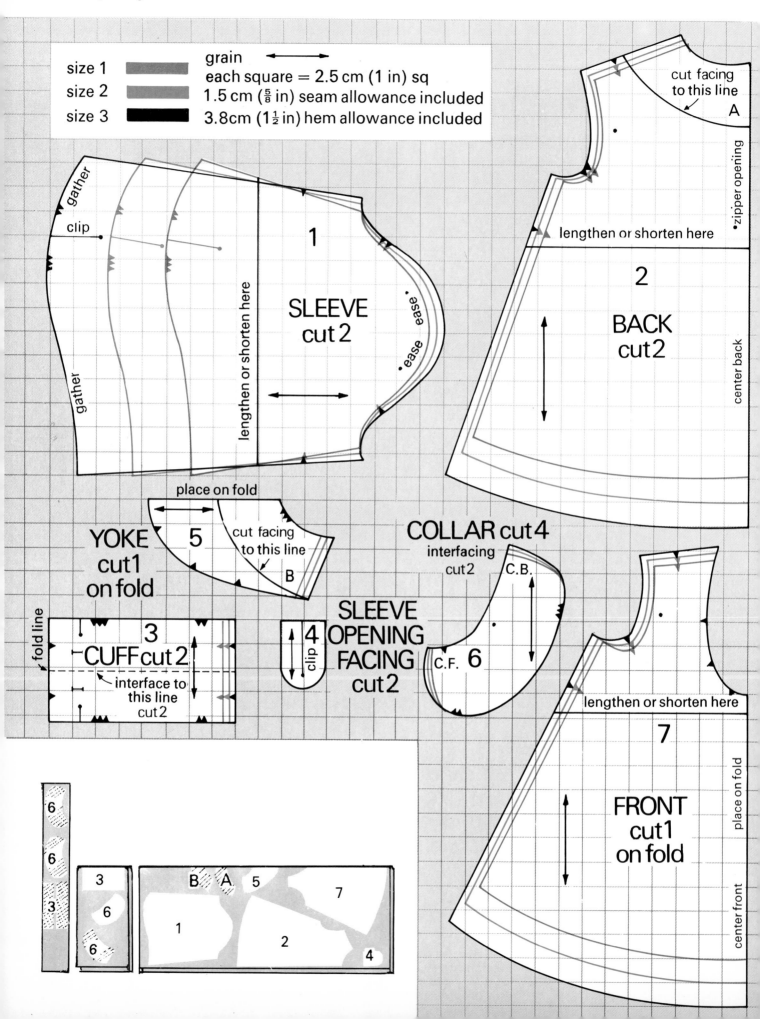

size 1
size 2
size 3

grain
each square = 2.5 cm (1 in) sq
1.5 cm (⅝ in) seam allowance included
3.8 cm (1½ in) hem allowance included

gather
clip
gather
SLEEVE
cut 2
lengthen or shorten here
ease
ease
ease

1

cut facing
to this line
A
zipper opening
lengthen or shorten here
2
BACK
cut 2
center back

place on fold
YOKE
cut 1
on fold
5
cut facing
to this line
B

COLLAR cut 4
interfacing
cut 2
C.B.
C.F. 6

fold line
3
CUFF cut 2
interface to
this line
cut 2

SLEEVE
OPENING
FACING
cut 2
clip
4

lengthen or shorten here
7
FRONT
cut 1
on fold
place on fold
center front

6
6
3
3
6
6
B A 5
7
1
2
4

Long Evening Dress

More basic know-how
Darts

Although their use is influenced by the vagaries of fashion – they are not found in loose unfitted clothes – darts are essential whenever shape is required in a garment. Darts give fullness at the bust, hip, shoulder or elbow and always point toward the fullest curve of the body. Darts are generally made on the wrong side of the garment; their size and position can be adapted if alterations are needed. Bust dart points should be in line with the point of the bust and should be altered if necessary. Dart positions should be marked with tailor's tacks. Darts can be shown either as lines or dots on the pattern. Working on the wrong side, fold the dart so that the markings coincide exactly. Pin and baste as shown, working from the seam edge to the point of the dart, tapering the stitching line to nothing at the point (fig. 1). Pull out the tailor's tacks, then stitch the dart in the same direction as the basting, taking the last stitches just past the folded edge of the fabric so that the thread forms a chain. Cut off thread and knot close to fabric (fig. 2). Press each dart after stitching (details are given in section on pressing). If using a thick fabric, e.g. tweed, slash the dart down the center and press open (fig. 3). Shoulder and elbow darts are narrower than darts on a bodice or skirt but are stitched in the same way.

Basic pattern alterations

Because figures vary so much in height and general proportions, pattern companies make patterns for various figure types, including teen, junior miss, miss petite and half size for the short sturdy figure, to misses' for the tall, mature figure.

These figure type designations do not necessarily relate to age; a tall, well-built girl may require a misses' size, and a petite older woman can use an adapted teen pattern; the important

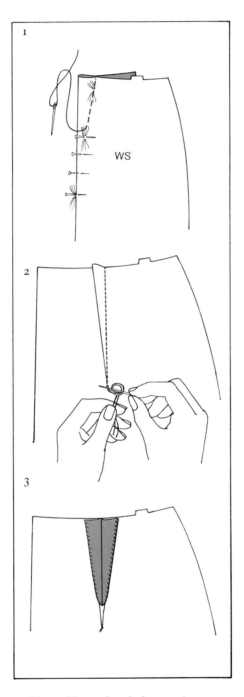

1. Pin and baste dart before sewing.
2. Stitch toward dart point and then knot securely. On heavy fabrics the darts should be slashed as shown.

thing is to know your figure.
Details of the various figure types are to be found in the pattern books in department stores, where there are usually trained assistants.

Taking accurate measurements

It is most important to have your own proportions accurately measured. The specific measurements given on the pattern envelope are actual body measurements.

The patterns do include a built-in allowance for ease, and where necessary they also include any extra fullness demanded by current fashion. There are fashion trends in fit and figure as well as in length and styling. Pattern manufacturers follow fashion trends very closely, so if you select a pattern that is right for your figure size, very little alteration should be necessary to give the correct fit.

General rules for altering patterns

When shortening or lengthening a garment, try to keep all the main lines of the pattern intact (i.e. style lines and hip, bust and elbow).

Try to preserve the proportions of the pattern and to disturb the outline as little as possible.

Remember that an alteration to one part of a garment affects the pieces adjacent to it.

An alteration which entails an addition to a pattern must be made before the garment is cut out.

Testing patterns

Remember to take account of current fashion trends, both of style and fit, when testing patterns for length and width.

With the exception of the sleeves, the best method of testing a pattern is to pin together one half and try it on in order to determine the length in relation to the figure.

A sleeve pattern would tend to tear if pinned together for fitting; instead, take the outer arm measurement from shoulder to elbow and down to the wrist, with the arm bent. Compare this measurement with the pattern, taking into account an extra style fullness.

Most patterns give instructions for

lengthening or shortening bodices, sleeves and skirt. These are repeated here with diagrams, followed by some of the less common alterations which are often necessary.

Shortening and lengthening

Bodice too long This causes creases above the waistline (fig. 1a).
To shorten, make a horizontal tuck on the pattern and pin it down on paper (fig. 1b and c). Straighten the seam lines as shown (fig. 1b and c).

Bodice too short This causes creases at the side seams, and the bodice rides above the waistline (fig. 2a).
To lengthen the bodice, crease and cut across the pattern horizontally. Spread it by the required amount and pin the pattern to paper (fig. 2b and c). Remember that if the style allows for a bloused effect in the bodice or sleeve this fullness must be retained.

Sleeve too long Make a horizontal tuck on the pattern and pin it down onto paper (fig. 3).

Sleeve too short To lengthen, crease and cut across the pattern horizontally. Spread it by the required amount and pin the pattern onto paper (fig. 4).

Skirt too long To shorten, make a horizontal tuck in the pattern and pin it down on paper (fig. 5).

Skirt too short To lengthen, crease and cut across the pattern horizontally. Spread it by the required amount and pin the pattern to paper (fig. 6).

Alterations for unusual figure variations

Square shoulders Square shoulders cause creasing across the neckline (fig. 7a and b).
Pin the bodice down on paper to armhole level. Cut the new shoulder line allowing the required amount, 1·3 to 2 cm ($\frac{1}{2}$ to $\frac{3}{4}$ in) at the armhole tapering to nothing at the neck (fig. 7c and d).
Raise the line at the underarm to maintain the original size of the armhole (fig. 7e and f).
Note This type of figure often requires a larger armhole, in which case omit the addition at the underarm but

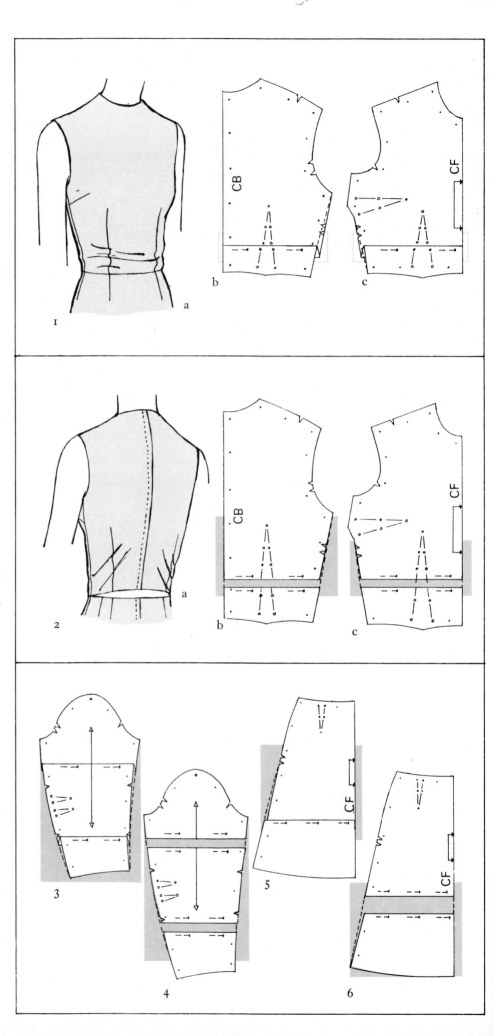

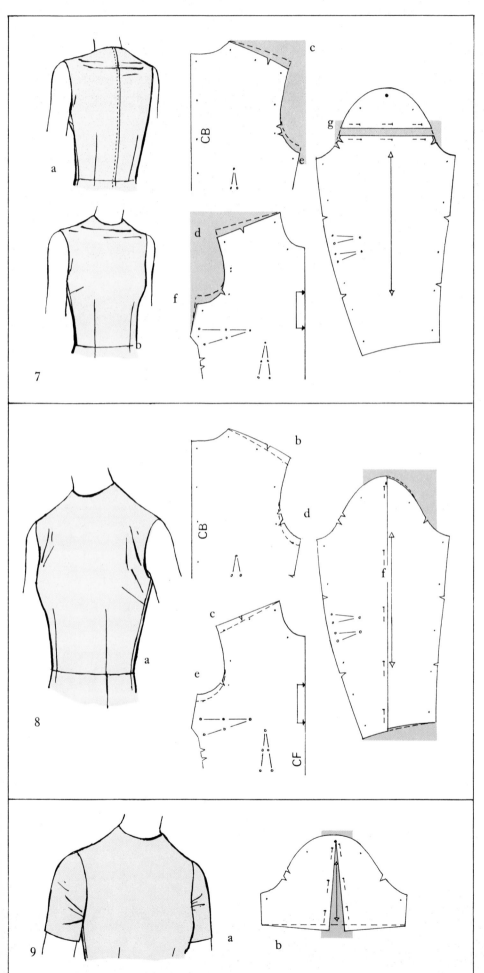

increase the cap of the sleeve as shown to make it fit into the larger armhole with the correct amount of ease (fig. 7g).

Sloping shoulders These cause folds at the armhole (fig. 8a).

Draw a line from the armhole tapering to nothing at the neckline and cut away the required amount of fabric (fig. 8b and c).

Cut away the same amount at the underarm to retain the original armhole size and sleeve cap (fig. 8d and e).

Note This type of figure often has thin arms so it may be necessary to decrease the sleeve width by making a lengthwise fold down the center of the sleeve (fig. 8f).

In this case do not cut away at the bodice underarm.

Large upper arm This causes creases at the underarm and across the top of the arm (fig. 9a).

Slash the pattern through the center from the hem to the top of the arm. Pin the pattern to a sheet of paper, spreading the pattern pieces apart by the required amount. Draw around the spread-out pattern to give the new sleeve shape (fig. 9b).

Round shoulders This causes the neckline and the collar to stand away from the back neck (fig. 10a p. 52).

Slash the pattern about $11 \cdot 5$ cm ($4\frac{1}{2}$ in) down from the neck at the center back to the armhole. Do not cut away (fig. 10b). Raise the neck the required amount, 2 cm to $2 \cdot 5$ cm ($\frac{3}{4}$ in to 1 in) (fig. 10c) and pin to paper.

Restore the neck to its original measurement using the lengthened, curved line if the design has a center back seam (fig. 10d), or using the straight line if the pattern is cut on the fold (fig. 10e), taking the extra fullness into a dart at the neckline (fig. 10f).

Alternatively, slash across from the center back to the armhole, then slash down from the center of the shoulder. Raise the back neck and spread the shoulder to make a shoulder dart (fig. 10g).

Hollow or sway back This causes horizontal wrinkles below the waist (fig. 11a).

On the back skirt pattern, cut away about 2 cm ($\frac{3}{4}$ in) from the center

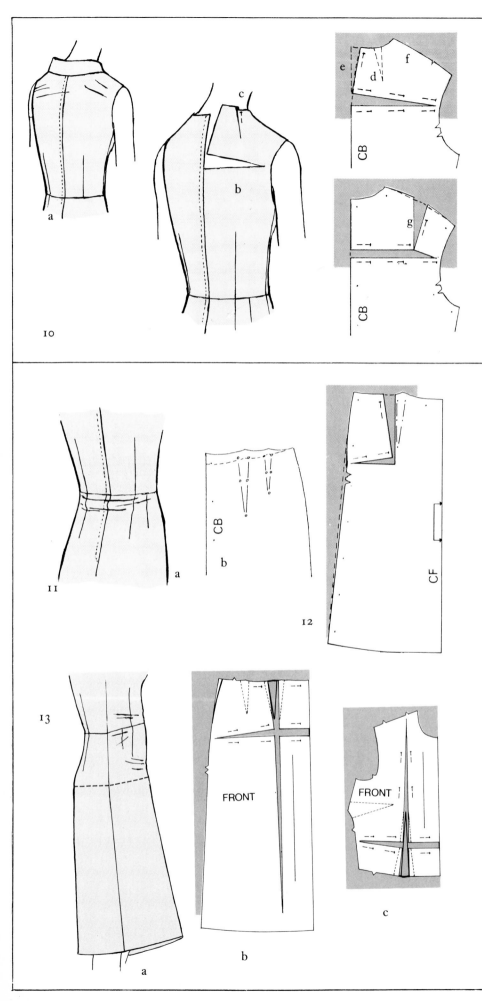

back, sloping to nothing at the side seam (fig. 11b). This alteration can be done at the fitting stage if you prefer.

Large waist On some designs it is not practicable to adjust the waist measurement by altering the side seams – for example:
(**A**) In a design with no side seams.
(**B**) Where a design has a one-sided effect.
(**C**) If folds come from the side seam, or a pocket or other style feature crosses it.
To increase the front waist measurement, slash the skirt pattern down from the center of the waistline and across to the side seam at approximately hip level. Spread the pattern to give the required amount at the waist and pin to paper (fig. 12).

High abdomen This figure type causes the skirt to rise up at the hem and the skirt to crease horizontally around hip level (fig. 13a).
Slash down from the center of the waistline and across to the center front line of the pattern at approximately hip level (fig. 13b). Do not cut away. Spread the pattern as shown to give extra width and height. Pin to paper. Re-draw the waistline and the center front line. A bodice can be enlarged in the same way (fig. 13c).

Long evening dress

This figure-skimming style is flattering to all age groups and easy and comfortable to wear. It can be dressed up for formal occasions or left simple and uncluttered. The full-length version shown here is made up in luxurious pure silk and is fully underlined for a smooth shape. You can add a belt if you wish. The dress is easily adaptable and can also be made in other lengths to wear as a day dress or as a tunic over slacks.
*Techniques included: inset tab fastening, underlining.

Measurements

The pattern is given in women's sizes 10, 12, 14 and 16. Each size is indicated on the graph pattern by a cutting line of a different color.

The pretty lining in this evening dress is what gives the undergarment its professionally made appearance.

Making the pattern

Draw up the pattern to scale from the graph pattern given here. One square represents 2·5 cm (1 in) square.

Suggested fabrics

Silk, poplin, linen, wool and cotton mixtures, fine wool, wool crêpe.

You will need:

90 cm (36 in) fabric, with nap, all sizes 3·50 m (3⅞ yd).
90 cm (36 in) interlining fabric, all sizes 3·50 m (3⅞ yd) or 120 cm (48 in) fabric, with nap, all sizes 3·50 m (3⅞ yd).
120 cm (48 in) interlining fabric, all sizes 3·50 m (3⅞ yd).
90 cm (36 in) interfacing (optional), all sizes 70 cm (¾ yd).
Seven 1·5 cm (⅝ in) buttons.
Sewing thread to match fabric.
Graph paper for pattern.

Cutting out

No seam allowance is included on the pattern so add 1·5 cm (⅝ in) for seams and 6·5 cm (2½ in) hem allowance.
Note If using wool crêpe do not underline. If you are underlining the dress cut out each pattern piece in lining fabric. The lining fabric should relate well to the main dress fabric, so it is advisable to select lining and main fabric at the same time, comparing the two. The color of the lining should not be deeper than the color of the fabric. Lining can also be used to give body to loosely woven fabrics.
If you do not wish to underline the dress, cut out and apply interfacing to the tab, wrap facing and collar sections (see Facings).

To make the dress

*Underlining the fabric Baste each lining piece to the corresponding dress piece with wrong sides together,

raw edges even; the facings are not underlined. First work a line of basting through the center, then baste all around each piece, close to the edge. Then treat as one piece of fabric (all pattern markings should be indicated with tailor's tacks).

*Inset tab fastening 1. Pin and baste the tab to the tab facing with right sides together and with the facing uppermost. Starting at the top, stitch down the right side, turn and stitch to the point. Fasten off securely at the point. Trim the seam allowance to 6 mm (¼ in). Turn the tab right side out and baste firmly along the stitched edge, rolling the facing under slightly to prevent it showing. Carefully press this edge on the wrong side of the tab making sure that the basting stitches do not make impressions on the fabric.

2. Pin, baste and stitch the center front seam of the dress from the pointed end of the tab stitching line to the hem. Clip into the seam allowance, finish the seam by overcasting and press open. Pin, baste and stitch the raw edge of the tab to the right dress front on the tab stitching line. Do not stitch along the neckline. Spread the corner on the dress so that you can stitch comfortably toward the pointed end of the tab. Make sure that the point of the tab is in line with the center front seam. Trim seam and press carefully. Fold under the seam allowance on the facing and pin it over the seamline on the point of the tab. Slip-stitch in place. Remove the basting and press the tab.

3. With right sides together, pin and baste the facing to the wrap extension on the left side of the dress. Stitch along the front edge of the wrap

Follow the pattern layout below when placing the pieces on the fabric.

extension but leave the lower edge and the neck edge unstitched. Trim the seam allowance and turn the facing inside the dress. Baste along the stitched edge and press.

4. Topstitch the tab 6 mm (¼ in) from the seamline, pivoting the machine needle carefully at corners and point. Overcast the raw lower edge of the wrap extension and sides of facing to finish.

Darts, shoulder and side seams

5. Pin and baste the shoulder and bust darts, shoulder and side seams, matching notches and seamlines. Baste waist darts if any. Try on dress and adjust fit if necessary.
Stitch and press darts.
Stitch shoulder and side seams. Press and finish seams.

Armholes 6. Cut 4 cm (1½ in) wide bias strips to length of armholes, plus 8 cm (3 in). Curve the bias strips to follow the curve of the armholes by placing the bias strip on an ironing board and pressing around the outer edge, gently stretching this into a curve. Press in the fullness on the inner edge of the curve so that the binding will be flat. Turn in 1·3 cm (½ in) seam allowance at one end of the bias strip. With right sides facing, starting at the armhole seamline, pin the inner curved edge of the bias strip around the armhole seamline. Ease the fullness of the strip into the underarm curve. Overlap the other end of the bias strip as shown, but do not trim and stitch until the binding is complete to prevent it from dragging. Baste and stitch the bias binding in place along the seamline. Snip into the seam allowance on the dress only, then turn binding to the inside. Roll the seam edge slightly to the inside to prevent the bias from showing and baste in place.
Turn under the raw edge of the binding and slip-stitch to the dress. Slip-stitch the ends of the binding. Press carefully. Repeat for second armhole.
Collar 7. Interface one section of collar if fabric requires it. Place the top and under-collar pieces together, with right sides facing. Pin, baste and stitch along the upper curved edge. Trim the seam allowance to 6 mm (¼ in) and turn to the right side. Baste along the stitched edges and press.
Baste the front facings to the dress along the neckline. With right sides

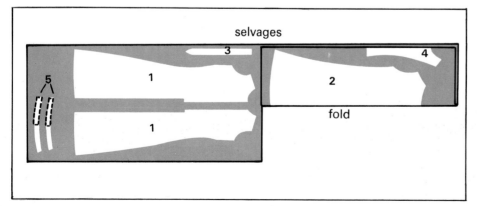

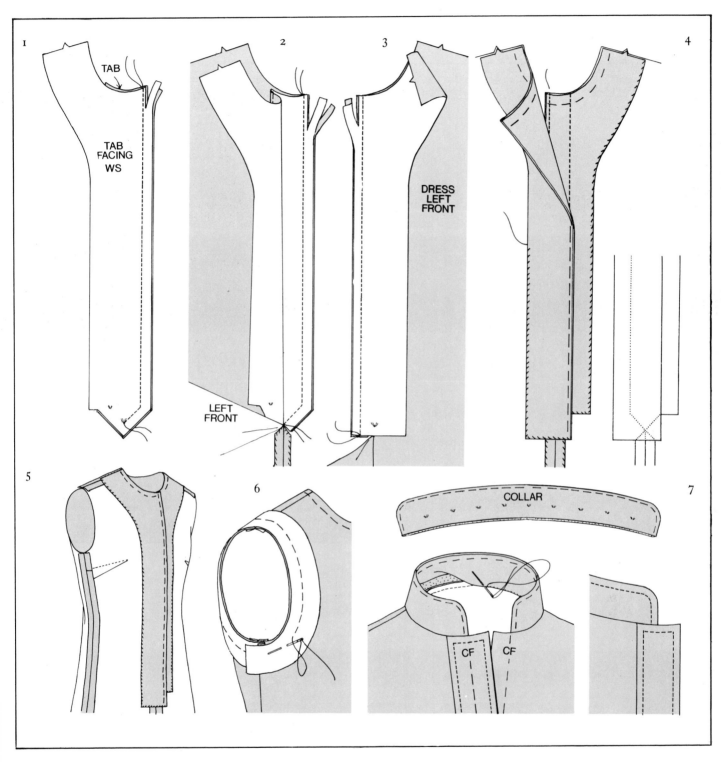

together, raw edges even, pin and baste the outer-collar band to the neckline. Baste, stitch and trim the seam allowance. Turn under the seam allowance on the inner collar band, lay it over the stitching line to cover the machine stitches and slip-stitch in place. Make tiny stitches, as the inner edge of the band will show if the neck of the dress is unbuttoned. Topstitch around the outer edge of the collar making sure that the stitches line up with the topstitching on the tab.

Fastenings 8. Mark the position for the first buttonhole 6 cm (2¼ in) down from the neck edge of the tab. Space the remaining five buttonholes at 8 cm (3 in) intervals down the tab. Work vertical buttonholes either by hand or by machine in positions marked, making one horizontal buttonhole halfway down collar. Sew on buttons to correspond.

*Finishes for underlined garments Seam allowances should be overcast by hand. Catch facings lightly to seamlines by hand. To stop the lining folding up inside the hem, prick stitch fabric and lining together just below the hemline before the hem is turned up and finished. When sewing the inner edge of hems and bias facings to an underlined dress make sure that you do not sew through to the outside fabric, but only catch the lining fabric to give the outside a smooth finish.

Hem 9. Check that the length of the dress is correct and that the hem is even. Add a line of basting along the hemline. Turn up and stitch hem (see Hems).

Graph pattern for long dress

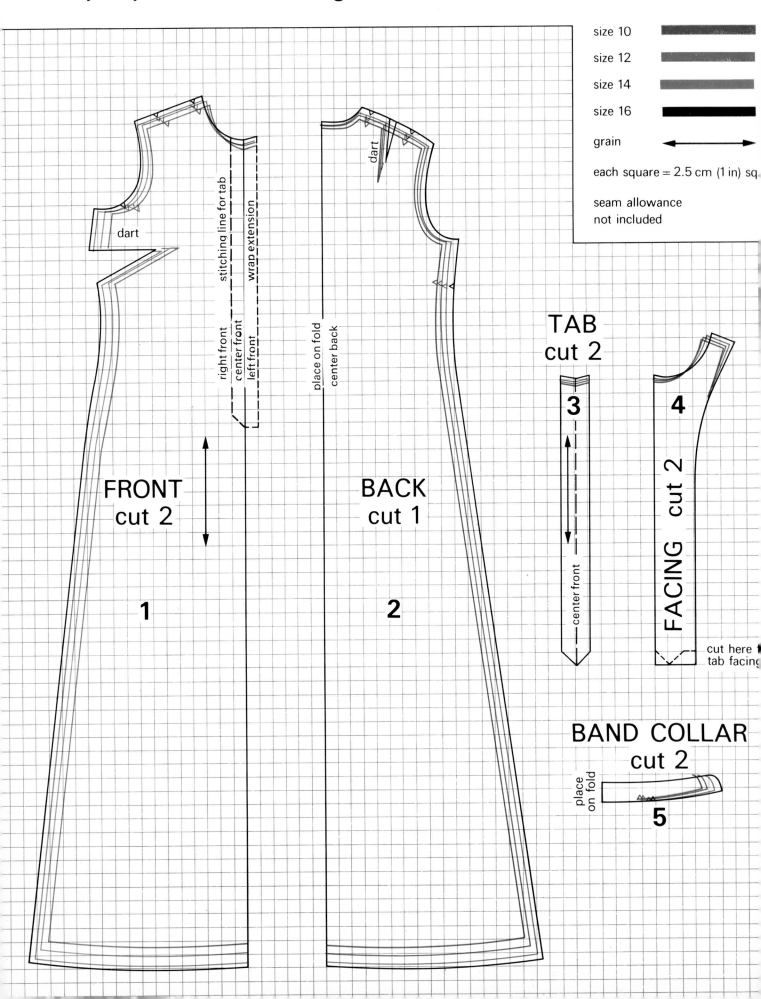

size 10

size 12

size 14

size 16

grain

each square = 2.5 cm (1 in) sq.

seam allowance
not included

dart

stitching line for tab

wrap extension

right front

center front

left front

place on fold

center back

dart

FRONT
cut 2

1

BACK
cut 1

2

TAB
cut 2

3

center front

FACING cut 2

4

cut here
tab facing

BAND COLLAR
cut 2

place
on fold

5

Skirt with Flare

More basic know-how
Waistbands and belts
*Techniques included: stab stitch, catch stitch, ladder stitch.

Waistbands

A properly sewn and fitted waistband never stretches, wrinkles or folds over, nor is it too tight or so loose that it slips down to the hips.

Personal preference and the style of the garment determine the width and type of waist finish, and all waistbands need to be interfaced to prevent stretching, particularly where a loosely woven fabric is being used. Knits need an elastic section to ensure a proper fit. Grosgrain belting can be used for interfacing; it comes in various widths and is either plain or stiffened with small "bones" of plastic. If used in a washable garment, it should be pre-shrunk by washing and left to drip dry.

Unless the garment is gathered at the waist, the skirt is eased to the band to fit the curve of the body directly below the waist. For this reason the skirt waist measurement must be 2·5 cm (1 in) bigger than the waistband, which itself must be a comfortable fit. This is where personal preference comes in and it must be left to the individual to decide how much ease to allow. If the design has an overlapping waistband, the ends of the waistband should overlap by 3·8 cm to 5 cm (1½ in to 2 in) with the back extending under the front for side openings, the left extending under the right for front openings and the right extending under the left for back openings.

The waistband is applied after the zipper and zipper guard, if used, and before the lining. If a waistband is not desired, then the waist is finished by the addition of a shaped facing which should be interfaced with a firm non-woven or woven interfacing. This is applied after the zipper is sewn in and the lining basted in place.

Tailored waistband Cut the waistband with one long edge on the selvage; if this is not possible finish one long edge by overcasting by hand or machine. Make it 8 cm (3 in) longer

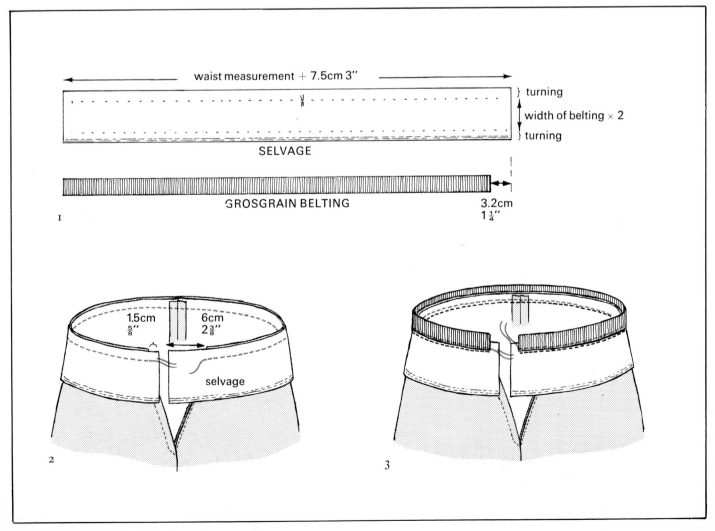

than the waist measurement and twice as wide as the belting, plus two seam allowances. Cut the belting 3·2 cm (1¼ in) shorter than the band (fig. 1). Ease the skirt onto the long cut edge of the waistband, leaving 6 cm (2⅜ in) underlap on the appropriate side. Baste through band and skirt and machine stitch (fig. 2).

Stitch the belting just above this line, placing it so that there is a 1·5 cm (⅝ in) seam allowance left at both ends (fig. 3). Turn in the seam allowance over the ends of the belting and fold the band over the belting (fig. 4). Baste.

Snip at the zipper, turn under along the underlap and baste along the length of the band. Hem the extension and the front ends (fig. 5).

Machine stitch or stab stitch carefully along the waistband seam; stitch through the skirt and inside waistband, not through the front of band (fig. 6). If you are lining the skirt, turn in the lining waist seam allowance and hem to waistband seam allowance along the stitching line.

Elasticized waistband This is used for knitted fabrics and gives a smooth finish in front and a slight gather at the back to take up the ease and prevent stretching. Because elastic is used the back darts can be made smaller, or left out altogether, and the difference between skirt and band can be as much as 6·3 cm (2½ in), comprising 1·3 cm (½ in) to ease in at the front and 5 cm (2 in) at the back.

Substitute the back half of the belting

with the elastic of the same width, cut 5 cm (2 in) shorter, and stitch a 5 cm (2 in) length of belting at the end to make the underlap (fig. 7).

Sew the waistband to the skirt as shown in fig. 2.

Sew the belting sections as in fig. 3 but do not sew the elastic (fig. 8). Fold the waistband over and finish as shown in figs. 4, 5 and 6.

Strong machine finished waistband
This is a useful finish for children's clothes, denims, etc., and on clothes on which a machine stitched effect adds to the style of the garment.

Lay the belting on the wrong side of the band and shape end if required. Catch stitch all around (fig. 9). See page 18 for technique.

Fold the band with right sides together along the center fold and machine stitch each end. Do not stitch through the belting. Trim the corner (fig. 10). Turn right side out and press. Using the un-interfaced side, lay the right side of the band on the wrong side of the garment, easing as before (fig. 11a).

Machine stitch and press the seam into the band (fig. 11b).

Turn in the remaining long edge over the belting and baste over the seam. Stitch all around band (fig. 11c).

If you like, make a buttonhole by machine or hand.

Faced waistline using fabric Some slacks or skirts are finished with a shaped facing, when comfort or style call for it. When there is a yoke to the

garment, this is interfaced and the facing cut to match the yoke and not itself interfaced. Otherwise the facing is interfaced before being sewn to the skirt. Use the weight of interfacing suitable for the garment fabric. The garment is completed before the facing is sewn in, any lining is basted in and any yoke seams pressed toward the waist.

Cut out the facing pieces, separate them and place the wrong side on the interfacing. Baste all around inside the sewing line and cut out. This ensures that the pieces match exactly (fig. 12).

Join the seams and trim back the interfacing; press open (fig. 13).

Finish the lower edge by overcasting raw edge to interfacing (fig. 14a), or trim the interfacing back 6 mm (¼ in), turn facing over interfacing and machine stitch down (fig. 14b).

Place the right side of the facing on the right side of the skirt, matching seams and easing garment to fit. Machine stitch (fig. 15).

Grade the seam (fig. 16a p. 60).

Snip through to the stitching line (fig. 16b).

Understitch the facing to the seam allowance to stop its rolling back (fig. 16c). Turn facing to the wrong side and press well. Fold under the end seam allowances, mitering slightly to avoid the zipper, and hem to the zipper tape (fig. 17a).

Catch the facing to the seams and darts (fig. 17b).

Sew hook and eye to the top of the facing to keep it in place and to prevent

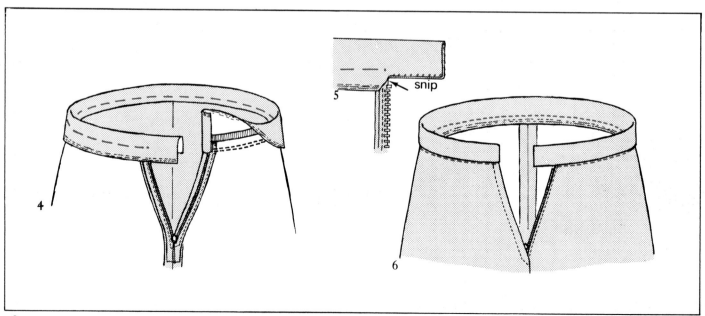

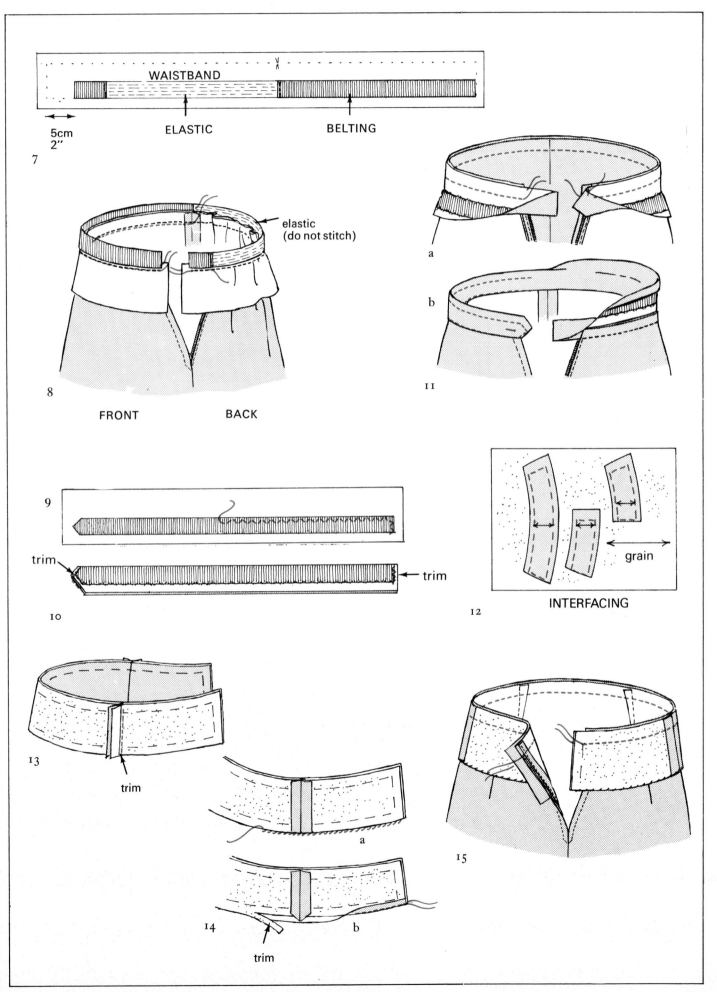

7

WAISTBAND

ELASTIC   BELTING

5cm
2"

8

elastic
(do not stitch)

FRONT   BACK

a

b

11

9

trim   trim

10

grain

12   INTERFACING

13

trim

14   **a**

b

trim

15

strain on the zipper (fig. 17c).

For a yoke facing, proceed as above but hem it all around the yoke seam to provide a neat finish (fig. 18).

Faced waistline using shaped belting It is possible to purchase shaped belting, but if this is not available, then shape a straight piece by pulling it under a medium hot iron, carefully stretching one side slightly as you go along.

When attaching the belting, be very careful to make sure that you attach the shorter, unstretched edge to the garment.

Fit the belting to the body, allowing 1·3 cm ($\frac{1}{2}$ in) extra at each end. Finish the garment as for the faced waistline and trim the waist seam to 1·3 cm ($\frac{1}{2}$ in), finishing the edge by overcasting (fig. 20).

Place the inside curve of the belting on the waist seamline on the right side as shown. Ease the skirt and baste. Machine stitch one line along the edge of the belting and a second line 3 mm ($\frac{1}{8}$ in) away (fig. 21).

Turn to the wrong side, fold under

the two short ends of the belting and finish as fig. 17.

Belts

A belt made of fabric is a good alternative to a purchased one in that it does not "break" the line of the garment. This is important if the figure is not all it should be, as the eye is drawn to the waist instead of taken away from it.

There are various interfacings which can be used to stiffen belts: buckram, plain grosgrain belting and boned grosgrain belting. The latter is not suitable if the belt is to be finished by topstitching.

Cut the interfacing 15 cm (6 in) longer than the waist measurement, shaping the end to a point or curve as desired (fig. 22a).

Cut two pieces of fabric the length and width of the interfacing plus seam allowances (fig. 22b).

Center the stiffening on the wrong side of one piece of fabric and catch stitch the seam allowances in place, snipping the corners so that the fabric will lie flat (fig. 23).

Press the raw edges of the other piece to the wrong side and lay it over the stiffening. Either baste in place if the belt is to be topstitched (fig. 24a), or ladder stitch together for a plain belt (fig. 24b).

Make a hole for the buckle 3·8 cm (1$\frac{1}{2}$ in) from the plain end, buttonhole stitch around or, alternatively, apply an eyelet (fig. 25a). (Eyelet kits are available in many colors and instructions are given with each set.)

Place the prong of the buckle through the hole and hem the edge down to the wrong side (fig. 25b).

Check for the correct position of the hole at the shaped end and make a hole (fig. 25c).

*****Stab stitch** Working on the right side, push the needle down vertically, and pull the needle through to the wrong side. Then push the needle up vertically and pull through to the right side. The stitches should be very small and evenly spaced.

*****Catch stitch** Used for attaching interfacing to facings.

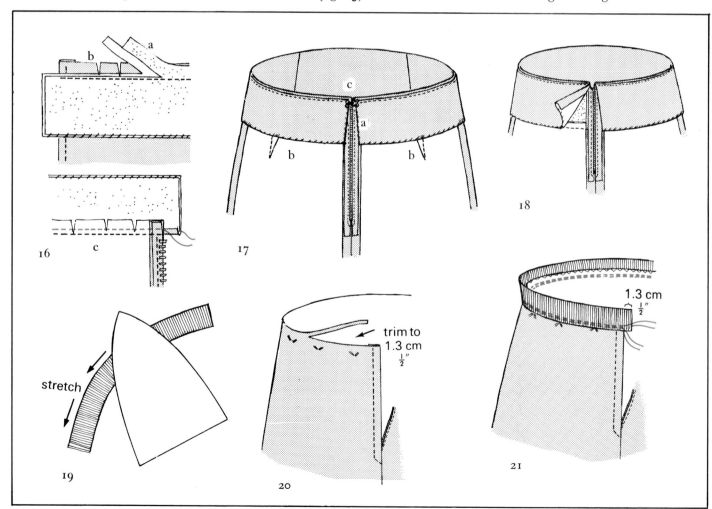

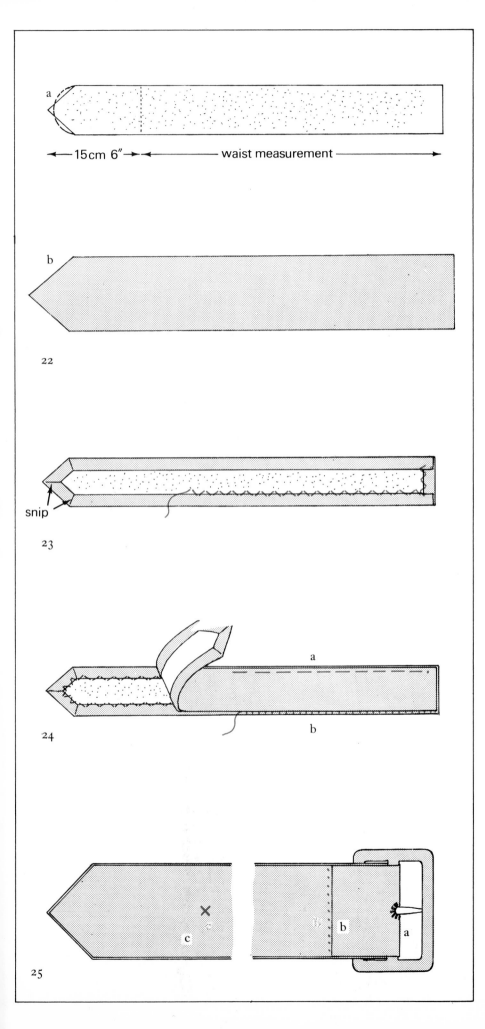

<- 15cm 6" -> <- waist measurement ->

22

snip

23

24

a

b

25

c

b

a

Working on the wrong side, pick up a thread of the fabric, then pick up a thread of the interfacing. The stitches must not go through to the right side.

*Ladder stitch Slip the needle through each fold of fabric in turn, creating a series of straight stitches which should be invisible.

Flared skirt

The line of this skirt is gently flared, emphasized by the texture of the corduroy from which it is made. The shape could not be easier to sew – just two pattern pieces and a narrow waistband, For an extra touch of luxury you can add a lining.
*Technique included: lining a skirt.

Measurements

The pattern is given in women's sizes 10, 12, 14 and 16. Each size is indicated on the graph pattern by a cutting line of a different color.

Making the pattern

Draw up the pattern to scale from the graph pattern given here.
One square represents 2·5 cm (1 in) square.

Suggested fabrics

Corduroy, pinwale corduroy, cotton blends, lightweight wools and wool mixtures, lightweight tweeds.

You will need:

90 cm (36 in) wide fabric, with nap, all sizes 3·10 m ($3\frac{3}{8}$ yd).
140 cm (54 in) wide fabric, with nap, all sizes 2·40 m ($2\frac{5}{8}$ yd).
90 cm (36 in) wide lining (optional), all sizes 1·60 m ($1\frac{3}{4}$ yd).
90 cm (36 in) wide woven interfacing, all sizes 30 cm ($\frac{1}{4}$ yd).
20 cm (8 in) zipper.
Sewing thread to match fabric.
Graph paper for pattern.

Cutting out

A seam allowance of 1·5 cm ($\frac{5}{8}$ in) has been allowed on all seam edges and a hem allowance of 6·5 cm ($2\frac{5}{8}$ in).

To make the skirt

Front 1. With right sides together, raw edges even and notches matching, baste and stitch the center front seam. Press the seam open.

A simple flared skirt is a practical addition to any wardrobe and, depending on the fabric it is made in, will be a suitable style for any occasion. Make this skirt and learn all about fitting waistbands and making belts.

Back 2. With right sides together, raw edges even and notches matching, baste and stitch the center back seam from the hem to the circle. Press the seam open. Baste around the opening as shown.

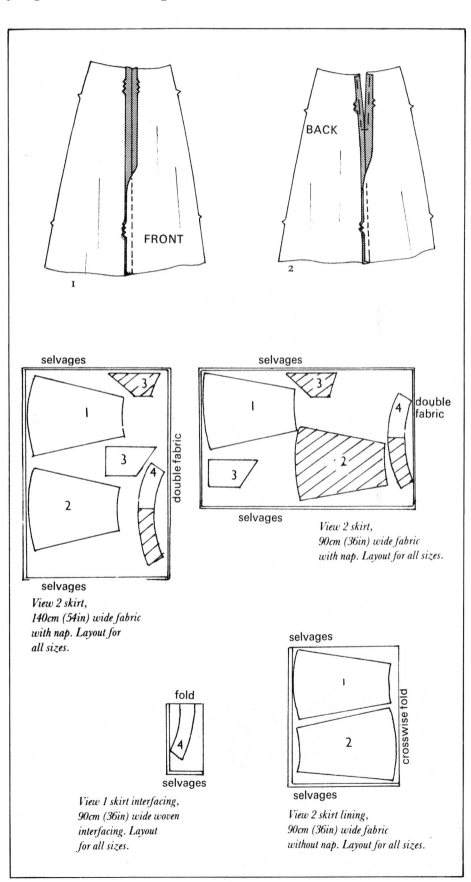

View 2 skirt, 140cm (54in) wide fabric with nap. Layout for all sizes.

View 2 skirt, 90cm (36in) wide fabric with nap. Layout for all sizes.

View 1 skirt interfacing, 90cm (36in) wide woven interfacing. Layout for all sizes.

View 2 skirt lining, 90cm (36in) wide fabric without nap. Layout for all sizes.

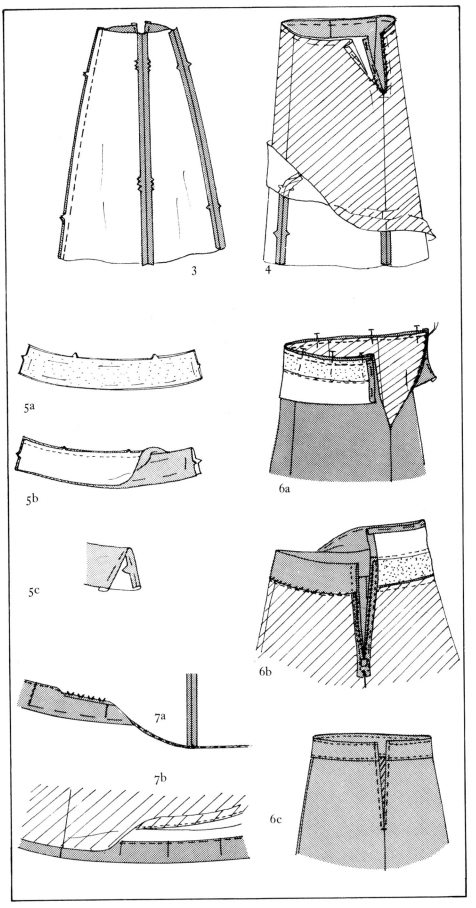

3

4

5a

5b

5c

6a

6b

7a

7b

6c

Side seams 3. With right sides together, raw edges even and notches matching, baste and stitch the front to the back at the side seams starting at the top. Press the seams open.

*Lining 4. Make the lining as for the skirt following steps 1, 2 and 3. With wrong sides together and center fronts and side seams matching, baste the lining to the skirt, around the waistline and center back opening. Slip-stitch the lining to the skirt at the back edge opening as shown.

Waistband 5. Baste the interfacing to the wrong side of the waistband. With right sides together and notches matching, baste and stitch the two waistband pieces together along the notched edge. Cut the interfacing close to the stitching and grade the seam allowance. Turn under 1·5 cm ($\frac{5}{8}$ in) seam allowance at the center backs on both waistband pieces. Baste as shown and press flat.

Turn the waistband right side out and baste close to the stitched edge. Press the stitched edge flat.

Attaching waistband 6. With right sides together, raw edges even, and center fronts, side seams and center backs matching, pin the waistband to the skirt. Stitch the entire waist. Cut the interfacing close to the stitching and grade the seam. Press the seam flat toward the waistband.

Insert the zipper at the center back opening from the circle to the top of the waistband.

Turn under 1·5 cm ($\frac{5}{8}$ in) seam allowance on the lower edge of the waistband facing. Baste and press flat. Sew the fold edge of the facing to the stitching line of the waistband and to the zipper tape at the center back, 6 mm ($\frac{1}{4}$ in) away from the teeth.

On the right side, topstitch 1 cm ($\frac{3}{8}$ in) from the top and waistline edges of the waistband (optional).

Hem 7. Try on the skirt and mark the hem. Turn up the hem and baste close to the fold edge. Trim the hem allowance to an even width and finish the raw edge either by overcasting or by turning under 6 mm ($\frac{1}{4}$ in) and machine stitching.

Take up any fullness with small darts and sew hem to skirt using invisible hemming stitch or catch stitch. Press the hem edge flat.

Note If using wool fabric, finish the raw edge by overcasting, gather up the fullness and lessen by shrinking, using a damp cloth.

Lining hem This is sewn separately from the skirt hem.

Mark the hem of the lining 2·5 cm (1 in) shorter than the skirt hem. Sew the lining hem in the same way as that of skirt hem.

Graph pattern for A-line skirt

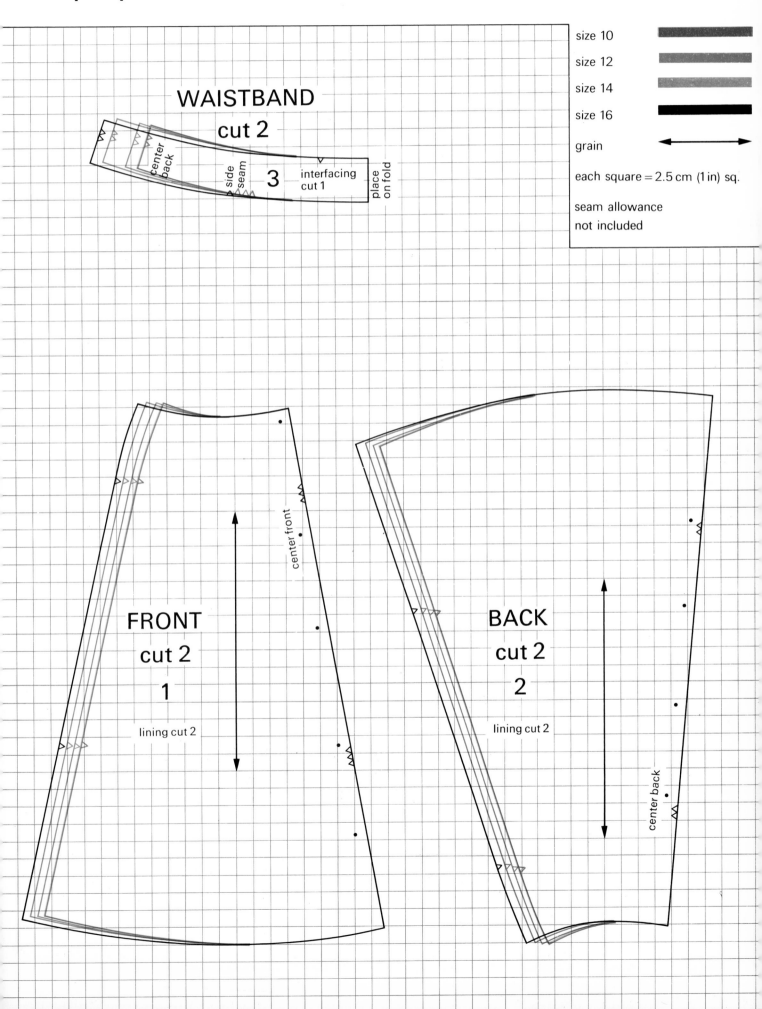

size 10
size 12
size 14
size 16

grain

each square = 2.5 cm (1 in) sq.

seam allowance
not included

WAISTBAND
cut 2

center back

side seam

3

interfacing cut 1

place on fold

FRONT
cut 2
1

lining cut 2

center front

BACK
cut 2
2

lining cut 2

center back

Man's Sportshirt

More basic know-how
Using knitted fabrics
Some commercial patterns are designed for a fabric with a specific amount of stretch (e.g. jersey). This is usually indicated on the pattern envelope.

Cutting out Pin and cut your fabric on a large flat surface and do not allow the fabric to hang over the edge. This prevents unwanted stretching. To straighten fabric, fold on a lengthwise rib; cut crosswise ends square with the end of the table. Hold ends together with basting.

Sewing Use a ballpoint machine needle and a synthetic thread. Test your machine stitching on a scrap of spare fabric to adjust stitch length before assembling your garment. A small zigzag or stretch stitch is the best to use. Otherwise, use a medium stitch length, stretching the fabric slightly as you sew.

Taping Where stretching is undesirable – e.g. on waists, necklines or shoulders – use cotton seam binding to hold the seam to its original length. Baste the binding to the seamline and stitch at the same time as you stitch the seam (fig. 1).

Buttonholes Back buttonholes with a lightweight but firm fabric.

Finishing This is often unnecessary as knits do not fray. If seam allowances curl, stitch them together with two rows of stitching (fig. 2).

Pressing Adjust iron temperature according to the fiber of the fabric. Always test on a spare scrap of fabric. Use a damp pressing cloth made of thin cotton. The ironing board should be softly padded to prevent impressions of seams and darts being made on the right side.
Darts should be slashed and then pressed open very carefully.

Shirt
Here's a shirt that is made for a sporting life, or for casual weekend wear. It has a front buttoning placket opening, trim collar and neatly fitting short sleeves. This design is easy to make and is only suitable for use with stretch fabrics.

Measurements
The pattern and instructions are given to fit chest sizes 87 cm (34 in), 92 cm (36 in), 97 cm (38 in) and 102 cm (40 in). Each size is indicated on the graph pattern by a cutting line of a different color.

Making the pattern
Draw up the pattern to scale from the graph pattern given here.
One square represents 2·5 cm (1 in) square.

Suggested fabrics
Cotton jersey, synthetic knits, stretch terry cloth.

You will need:
150 cm (60 in) wide fabric, with nap, all sizes, 1·30 m (1⅜ yd).
90 cm (36 in) woven interfacing; all sizes, 70 cm (¾ yd).
Sewing thread to match fabric.
Four 1 cm (⅜ in) buttons.
Graph paper for pattern.

Cutting out
No seam allowance is included on the pattern so add 1·5 cm (⅝ in) to all seam edges and 4 cm (1½ in) hem allowance.

To make the shirt
Front opening 1. Baste interfacing to wrong side of front bands on notched side and catch stitch to fold line.
On the un-notched edge, turn under 1·5 cm (⅝ in) seam allowance and baste. On the shirt front, stay stitch around inner corners of front opening.
With right sides together and notches matching, baste and stitch left front band to left front to circle and right front band to right front to circle, taking 1·5 cm (⅝ in) seam allowance. Trim interfacing close to stitching line

Working with stretch fabrics requires the use of special techniques, and this sportshirt provides the perfect opportunity to acquire these skills.

1. Tape stitched to seam to retain the original length. 2. Finish seams by sewing edges together and trimming.

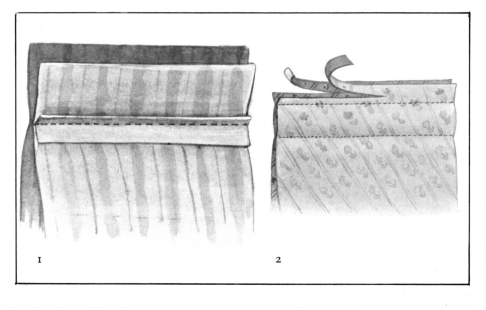

1   2

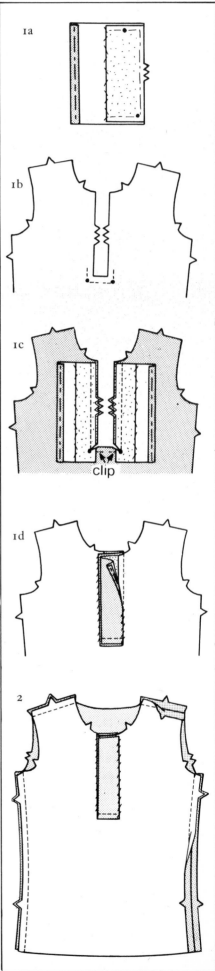

1a

1b

1c

clip

1d

2

and grade seam allowance. Clip to inner corners as shown.

Fold band to inside along fold lines, so that left band is over right band on the outside. Working on the wrong side, baste and stitch the bands to the shirt front across lower edges, taking

1·5 cm ($\frac{5}{8}$ in) seam allowance as shown. Slip-stitch bands on the inside to stitching line.

Shoulder and side seams 2. With right sides together and notches matching, baste and stitch shoulder and side seams. Press seams open.

Collar 3. Baste interfacing to wrong side of collar and collar band. With right sides together, baste and stitch under-collar to upper collar around outer un-notched edges as shown. Trim interfacing close to stitching, grade seam and cut across corners.

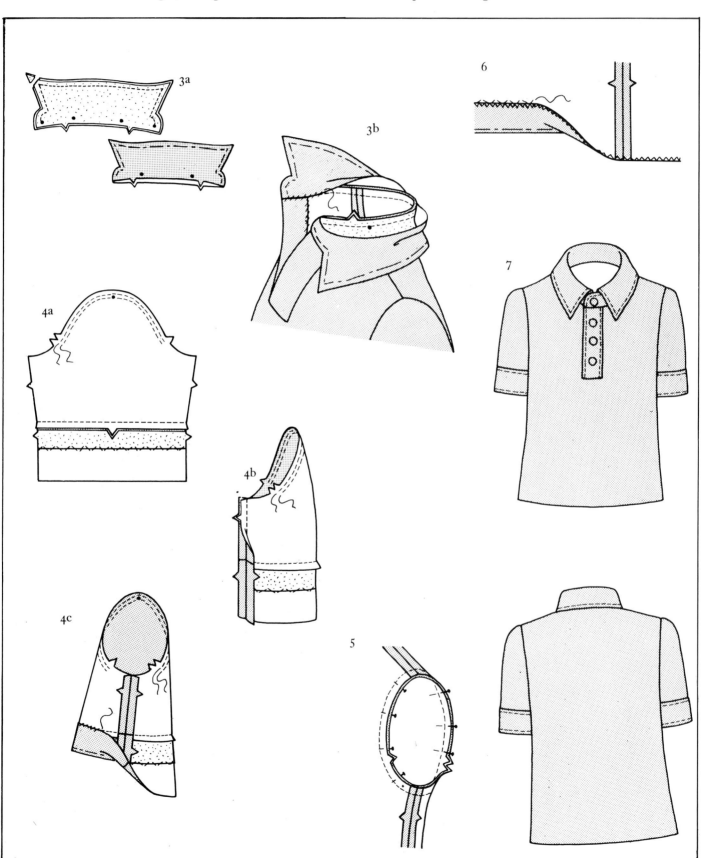

Turn collar to right side and baste around stitched edge. Press flat.
With right sides together, matching center backs, circles to shoulder seams, notches and circles to center fronts, baste and stitch interfaced collar section to neck edge. Trim interfacing close to stitching line, grade seam and clip curves. Press seam toward collar. On the inside, turn under seam allowance of upper collar and slip-stitch to stitching line, enclosing all thicknesses.

Sleeves and sleeve bands 4. Baste interfacing to wrong side of notched edge of sleeve band and catch stitch to fold line. With right sides together, and notches and underarm seams matching, baste and stitch interfaced band edge to lower edge of sleeve. Grade seam, trimming interfacing close to stitching line. Press seam toward band. Work two rows of gathering stitches around top of sleeve between notches. With right sides together, notches and seams matching, baste and stitch underarm seam. Press seams open. Fold band to inside along fold line and baste close to folded edge. Turn under seam allowance of band and slip-stitch to stitching line. Press. Repeat for second sleeve.

Setting in sleeves 5. With right sides together, matching underarm seams, notches and circle to shoulder seam, pin sleeve into armhole, easing in fullness between notches. Stitch seam with sleeve uppermost. Press seam toward sleeve and finish raw edges together. Repeat for second sleeve.

Hem 6. Try shirt on wearer and mark hem. Trim hem to an even depth. Turn hem up and baste close to folded edge. Finish raw edge with hand or machine overcasting. Sew hem to shirt using invisible hemming stitch. Press flat. Alternatively make a double machine-stitched hem.

To finish On the outside, topstitch collar and front bands 6 mm ($\frac{1}{4}$ in) in from outer edges and 6 mm ($\frac{1}{4}$ in) in from inner seamline of bands. Topstitch sleeve bands 6 mm ($\frac{1}{4}$ in) from outer and seam edges.

7. Mark buttonhole positions on left front along center front line and on collar band as indicated on pattern. Make hand-worked or machine buttonholes. Sew buttons on right front band to match buttonholes.

Graph pattern for shirt

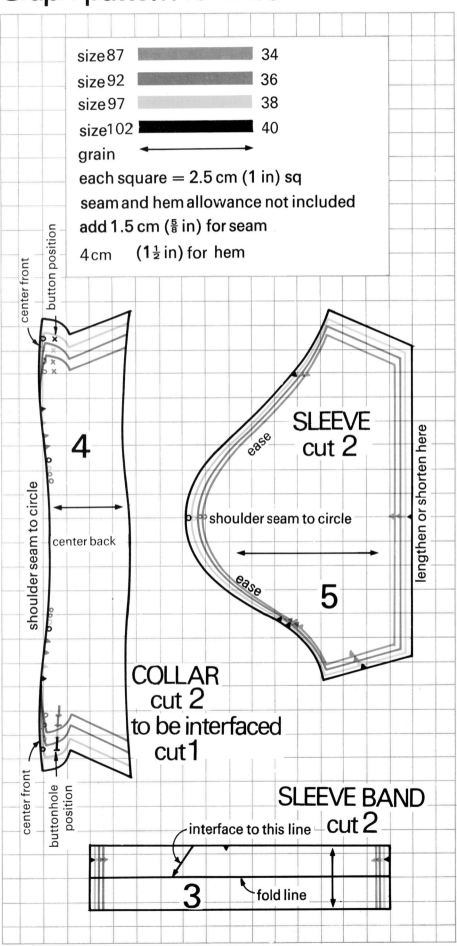

size 87		34
size 92		36
size 97		38
size 102		40

grain

each square = 2.5 cm (1 in) sq

seam and hem allowance not included

add 1.5 cm ($\frac{5}{8}$ in) for seam

4 cm (1$\frac{1}{2}$ in) for hem

69

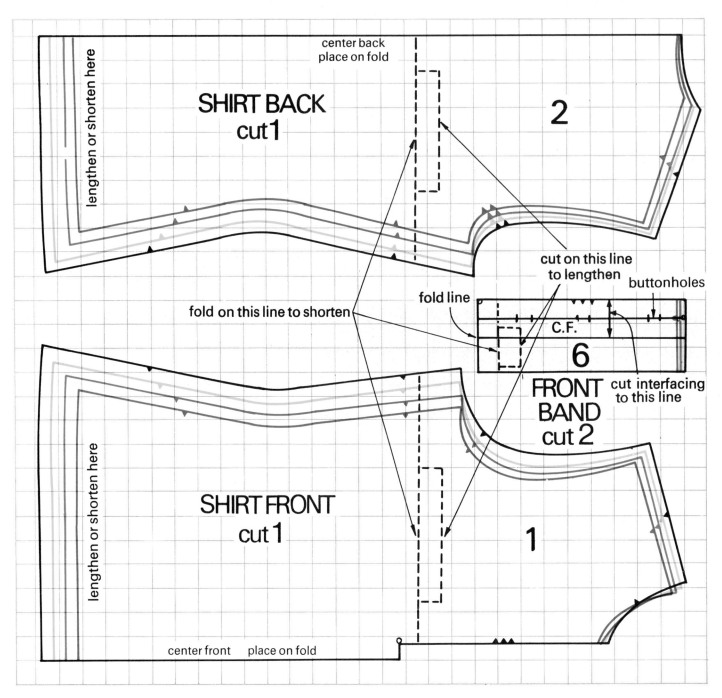

SHIRT BACK
cut 1

lengthen or shorten here

center back
place on fold

2

cut on this line
to lengthen

buttonholes

fold line

fold on this line to shorten

C.F.

6

FRONT
BAND
cut 2

cut interfacing
to this line

SHIRT FRONT
cut 1

lengthen or shorten here

1

center front   place on fold

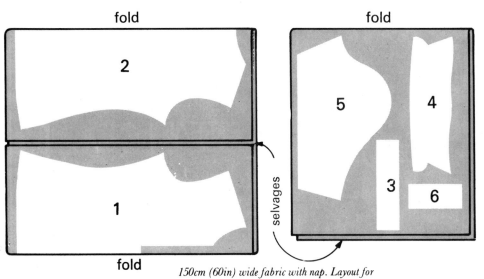

fold

2

1

fold

150cm (60in) wide fabric with nap. Layout for all sizes.

selvages

fold

5

4

3

6

selvages

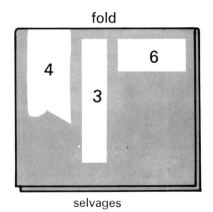

fold

4

6

3

90cm (36in) wide woven interfacing. Layout for all sizes.

Blouson Cover-up

More basic know-how
Using bias strips

To join bias strips Pull a thread at each end and cut on the straight grain. Place strips on a flat surface with right sides up and angles matching (fig. 1).

Place one strip on the other with right sides facing and the edges cut on the straight grain together so that bias cut edges cross each other 6 mm ($\frac{1}{4}$ in) from the pointed ends. Baste and stitch strips together 6 mm ($\frac{1}{4}$ in) in from the edge (fig. 2).

Press seam open and trim off points. When joining stripes, plaids or checks join the bias strips so that the pattern is not broken.

Rouleau Made from bias strips, this trimming is suitable for lacing, loop buttonholes, belt carriers, shoestring straps and bows. Cut a strip 2·5 to 3 cm (1 to 1$\frac{1}{4}$ in) wide from the true bias of the fabric. With right sides together, fold strip in half lengthwise and stitch 6 mm ($\frac{1}{4}$ in) in from the edge (fig. 1). Do not trim the seams, as the seam allowances make

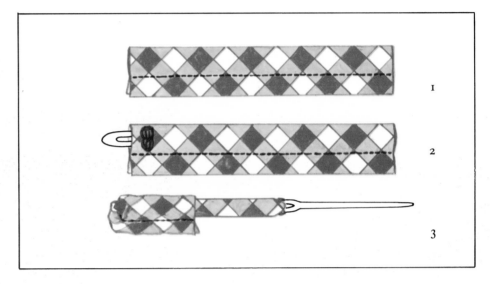

the filling. Sew end of tube onto eye of a large bodkin, or blunt-ended tapestry needle (fig. 2). Push this through the tube until it reaches the other end (fig. 3). Cut thread from tube to needle.

Note It is possible to make a wider rouleau for belts using this method.

Button loops
Cut the length of bias fabric required to fit the edge to be buttoned, plus

1. Rouleau is made from a bias strip stitched to make a tube. 2. Sew a bodkin to one end and 3. pull through.

3 cm (1$\frac{1}{4}$ in) extra for each loop. Make a rouleau as described above. Place the end of the rouleau to the edge of the garment on the right side. Pin in place. Make loops the size required to fit each button as shown. Leave approximately 6 mm ($\frac{1}{4}$ in) between the loops (fig. 1). Baste and stitch loops in place along the seamline before attaching the facing.

1. Join bias strips by matching the angles and stitching as shown in 2.

1. Loop buttonholes are made by sewing a length of rouleau along the opening.

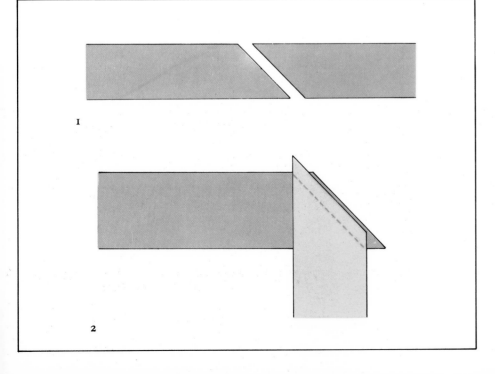

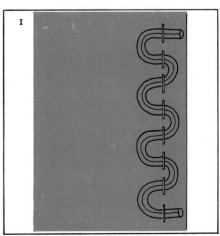

Jersey blouson top

This cool and comfortable blouson top in a soft knit can be worn with shorts or a skirt. You can cover it with a fine layer of netting.
*Technique included: thread button-loops.

Measurements

The pattern and instructions given here are to fit sizes 10, 12, 14 and 16.

Making the pattern

The measurements given on the pattern pieces are for a size 10. For sizes 12, 14 and 16, add to the blouse front and back seams, armhole edges and lower edge and to the sleeve top, side and lower edges, the measurements given in the chart.

Suggested fabrics

Cotton knits, stretch terrycloth, woolen jersey. Netting optional.

You will need:

140 cm (54 in) wide fabric, all sizes, 1·40 m (1½ yd) (for narrower widths allow an extra 90 cm (⅞ yd)).
Netting (optional), the same quantity as of main fabric.
3 mm (⅛ in) wide elastic, all sizes, 2·10 m (2¼ yd).
Sewing thread to match fabric.
One 6 mm (¼ in) button.
Graph or plain paper for pattern.

Cutting out

A seam allowance of 6 mm (¼ in) has been included on the neck edges and 1·5 (⅝ in) on all other seam edges. A lower hem allowance of 3.8 cm (1½ in) and a sleeve hem allowance of 2 cm (¾ in) have also been included.
Note If netting is being used, cut out the pattern pieces in the main fabric first. Then lay the netting over each piece. Pin and baste securely in place before cutting the netting to the shape. Treat as one fabric when sewing.

To make the blouson top

Keyhole neckline 1. Work two rows of stay stitching 3 mm (⅛ in) apart around the keyhole shape of the front neckline, the first row just outside the stitching line. Trim the fabric close to the stitching.
2. Cut a strip of bias fabric the length of the keyhole opening by 2·5 cm (1 in)

wide. (A particularly stretchy knit fabric can be cut on the straight or the bias grain.) With right sides together, baste and stitch the binding to the opening, taking 6 mm (¼ in) seam allowance.
Fold the binding over the opening edge, turn under 6 mm (¼ in) seam allowance and slip-stitch to the line of stitching. Press flat.
Side seams 3. With right sides together, and notches matching, baste and stitch the back to the front at the side seams. Work a second row of stitching 1 cm (⅜ in) away from the first and trim seam to stitching or

zigzag stitch raw edges together. Press seams toward back.
Sleeves 4. With right sides together, baste and stitch the underarm seam. Finish seam as for 3. Press seam toward back. Repeat for second sleeve.
5. With right sides together, and notches and underarm seams matching, baste and stitch the sleeve into the armhole. Finish seam as described but do not trim. Press seam toward sleeve. Repeat for second sleeve.

For summer wear make this jersey blouson top. It is loose fitting and has a rouleau-trimmed keyhole neckline.

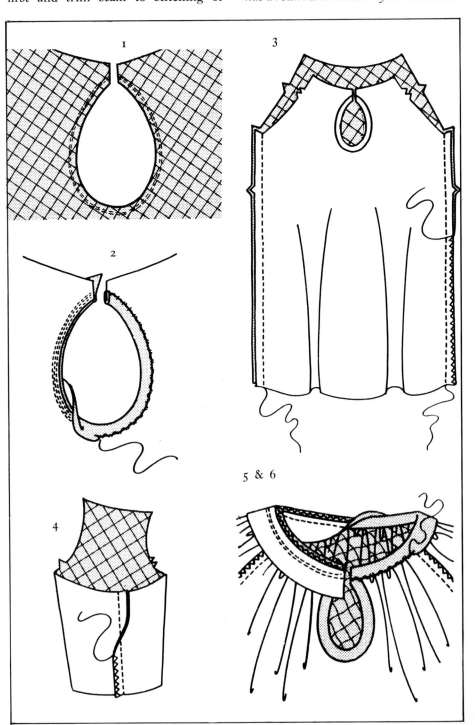

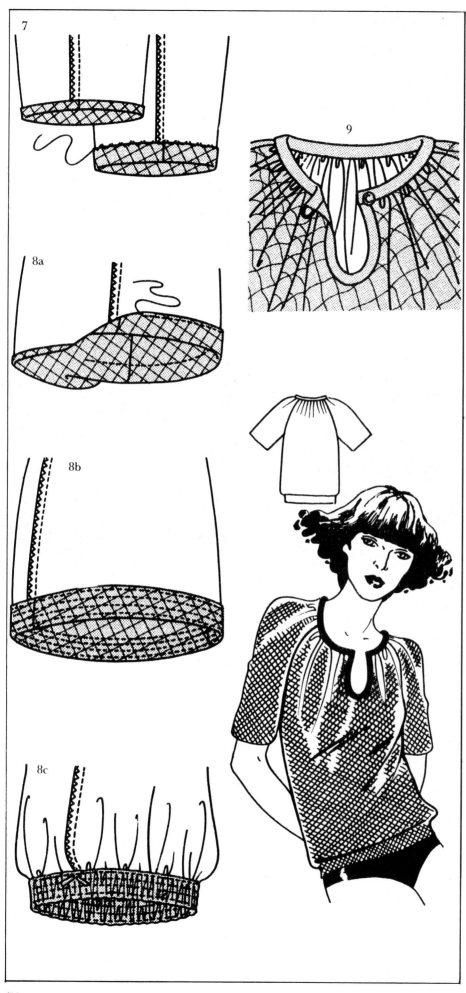

Neckline 6, 7. Work two rows of gathering stitches around the neckline. Draw the gathers up to 66 mm (26 in) for sizes 8 and 10, and 71 cm (28 in) for sizes 12 and 14.

Try on the blouse to check that the fullness is in the most becoming position.

Pin and baste a narrow strip of paper to the wrong side along the stitching line of the neck and machine stitch the gathers to this. Cut a strip of binding fabric 2·5 cm (1 in) longer than the neckline and 2·5 cm (1 in) wide.

On the short edges turn 1·3 cm ($\frac{1}{2}$ in) to the wrong side. Baste and stitch the binding to the neckline. Tear away the paper stay. Fold the binding to the wrong side, turn under 6 mm ($\frac{1}{4}$ in) and slip-stitch to the stitching line. Press binding flat.

Sleeve hems 8. At the lower edge of the sleeve hem, turn under 6 mm ($\frac{1}{4}$ in) and baste. Turn under a further 1·3 cm ($\frac{1}{2}$ in) and slip-stitch the hem to the sleeve. Press flat. Repeat for second sleeve.

Lower hem edge 9. Turn under and baste 6 mm ($\frac{1}{4}$ in) along the lower hem edge. Turn up the hem along the fold line, baste and press.

Machine stitch in place close to the fold, leaving an opening at one side to allow for elastic to be threaded through. Work another row of machine stitching 6 mm ($\frac{1}{4}$ in) below the first. Make a second casing for the elastic by working a further row of machine stitching close to the bottom edge and another row 6 mm ($\frac{1}{4}$ in) above.

Carefully unpick one or two stitches in the side seam of the lower casing to make an opening for the elastic to be threaded through. Cut two pieces of elastic long enough to fit the hips comfortably, plus 6 mm ($\frac{1}{4}$ in).

Thread the two lengths of elastic through the casings, overlap ends by 6 mm ($\frac{1}{4}$ in) and sew firmly to secure. Slip-stitch the openings to close.

To finish 10. Sew a button to the top of neck opening on left side.

*Work a loop on the right side to correspond. Length of loop should be diameter plus thickness of button. Make a foundation loop from a length of thread secured with a backstitch at each end. Repeat twice more. Work closely packed blanket or buttonhole stitches along this loop. (A larger version can be made for a belt.)

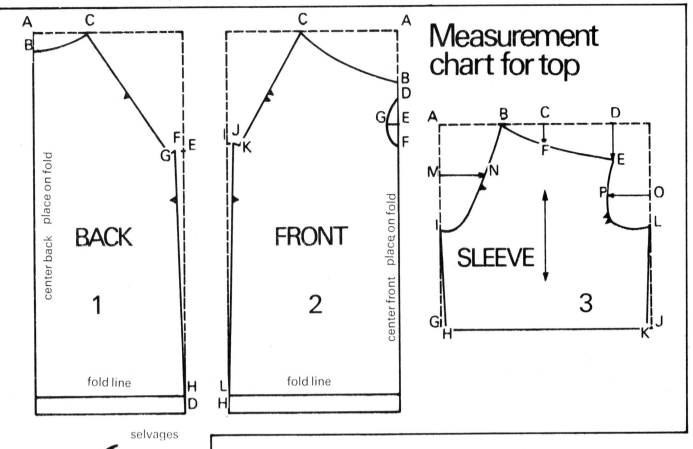

Measurement chart for top

(labels on diagrams: BACK 1, FRONT 2, SLEEVE 3; center back place on fold; center front place on fold; fold line; selvages)

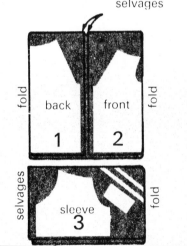

140cm (54in) wide fabric with nap. Layout for all sizes.

Measurement instructions for drafting the pattern			
Additional measurement chart in centimeters (inches in brackets)			
Size	12	14	16
Blouson front and back			
Side seams (width)	1 ($\frac{3}{8}$)	2·2 ($\frac{7}{8}$)	3·5 ($1\frac{3}{8}$)
Armhole edges	0·6 ($\frac{1}{4}$)	1·3 ($\frac{1}{2}$)	2·5 (1)
Lower edges (length)	1·3 ($\frac{1}{2}$)	2·5 (1)	3·8 ($1\frac{1}{2}$)
Sleeve			
Top edge	0·6 ($\frac{1}{4}$)	1·3 ($\frac{1}{2}$)	2 ($\frac{3}{4}$)
Side edges (width)	0·6 ($\frac{1}{4}$)	1·3 ($\frac{1}{2}$)	2 ($\frac{3}{4}$)
Lower edge (length)	0·6 ($\frac{1}{4}$)	1·3 ($\frac{1}{2}$)	2 ($\frac{3}{4}$)

Measurement instructions for drafting the pattern

Back (diagram 1)
Draw a rectangle measuring 27·5 cm by 66·5 cm ($10\frac{3}{4}$ in by $26\frac{1}{4}$ in).
A to B = 2·5 cm (1 in)
A to C = 10 cm (4 in)
Connect B to C.
D to E = 46·5 cm ($18\frac{1}{4}$ in)
E to F = 1·3 cm ($\frac{1}{2}$ in)
F to G = 1·3 cm ($\frac{1}{2}$ in)
C to G = 26 cm ($10\frac{1}{4}$ in)
D to H = 3·8 cm ($1\frac{1}{2}$ in) = fold line.

Front (diagram 2)
Draw a rectangle measuring 30·5 cm by 64·8 cm (12 in by $25\frac{1}{2}$ in)
A to B = 8 cm ($3\frac{1}{4}$ in)
A to C = 17 cm ($6\frac{3}{4}$ in).
Connect B to C.
A to D = 11·5 cm ($4\frac{1}{2}$ in)
A to E = 15 cm (6 in)
A to F = 19·3 cm ($7\frac{1}{2}$ in)
E to G = 2 cm ($\frac{3}{4}$ in)
Connect D to G and G to F.
H to I = 46·5 ($18\frac{1}{4}$ in)
I to J = 6 mm ($\frac{1}{4}$ in)
J to K = 1·3 cm ($\frac{1}{2}$ in)
C to K = 23 cm (9 in)
H to L = 2·8 cm ($1\frac{1}{2}$ in) = fold line.

Sleeve (diagram 3)
Draw a rectangle measuring 46 cm by 41·8 cm (18 in by $16\frac{1}{2}$ in).
A to B = 13 cm ($5\frac{1}{4}$ in)
A to C = 23 cm (9 in)
A to D = 38 cm (15 in)
D to E = 8 cm (3 in)
C to F = 3·8 cm ($1\frac{1}{2}$ in)
Connect B to F, F to E.
G to H = 1·3 cm ($\frac{1}{2}$ in)
H to I = 21 cm ($8\frac{1}{4}$ in)
J to K = 6 mm ($\frac{1}{4}$ in)
K to L = 21 cm ($8\frac{1}{4}$ in)
A to M = 10 cm (4 in)
M to N = 10 cm (4 in)
Connect B to N, N to I.
L to O = 6·5 cm ($2\frac{1}{2}$ in)
O to P = 9 cm ($3\frac{1}{2}$ in)
Connect E to P, P to L.

His 'n Her Nightshirt

This nightshirt pattern is easily adaptable to make a smart casual shirt for him or a shift dress for her.

Measurements

The woman's nightshirt is in sizes 10, 12, 14 and 16 and the man's version is in sizes 97 cm (38 in), 102 cm (40 in), 107 cm (42 in) and 112 cm (44 in).

Making the pattern

Draw up the desired pattern to scale from the graph patterns given here. One square represents 2·5 cm (1 in) square.

Suggested fabrics

Cotton, fine wool, cotton and wool mixtures.

You will need:

To make the woman's nightshirt: 115 cm (45 in) fabric, all sizes, 3·1 cm ($3\frac{3}{8}$ yd).

To make the man's nightshirt: 115 cm (45 in) fabric, all sizes, 3·40 m ($3\frac{5}{8}$ yd).

For either:

Four 1·5 cm ($\frac{5}{8}$ in) buttons.

Sewing thread to match fabric.

Graph paper for pattern.

Cutting out

There are no seam allowances included on the pattern. When cutting out add 1·5 cm ($\frac{5}{8}$ in) to all edges.

To make the nightshirts

Seams and hem 1. With right sides together, baste and stitch the back and front pieces at the side and the shoulder seams. Press the seams open.
2. On the lower edge of the nightshirt make a narrow hem by turning over 3 mm ($\frac{1}{8}$ in) and topstitch. Trim away the excess fabric close to the stitching. Turn up 3 mm ($\frac{1}{8}$ in) and hem as shown. Press the hem flat.

Sleeves 3. With right sides together, baste and stitch the sleeve seam. Press the seam open. Work two rows of gathers around the cap of the sleeve between the notches, and the bottom of the sleeve as shown.
4. With right sides together, baste and stitch the short ends of the cuff to form a circle. Press the seam open.
5. With right sides together and seams matching, pin the sleeve to one edge of the cuff, drawing up the gathers to fit evenly. Baste and stitch. Press the seam down toward the cuff.
6. Turn under the seam allowance on the raw edge of the cuff and stitch it to stitching line neatly and carefully.
7. With right sides together, matching notches, underarm seams and balance mark to shoulder seam, pin the sleeve to the armhole, drawing up the gathers evenly on the cap. Baste and stitch the sleeve to the armhole with the sleeve uppermost. Press the seam toward the sleeve. Repeat steps 3-7 for second sleeve.

Make these nightshirts in cool cotton.

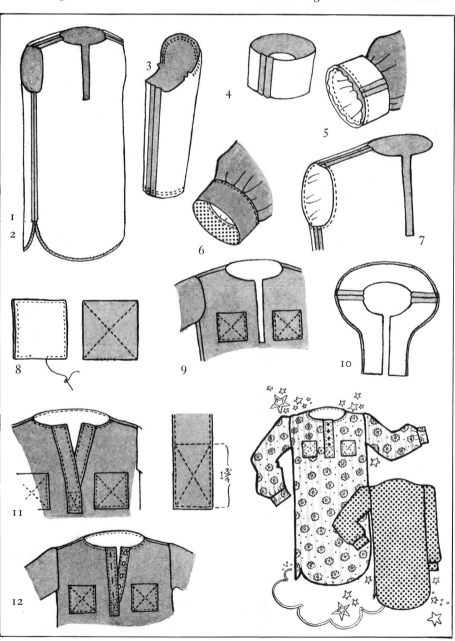

Pocket 8. Place the pocket pieces together with right sides facing. Baste and stitch around the three seam edges, leaving an opening for turning the pocket right side out. Grade the seams and cut across the corners. Turn the pocket right side out and baste around all edges. Slip-stitch the opening to close. Press flat. Topstitch the pocket with diagonal lines as shown. Repeat for second pocket.

9. Baste and stitch the pockets to the nightshirt.

Neck facing and opening 10. With right sides together, baste and stitch the back and front neck facings at the shoulder seams. Press the seams open. Finish the raw edges of the facing by turning under 3 mm ($\frac{1}{8}$ in) and top-stitching by machine. Press the edges flat. Mark the center fold on the front facing with basting stitches.

Tab fastening 11. With right sides together baste and stitch the straight edge of the neck facing to the center front opening. Grade the seams and press toward the center front.

With right sides together fold the facing along the basted fold line. With right sides together and shoulder seams matching, baste and stitch the facing to the nightshirt around the neck edge. Grade the seam allowances, clipping on curves and across corners where necessary.

Turn the facing to the wrong side and baste around the neckline and along the front fold line indicated on the pattern.

12. On the inside, overlap the tab ends, right over left for the woman's shirt and left over right for the man's. Clip 6 mm ($\frac{1}{4}$ in) into inner corners, then with right sides together baste and stitch the lower edges of the tab to the lower end of the opening.

Topstitch around the neck and all around each tab 1 cm ($\frac{3}{8}$ in) in from the edge. Stitch across the base of both tabs as shown.

Work four buttonholes at equally spaced intervals down the center of the front tab. Center and sew buttons in position on the undertab.

Short sleeves If short sleeves are desired, cut down the sleeve pattern to 12·5 cm (5 in) plus 1·5 cm ($\frac{5}{8}$ in) hem below the underarm.

Finish the sleeve hem as explained in step 2.

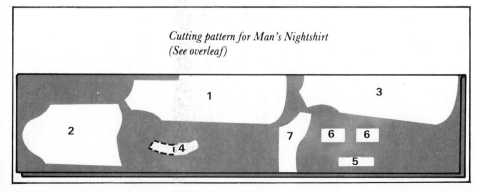

Cutting pattern for Man's Nightshirt (See overleaf)

Graph pattern for men's nightshirt

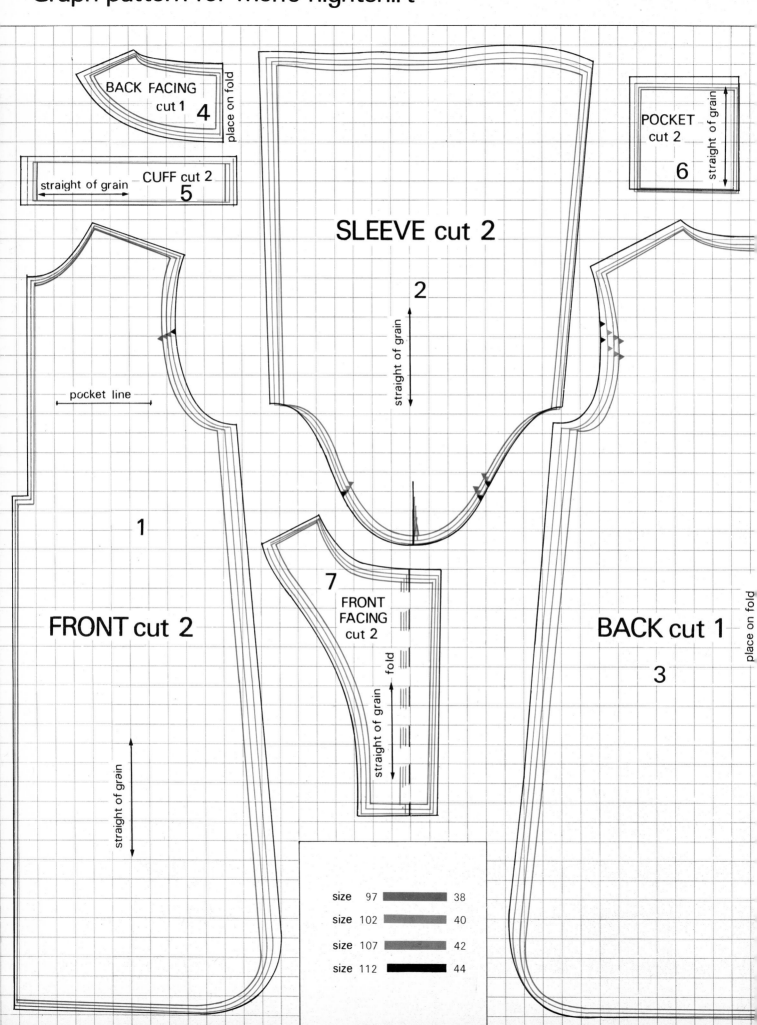

BACK FACING
cut 1   4

place on fold

CUFF cut 2
straight of grain   5

POCKET
cut 2
straight of grain
6

SLEEVE cut 2

2
straight of grain

pocket line

1

FRONT cut 2
straight of grain

7

FRONT
FACING
cut 2
straight of grain   fold

BACK cut 1

3

place on fold

size	97		38
size	102		40
size	107		42
size	112		44

Graph pattern for women's nightshirt

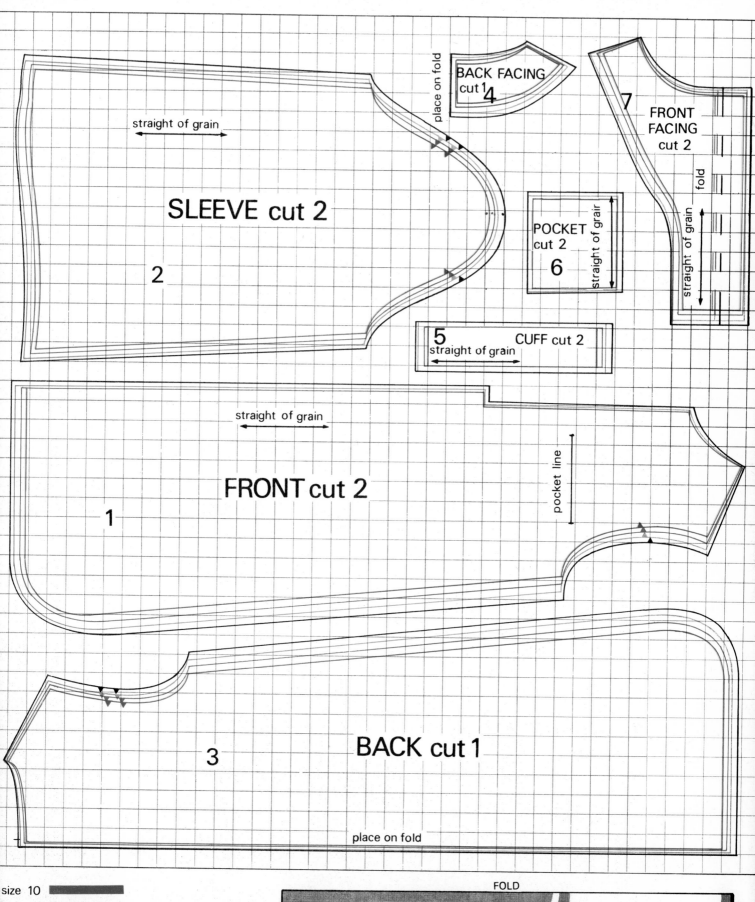

straight of grain

SLEEVE cut 2

2

place on fold

BACK FACING
cut 1 4

7 FRONT FACING cut 2

fold

straight of grain

POCKET
cut 2
6

straight of grain

5 CUFF cut 2
straight of grain

straight of grain

pocket line

FRONT cut 2

1

BACK cut 1

3

place on fold

size 10
size 12
size 14
size 16

each square=1 in (2.5 cm) sq

seam allowance not included

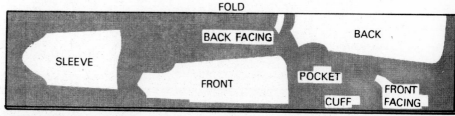

FOLD

SLEEVE

BACK FACING

BACK

FRONT

POCKET

CUFF

FRONT
FACING

115 cm (45 in) wide fabric without
nap. Layout for all sizes

selvages

Summer Separates

A raglan-sleeved blouse with open-or-closed collar and matching button-down skirt make this an ideal summer outfit which splits into useful separates. Make top and skirt to match or use contrasting or mix and match fabrics.
*Techniques included: raglan sleeves, gathered pockets, tie belt.

Measurements
The pattern is given in women's sizes 10, 12, 14 and 16. Each size is indicated on the graph pattern by a cutting line of a different color.

Making the pattern
Draw up the pattern to scale from the graph pattern given here. One square represents 2·5 cm (1 in) square.

Suggested fabrics
Cotton and synthetic blends, mix and match cottons, gingham, seersucker.

You will need:
To make the two-piece:
90 cm (36 in) wide fabric, all sizes, 5·20 m (5⅝ yd) or,
115 cm. (45 in) wide fabric, all sizes, 4·80 m (5¼ yd).
90 cm (36 in) wide woven interfacing, all sizes, 1 m (1 yd).
Twelve 1 cm (⅜ in) buttons.

To make the blouse:
90 cm (36 in) wide fabric, all sizes,

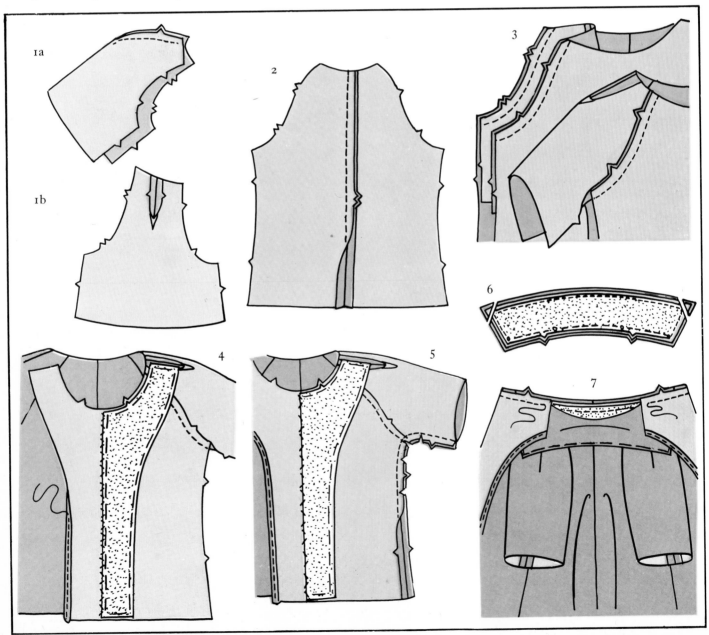

3 m ($3\frac{1}{4}$ yd) or,

115 cm (45 in) wide fabric, all sizes, 2·30 m ($2\frac{1}{2}$ yd).

To make the skirt:

90 cm (36 in) wide fabric, all sizes, 2·70 m ($2\frac{7}{8}$ yd) or,

115 cm (45 in) wide fabric, all sizes, 2·50 m ($2\frac{3}{4}$ yd).

Two hooks and eyes.

Sewing thread to match fabric.

Graph paper for pattern.

Cutting out

A seam allowance of 1·5 cm ($\frac{5}{8}$ in) has been allowed on all seam edges and a hem allowance of 6·5 cm ($2\frac{5}{8}$ in).

To make the blouse
Front and back, *raglan sleeves

1. With right sides together, and notches matching, baste and stitch shoulder darts of sleeves. Press darts open.

2. With right sides together and notches matching, baste and stitch center back seam. Press seam open.

3. With right sides together and notches and neck edges matching, baste and stitch front and back sleeve to front and back bodices, having the sleeve uppermost. Ease in fullness between notches. Press seams toward sleeve.

Repeat for second sleeve.

To finish outer edge of front facing, turn under 6 mm ($\frac{1}{4}$ in) and stitch.

4. Baste interfacing to wrong side of front bodice and neck edge. Catch stitch interfacing to fold line.

5. With right sides together and notches matching, baste and stitch the side seams and underarm seams. Clip curves and press seams open.

Collar 6. Baste interfacing to wrong side of one collar piece. With right sides together, matching center backs and circles at center fronts, baste and stitch collar facing to collar around outer edge to center fronts. Trim interfacing close to stitching. Grade seam and cut across corners. Turn right side out, baste close to stitched edges and press flat.

7. With right sides together, matching center backs, circles to shoulder darts, notches and circles at center front, pin and baste under-collar and inter-

A loose fitting top and button-down skirt make this outfit the perfect choice for summer holiday wear.

facing to back neck edge from shoulder to shoulder and stitch. Pin and baste the under and top collar to the front neck edge from shoulder to center fronts as shown. With right sides together and notches matching, fold front facing over the collar to shoulder and baste.

Stitch from shoulders to front edges through all thicknesses.

Trim interfacing close to stitching. Grade seam, clip curves and cut across corners. Turn facing to inside and baste along folded edge.

8. On the inside, clip back neck seam allowance to circle at shoulder. Press seam toward collar.

9. Turn under 1·5 cm ($\frac{5}{8}$ in) seam allowance on the top collar and slip-stitch to stitching line as shown. Turn under seam allowance of facing and catch stitch to shoulder dart.

Sleeve hems 10. Finish the lower edge of the sleeve with hand or machine overcasting. Turn up hem allowance and baste along folded edge. Sew hem to sleeve using invisible hemming stitch.

Repeat for second sleeve hem.

Blouse hem 11. Turn out the front facing at lower edge. Turn 6 mm ($\frac{1}{4}$ in) to inside around lower edge and

90cm (36in) wide fabric with nap. Layout for all sizes.

90cm (36in) wide woven interface for all sizes.

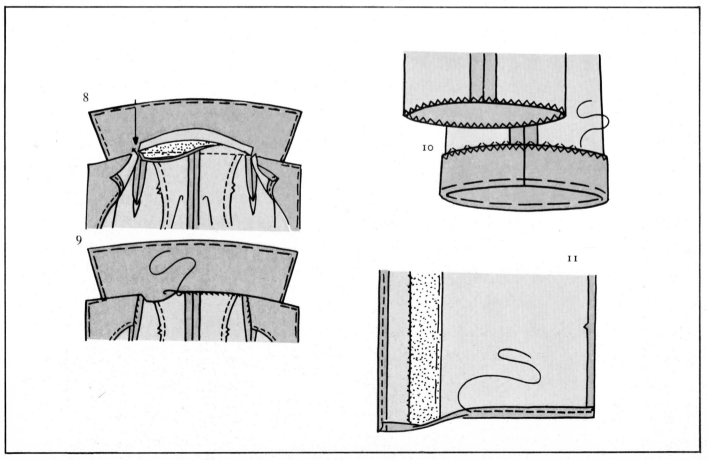

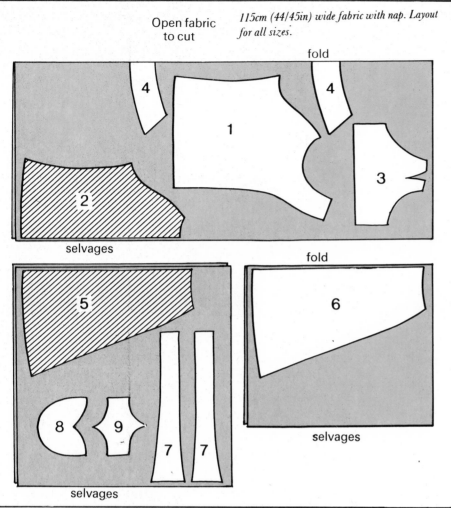

Open fabric to cut

115cm (44/45in) wide fabric with nap. Layout for all sizes.

fold

4   4

1

2

3

selvages

fold

5

6

8   9

7   7

selvages

selvages

then a further 1 cm ($\frac{3}{8}$ in). Baste and press flat.

Fold facing to inside. Topstitch 6 mm ($\frac{1}{4}$ in) in from lower edge, front edge and collar as shown.

To finish 12. Make hand-worked or machine buttonholes on right front as indicated on pattern. Sew buttons to left front to correspond with button-holes.

To make the skirt

Front facing and side seams 13. Baste interfacing to wrong side of skirt fronts. Catch stitch to fold line. To finish raw edge of facing, turn under 6 mm ($\frac{1}{4}$ in) and machine stitch. Turn facing to inside and baste along folded edge.

With right sides together and notches matching, baste and stitch side seams. Press seams open.

Gathered pockets 14. Stay stitch inner corner of pocket. Work two rows of gathering stitches along top edge of pocket. Draw up gathers until pocket fits welt as shown.

15. With right sides together, baste and stitch pocket welt to pocket. Trim and press seam toward welt.

16. With right sides together and

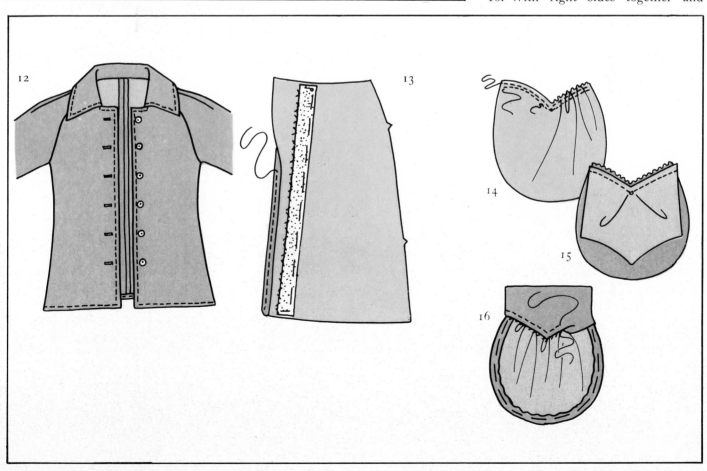

Graph pattern for separates

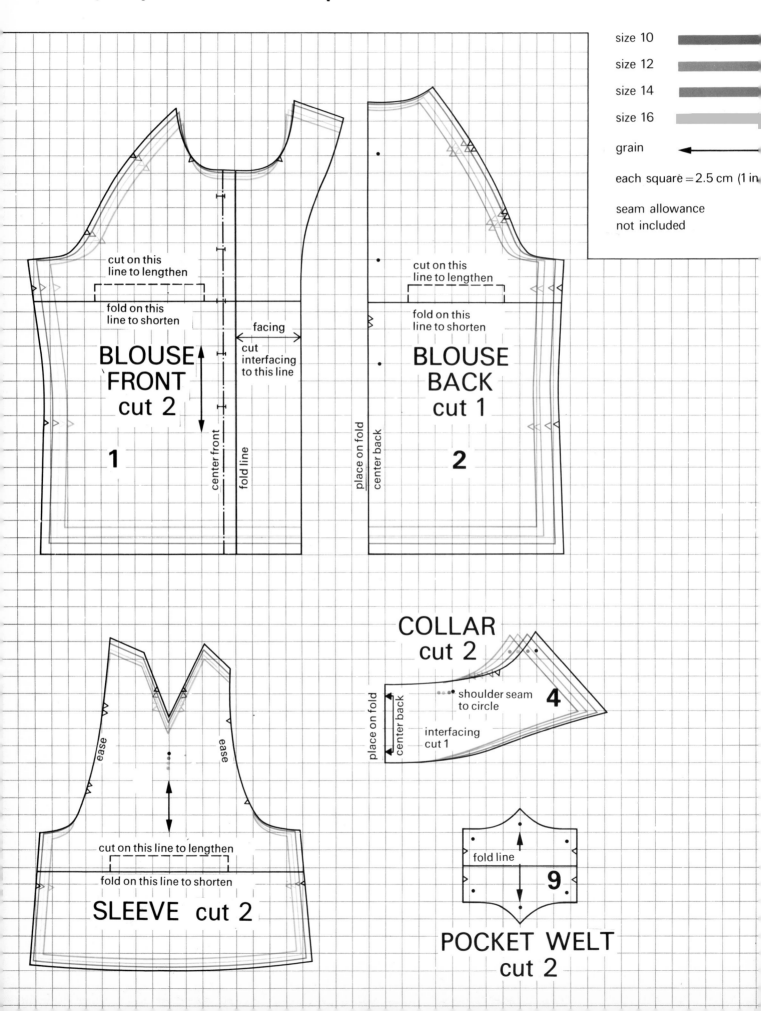

size 10
size 12
size 14
size 16

grain

each square = 2.5 cm (1 in

seam allowance
not included

cut on this
line to lengthen

fold on this
line to shorten

facing

cut
interfacing
to this line

BLOUSE
FRONT
cut 2

center front

fold line

1

cut on this
line to lengthen

fold on this
line to shorten

BLOUSE
BACK
cut 1

place on fold

center back

2

COLLAR
cut 2

place on fold

center back

shoulder seam
to circle

interfacing
cut 1

4

ease

ease

cut on this line to lengthen

fold on this line to shorten

SLEEVE cut 2

fold line

9

POCKET WELT
cut 2

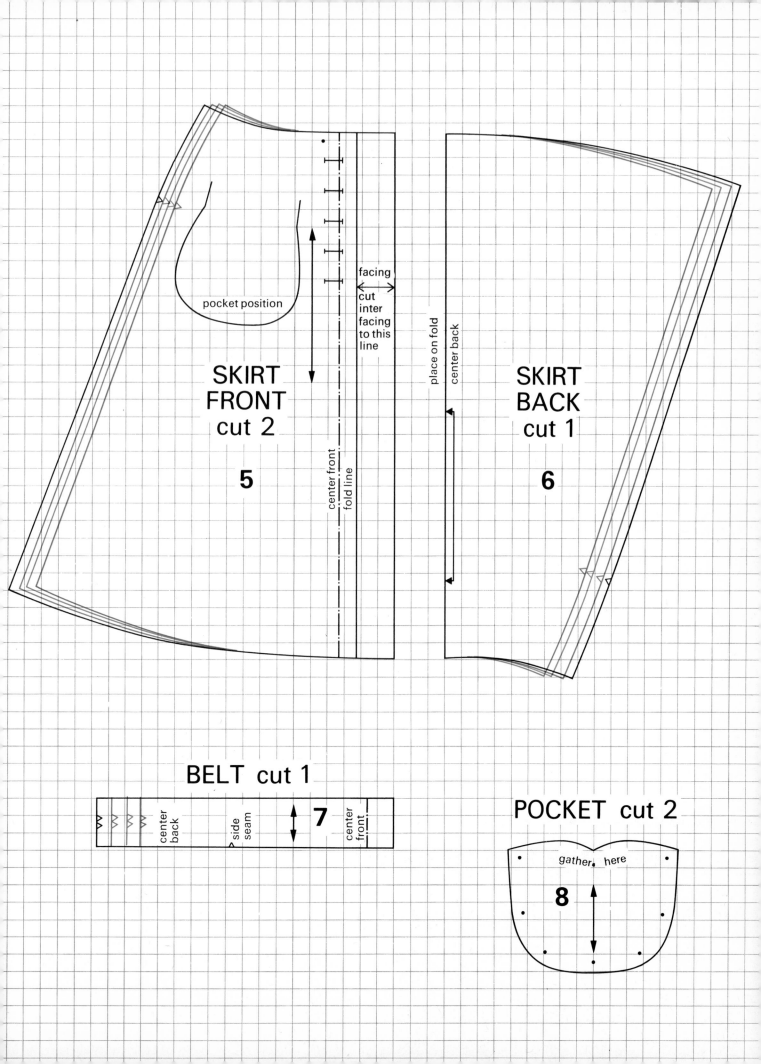

SKIRT
FRONT
cut 2

5

pocket position

facing
cut
inter
facing
to this
line

center front

fold line

SKIRT
BACK
cut 1

6

place on fold

center back

BELT cut 1

center
back

side
seam

7

center
front

POCKET cut 2

gather here

8

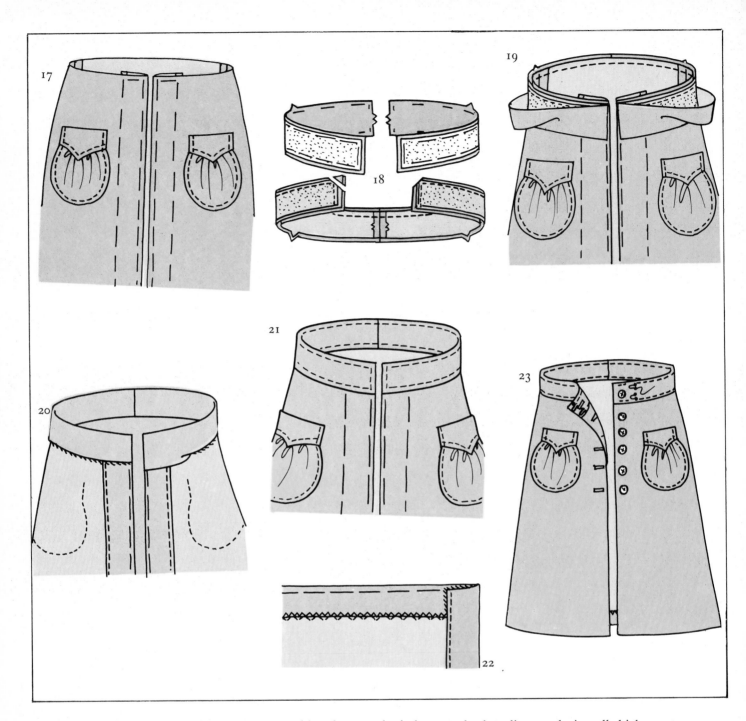

notches matching, fold welt along fold line. Baste and stitch outer edges of welt. Trim seam and cut across corners. Turn right side out. Turn under seam allowance of welt facing and slip-stitch to stitching line. On right side, topstitch 6 mm ($\frac{1}{4}$ in) away from inner shaped seam of welt as shown. Turn under seam allowance around outer edge of pocket and baste. Repeat for second pocket.

17. Baste pockets in positions indicated on pattern and topstitch 6 mm ($\frac{1}{4}$ in) in from outer edges of pockets as shown.

Waistband 18. Baste interfacing to wrong sides of waistband pieces. With right sides together and notches

matching, baste and stitch center back seams of waistband and waistband facing. Press seams open. With right sides together, baste and stitch waistband facing to waistband along unnotched edge and ends. Trim interfacing to stitching line, grade seam and cut across corners. Turn right side out, baste stitched edges and press.

19. Placing right sides together and matching center backs, notches to side seams and center fronts, baste and stitch waistband to skirt. Trim interfacing close to stitching and grade seam allowance. Press seam toward waistband.

20. On the inside, turn under seam allowance and slip-stitch to stitching

line, enclosing all thicknesses.

21. On the outside, topstitch around all edges of waistband.

Skirt hem 22. Try on skirt and mark the hem. Turn out front facing at lower edge. Trim hem allowance to an even width, turn up hem and baste close to folded edge. Finish raw edge with hand or machine overcasting. Sew the hem to the skirt using invisible hemming stitch. Turn facing to inside and slip-stitch to hem as shown. Press flat.

To finish 23. Make hand-worked or machine buttonholes on right front. Sew buttons to left front to correspond with buttonholes. Sew hooks and eyes to waistband as shown.

Classic Shirt

Classic shirt

A timeless style that changes its look with the way you wear it. This version, in supple synthetic crêpe, would look just as good in fine cotton, silk or wool. For a different look you could make it without a collar, finishing the neck with the collarband on its own.

*Techniques included: collar and collarband, sleeve opening with wrap extension.

Measurements

The pattern is given in women's sizes 10, 12, 14 and 16. Each size is indicated on the graph pattern by a cutting line of a different color.

Making the pattern

Draw up the pattern to scale from the graph pattern given here. One square represents 2·5 cm (1 in) square.

Suggested fabrics

Synthetic crêpe, voile, gingham, silk, wool and cotton mixtures or a fine cotton and polyester blend.

You will need:

90 cm (36 in) fabric with nap, all sizes, 3·10 m (3⅜ yd).
90 cm (36 in) woven interfacing, all sizes, 40 cm (⅜ yd).
Nine 1 cm (⅜ in) buttons.
Sewing thread to match fabric.
Graph paper for pattern.

Cutting out

No seam allowance is included on the pattern so add 1·5 cm (⅝ in) for seam and hem allowances in cutting out the shirt.

To make the shirt

Facings 1. Finish the outer edges of the facings. Placing right sides together pin, baste and stitch the facings to the front edges. Do not stitch them along the neck and hem edges. Turn the facings to the inside, baste close to the stitched edge and press.

Shoulder and side seams 2. Baste and stitch underarm darts on each front section. Press. Baste and stitch the shoulder seams, making flat fell seams stitched on the outside of the shirt. Baste and stitch the side seams as far as circle on pattern so that the folded edge of the flat fell seam lies toward the front.

Hemming the tails 3. Snip into the front side seam allowance at the bottom of the seams and trim the front seam allowance for flat fell seaming.

Fold the back seam allowance over the trimmed front seam. Pin and baste.

Pin and baste the hem on the front and back to the wrong side. Where the side seam and front hem merge, pin the folded edge of the back hem in line with the side seam. Machine stitch both hems, continuing the stitching into the folded flat fell seam edge so that you stitch the hem and flat fell side seam in one operation.

Stitch across the top of the hem to hold it firmly in place.

*Collar and collarband 4. Pin and baste interfacing to wrong side of one collar piece and to one collarband piece. The interfacing should go on the piece that will be uppermost.

5. Place the top (interfaced) and under-collar pieces together, with right sides facing. Pin, baste and stitch along the front edges and the upper curved seam. Trim the seam allowance to 6 mm (¼ in), trim across the corners and turn right side out. Baste along the stitched edges and press. Topstitch 6 mm (¼ in) from the edge if you wish.

Matching all markings, place the collar between the inner and outer collarband pieces and stitch with right sides together, leaving the lower edge open.

6. Trim the seam allowance on the stitched edges of the collarband to 6 mm (¼ in) and turn right side out. Baste along the stitched edges and press.

Stitching on the collar 7. Baste the front facing to the shirt along the neckline. Pin the inner collarband along the inside of the neckline with the raw edges even. Baste, stitch and trim the seam allowance.

Turn under the seam allowance on the outer collarband; lay it over the stitching line to cover the machine stitches. Slip-stitch in place neatly.

*Sleeve openings with wrap extensions and sleeve seams 8. Cut a straight strip of fabric, 4 by 20 cm (1½ by 8 in). Cut the sleeve opening along the marked line. Pin and baste the fabric strip along the opening with the right side of the strip to the wrong side of the sleeve. Stitch along the opening taking 6 mm (¼ in) seam allowance on the facing but tapering toward the point. At the point pivot the work on the needle, ease the fold to the back of the needle and stitch along the other side. Press the seam toward the strip.

Fold in the long raw edge of the strip, pin and baste it over the seam on the outside of the sleeve and topstitch. Press the wrap to the inside of the sleeve. Repeat for second sleeve. Pin, baste and stitch the sleeve seams with flat fell seams.

Add two rows of gathering stitches around the lower edge of each sleeve.

Cuffs 9. Pin and baste interfacing to the wrong side of each cuff. Catch stitch to fold line.

Placing right sides together, fold cuff lengthwise and stitch each side up to the seam allowance at the top edge. Trim the seam allowance and turn right side out. Edge baste and press.

10. Placing right sides together, pin the cuff to lower end of sleeve, so that interfaced half will be the upper half of the cuff. Pull up the gathers on sleeve until they fit the cuff. Baste, distributing the gathers evenly and stitch. Trim interfacing close to the stitching. Trim seam and press toward cuff.

11. Turn under the remaining raw edge on cuff, pin and slip-stitch over the seam on the inside. Attach second cuff in the same way. Topstitch cuffs 6 mm (¼ in) from the edge if you wish.

Setting in the sleeves 12. Make two rows of running stitches around the top of each sleeve, one on each side of the seamline. Carefully draw up the ease, which is approximately 4 cm (1½ in), and wind the gathering threads onto a pin. Shrink in the fullness, using a sleeve board; steam will help if the fabric does not mark.

13. Pin sleeves into armholes, right sides facing, matching seams and notches. Any fullness on the sleeves should be evenly distributed. Baste in the sleeves and stitch. Press seams toward the shirt and trim for flat fell seaming. Complete flat fell seams and press.

To finish 14. Make hand-worked or machine buttonholes in positions marked on front of shirt, also making one buttonhole on collarband and on each cuff. Sew on buttons to correspond.

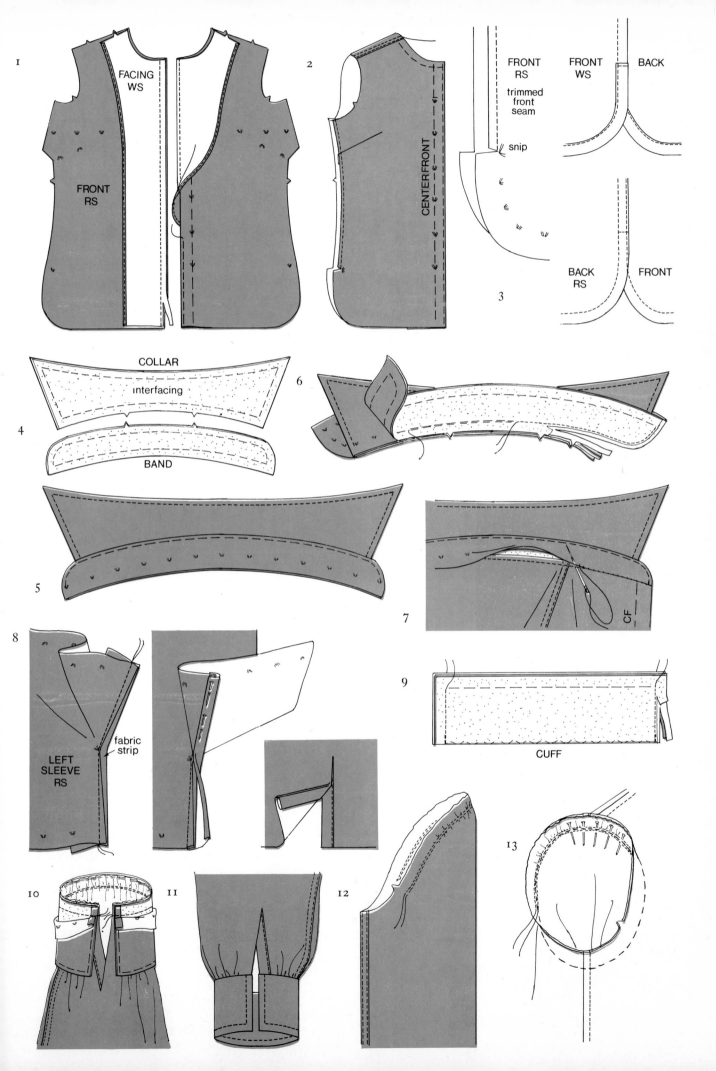

1

FACING
WS

FRONT
RS

2

CENTERFRONT

3

FRONT
RS

trimmed
front
seam

snip

FRONT
WS

BACK

BACK
RS

FRONT

4

COLLAR

interfacing

BAND

6

5

7

CF

8

LEFT
SLEEVE
RS

fabric
strip

9

CUFF

10

11

12

13

Graph pattern for shirt

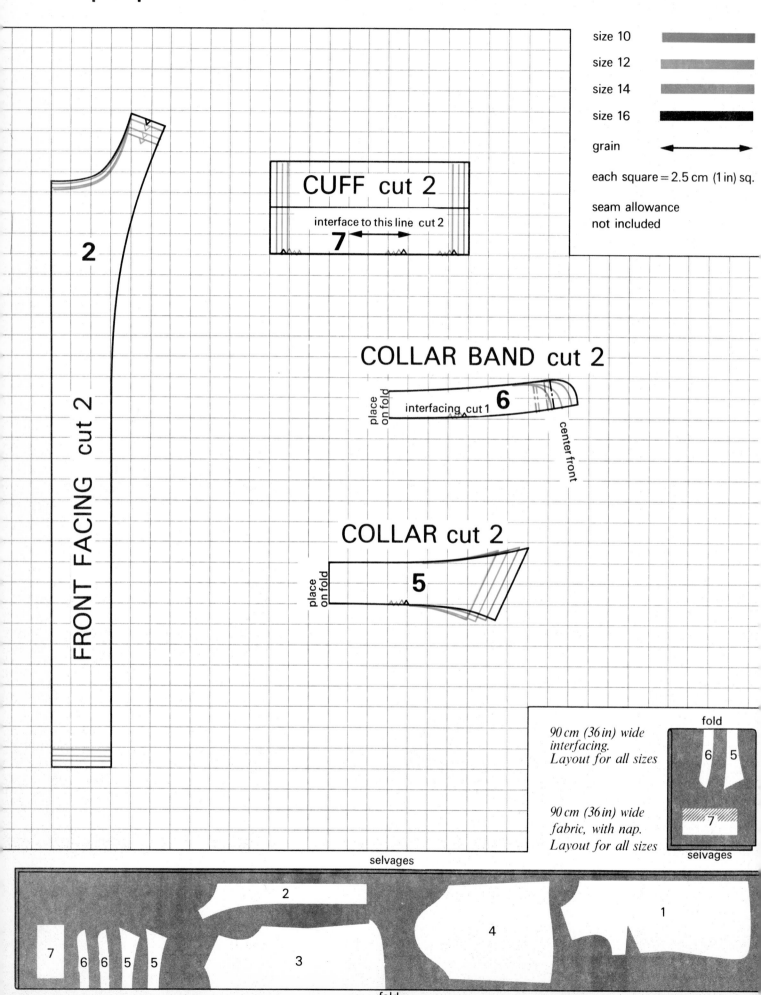

size 10

size 12

size 14

size 16

grain

each square = 2.5 cm (1 in) sq.

seam allowance
not included

CUFF cut 2

interface to this line cut 2

7

2

FRONT FACING cut 2

COLLAR BAND cut 2

place
on fold

interfacing cut 1 **6**

center front

COLLAR cut 2

place
on fold

5

90 cm (36 in) wide
interfacing.
Layout for all sizes

fold

6 5

90 cm (36 in) wide
fabric, with nap.
Layout for all sizes

7

selvages

selvages

2

1

4

7

6 6 5 5

3

fold

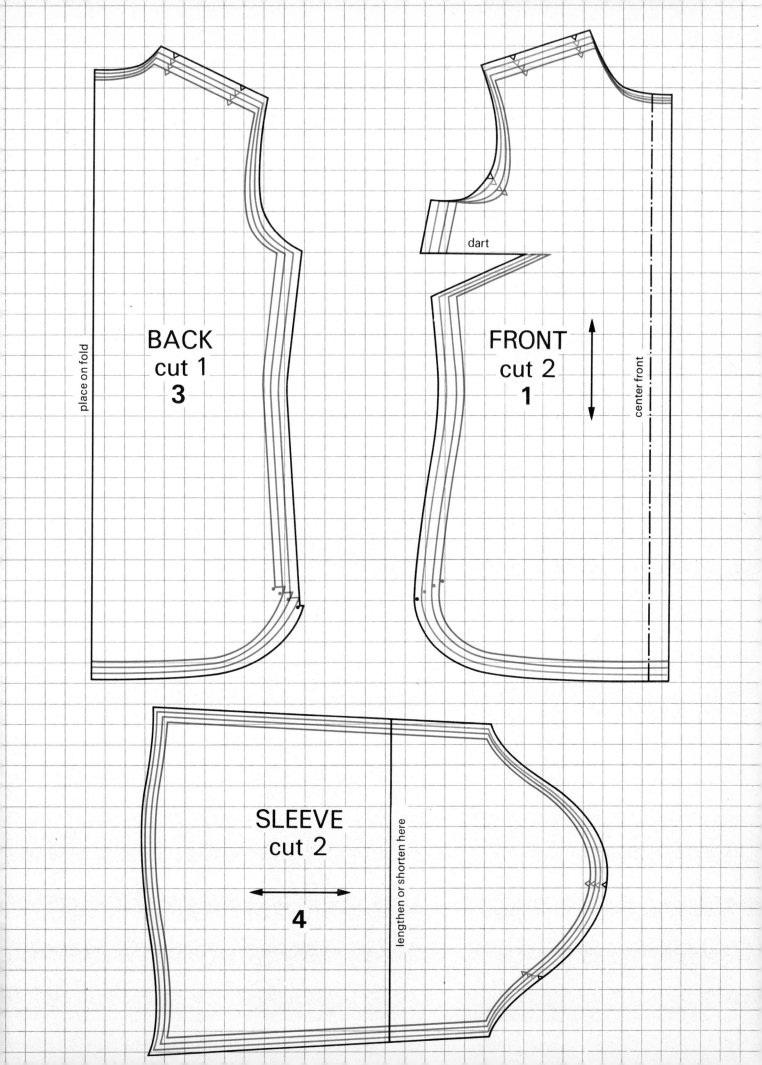

BACK
cut 1
3

place on fold

FRONT
cut 2
1

dart

center front

SLEEVE
cut 2

4

lengthen or shorten here

Knife-pleated Skirt

More basic know-how
Working with pleats

Pleats are folds of fabric which provide controlled fullness in certain parts of a garment. They can be placed either singly or in a series, and can be pressed flat or left unpressed, as the style of the garment dictates. Pressed pleats give a smooth, slimming line to a garment and unpressed pleats a softer, fuller shape.

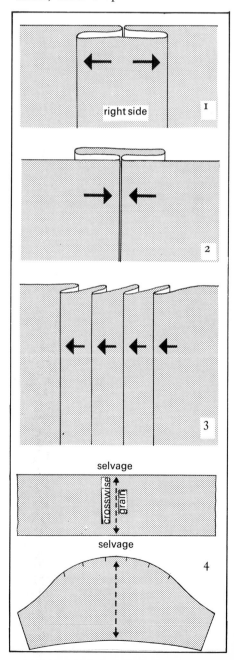

1. *Knife pleats.* 2. *Inverted pleat.*
3. *Box pleats.* 4. *Unpressed pleats.*
5. *Making a contrast fabric
inverted pleat.* 6. *Top-stitching
pleats.*

Fabrics

The type of fabric determines how the pleats hang, so choose it carefully. Consider the grain and check the layout given with the pattern, remembering that pleats on the lengthwise grain hang well, while those on the crosswise grain tend to stand out.

Never try to save fabric by cutting one skirt pattern piece on the lengthwise grain and the other on the crosswise grain of the fabric – the effect can be disastrous.

Any firmly woven fabric such as wool, gabardine or linen will hold a pleat well, but pleats in loosely woven fabrics, knits and silk look better if they are topstitched.

Patterns for pleated skirts should be bought by the hip measurement and patterns with pleated bodices by the bust measurement. If any alteration in width is required, distribute it evenly throughout all the pleats to keep them uniform. When tapering

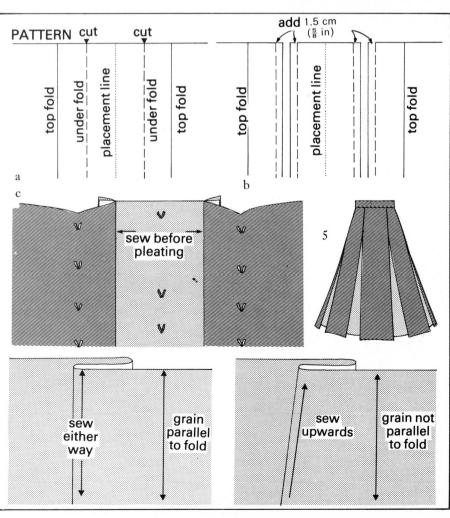

pleats to fit the waistline, keep the top fold on the same grain and make any adjustment to the under fold, remembering to distribute alterations evenly.

Types of pleat

Box pleats These are made by making two equal folds and turning them away from each other, the under folds meeting in the center beneath the pleat (fig. 1 p. 92).

Inverted pleats Inverted pleats are the reverse of box pleats. Two folds of equal depth are turned toward each other to meet at the center, the fullness lying underneath (fig. 2).

Knife pleats These are narrow folds running in one direction (fig. 3).

Unpressed pleats Unpressed pleats can be folded in the same way as pressed pleats, but the unpressed ones are left to hang free so they may fall in their own natural line.

If a bunchy effect is required for a particular design, the fabric should be cut on the crosswise grain. Sometimes it is best to cut a pleated sleeve crown this way (fig. 4).
A bunchy effect is not generally suitable for unpressed pleats on a skirt, so cut on the lengthwise grain.

Contrast fabric inverted pleat Inverted pleat underlays can look attractive in a contrast fabric. If the pattern does not have a separate piece for the underlay, adjust it as follows.
Cut the pattern on the under fold line and add 1·5 cm ($\frac{5}{8}$ in) seam allowance to all cut edges.
Sew the contrast fabric to the under fold line before making the pleat (fig. 5).

Topstitching pleats It is possible to make a fashion feature of topstitched pleats. Baste the pleats before stitching. A bold effect is required, so use a large needle in the sewing

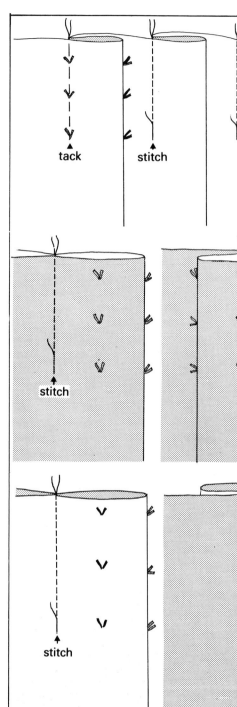

7. *Marking pleats.* 8. *Pinning pleats.* 9. *Basting pleat folds.* 10. *Stitching knife pleats.* 11. *Stitching box pleats.* 12. *Stitching inverted pleats.* 13. *To reduce bulk on inverted pleats, cut away fabric as shown.* 14. *To hem a pleated skirt, snip the seam as shown and turn up hem to this depth.*

machine, set the machine to the longest stitch and use buttonhole twist for top and bobbin thread.
Before working the topstitching on a garment, take a spare piece of the fabric, make some pleats and practice the stitches, adjusting the tension

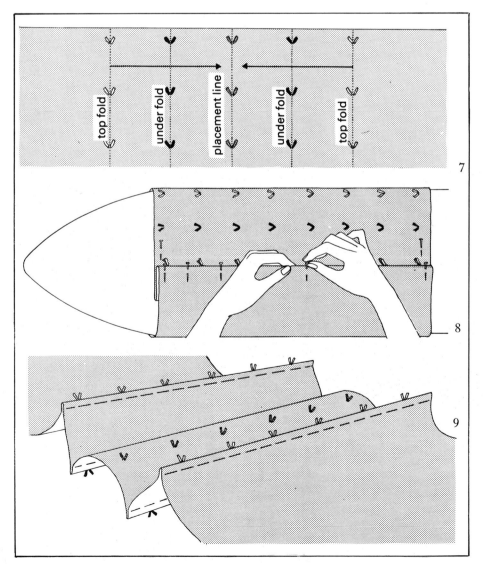

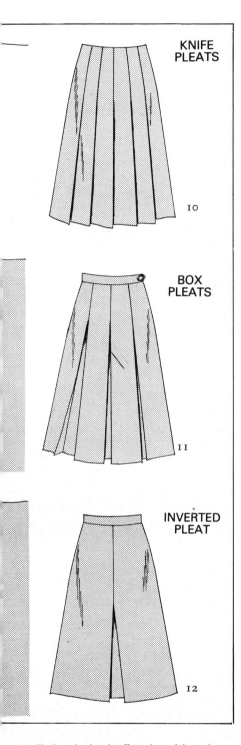

KNIFE
PLEATS

10

BOX
PLEATS

11

INVERTED
PLEAT

12

The best stage at which to work the topstitching is before the skirt is sewn onto the waistband or the bodice, and after the hemline is finished.

The general construction of pleats

All pleats should be shaped with precision, so always transfer the pattern markings accurately, using different colored tailor's tacks for the top and under folds and for the placement line (fig. 7). Lay the fabric on a flat surface. An ironing board is ideal, as the fabric can be pinned to the cover when the initial folding takes place. Pin each pleat at the upper and lower ends and then along the length, keeping it free from the under layer (fig. 8).

Beginning at the lower edge, baste the pleat folds on the right side, then turn the fabric over and baste the folds on

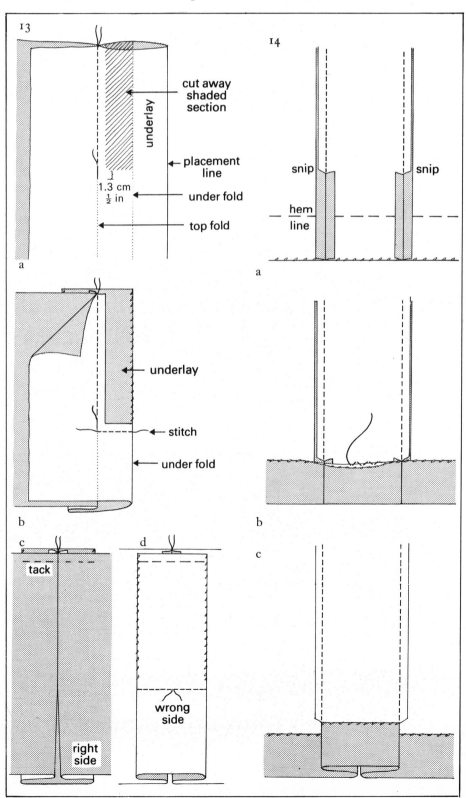

until the desired effect is achieved.

For fine fabrics which do not hold a pleat well it is best to topstitch along both top and under folds for the entire length of the pleat.

As long as the pleat is on the straight grain of the fabric, it can be stitched either from the top or the bottom. If the grain is not straight it is better to stitch from the bottom of the pleat upward to avoid stretching the fabric (fig. 6).

If the fabric is stretched it will create a slight fullness at the hem which means that the pleat will not hang straight.

the wrong side (fig. 9). Baste down any which are to be topstitched. Baste across pleats at waistline and baste up the garment for fitting.

Fitting When the skirt is basted, try it on to make sure that the pleats hang straight. If the skirt is tight over the hips or stomach, adjust each pleat under fold until it hangs correctly. However, the problem should not arise if the pattern has been adjusted properly before cutting out.

If the pleats spring open at the hem, raise the waistline. Pin the skirt to a length of tape fastened around the waist, and raise the fabric until the pleats hang straight. Re-pin tape to new waistline and adjust the under folds evenly.

If the pleats overlap at the hem, lower the waist slightly in the same way and adjust the pleat under folds evenly.

Finishing the pleats When finishing pleats always work with the front and back of the skirt separated. Mark any fitting alterations before unbasting the side seams and starting work on the pleats.

Stitch knife pleats on the wrong side for a smooth effect, making sure to finish them securely at the lower end (fig. 10). Stitch box pleats on the right side for desired length and press pleat flat (fig. 11). Stitch inverted pleats on the wrong side and press flat (fig. 12). If inverted pleats are being made in a heavy fabric, a section of the under fold can be cut away as shown, to reduce bulk (figs. 13a-d).

Machine stitch pleat to the length required and cut away half the under pleat as shown. Finish the outside raw edge and machine stitch across each side of the pleat, keeping the fold away from the background fabric. Baste across the top of the pleat.

Hemming pleated skirts Run a line of basting stitches along the hemline. Trim the hem evenly and overcast the raw edge. Measure the hem depth above the hemline and snip seams at this point. Press the seam flat above the snip and open below it (fig. 14). Slip-stitch hem, re-baste pleats and press. (Also see Hems.)

Knife pleated skirt
Flattering to any figure, this skirt has

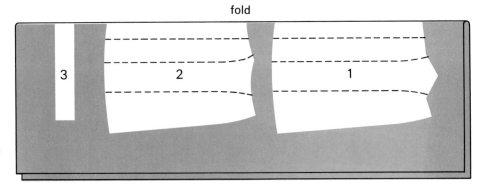

fold

3 2 1

selvages

slim elegant lines with roomy knife pleats at the back and front to give ease of movement. It can be made in any crisp fabric that pleats well.

Measurements
The pattern is given in women's sizes 10, 12, 14 and 16. Each size is indicated on the graph pattern by a cutting line of a different color.

Making the pattern
Draw up the pattern to scale from the graph pattern given here. One square represents 2·5 cm (1 in) square.

Suggested fabrics
Wool, worsted, gabardine, linen, firmly woven tweed

You will need:
140 cm (54 in) wide fabric, all sizes, 1·80 m (2 yd) or
1 m (1 yd) 2·5 cm (1 in) wide belting.
18 cm (7 in) zipper.
Two hooks and eyes.
Sewing thread to match fabric.
Graph paper for pattern.

Cutting out
No seam allowance is included on the pattern so add 1·5 cm ($\frac{5}{8}$ in) for seams, but add a 2 cm ($\frac{3}{4}$ in) allowance at the waist edge and a 2·5 cm seam allowance for zipper on skirt back. Add 6·5 cm ($2\frac{1}{2}$ in) hem allowance.

To make the skirt
Preparing the pleats 1. Mark the pleat lines on the back and front skirt sections with tailor's tacks. Connect the balance marks with horizontal lines of basting.
2. Lay the pleats from right to left on the outside of the skirt. Fold, pin and baste them securely down the edge.

Then press the pleats very lightly. With the right sides facing, raw edges even, pin and baste the side seams. Try on the skirt to check the fit (see Basic pattern alterations). When you have made any necessary adjustments, fit the skirt again with the basting at the pleat hems removed. The pleats should hang straight and closed, not jutting forward and pulling open. If you see the pleats spreading, fan-like, toward the side seams, lift the skirt and pleats into the waist until the pleats hang straight. If one pleat is hanging badly this will need to be pulled up from the inside.

Topstitch each pleat 2 mm ($\frac{1}{16}$ in) from the edge as far as the hip line of the skirt.

Seams and zipper 3. Stitch all the seams, starting at the top and working downward. Leave the left side seam open from the circle to the waist edge for inserting the zipper. Insert the zipper using the concealed method (see Zippers).

Waistband 4. Pin, baste and stitch the waistband to the skirt, making sure that all the pleats are caught flat and firmly into the stitching line. Trim and press the seam upward. Apply the stiffening and finish the waistband (see Waistbands and belts). Sew on hooks and eyes.

Hem 5. Try on the skirt to check the length; mark and stitch the hem (see Hems and also Working with pleats). When turning up the hem, make the hem at the inner crease of the pleat about 6 mm ($\frac{1}{4}$ in) shorter; this keeps the inside of the pleat from showing on the right side.

Give pleats a final pressing; carefully press under the pleats on the wrong side to remove any inpressions on the fabric.

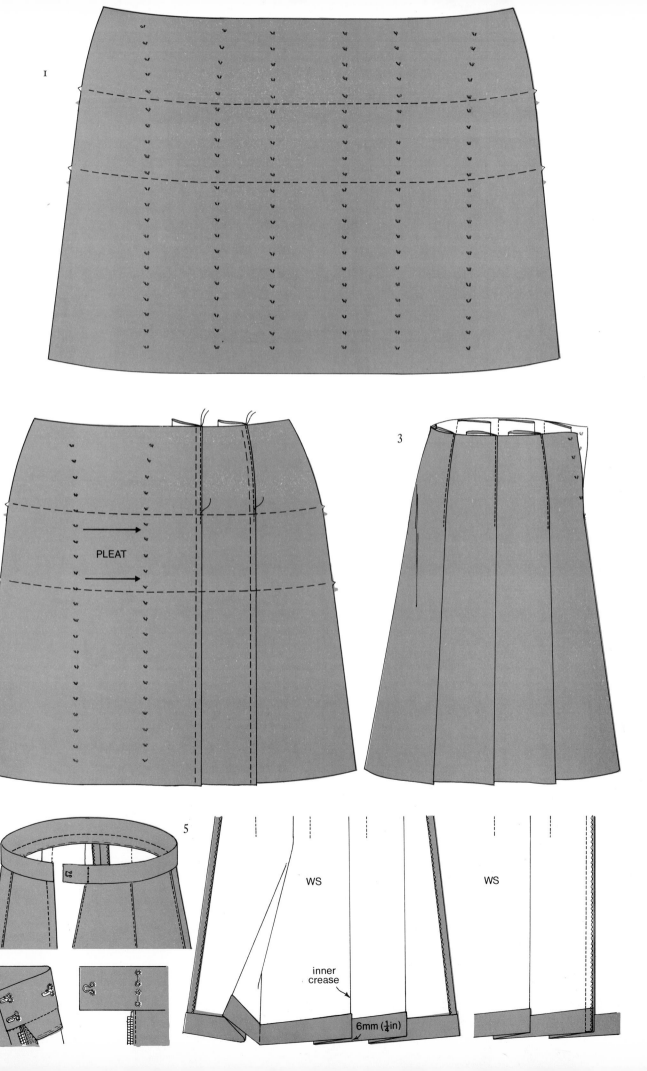

1

2

PLEAT

3

4

5

WS

WS

inner
crease

6mm (¼in)

Graph pattern for pleated skirt

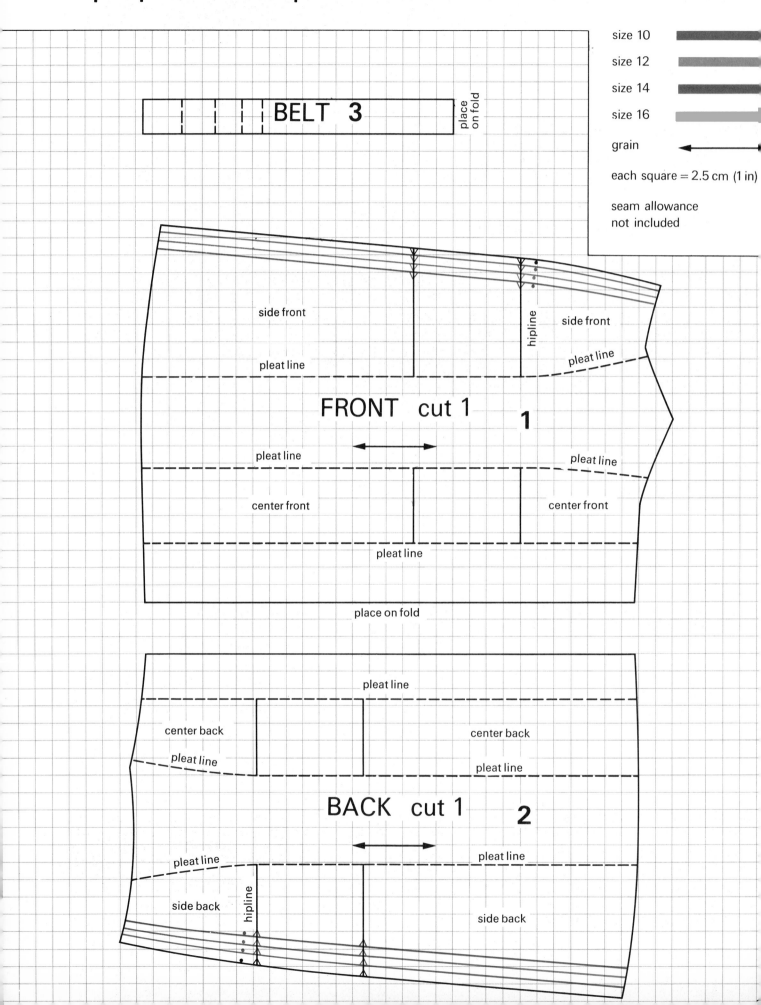

size 10

size 12

size 14

size 16

grain

each square = 2.5 cm (1 in)

seam allowance
not included

BELT 3

place on fold

side front

side front

hipline

pleat line

pleat line

FRONT cut 1

1

pleat line

pleat line

center front

center front

pleat line

place on fold

pleat line

center back

center back

pleat line

pleat line

BACK cut 1

2

pleat line

pleat line

side back

hipline

side back

Unisex Jackets

More basic know-how
Bound buttonholes

Fabric-bound buttonholes are not difficult to make and give a good-looking finish to lightweight jackets, dresses or suits. Any firmly-woven fabric is suitable as long as it is not too thick.

Size and spacing The buttonhole length is determined by the size of the button used, so buttons should be purchased before making buttonholes. To establish the buttonhole length needed, measure the diameter of the button, then add its thickness. Button positions are marked on the pattern. However, if you have had to lengthen or shorten the pattern or are using a different sized button than the one specified, you must alter the buttonhole spacing accordingly. For button-down styles the final buttonhole should be placed about 10 cm (4 in) above the hemline.

Making bound buttonholes Before embarking on your finished work, try out the method using spare scraps of your fabric to perfect the technique. Each buttonhole requires a piece of fabric cut either on the bias or on the straight grain, 2·5 cm (1 in) longer than the opening and approximately 5 cm (2 in) wide. Mark the buttonhole lines on the garment (fig. 1). Place the square of fabric on the right side of the garment and baste (fig. 2). On the wrong side, machine-stitch the outline of the buttonhole using a small stitch size. Pivot the needle at

1. Marking position for buttonhole.
2. Fabric for binding pinned in place.
3. Stitching the buttonhole outline.
4. Clipping the buttonhole.
5. Turning binding to wrong side.
6, 7. Fold binding to meet in the center and overcast the opening.
8. Secure rolled edge with prick stitch.
9. Slipstitch facing to finished buttonhole. 10. Finished buttonhole.

the corners to shape a perfect rectangle. Do not start at a corner (fig. 3); overlap beginning and end of stitching slightly to secure.

With small pointed scissors cut down the center through both thicknesses to within 6 mm ($\frac{1}{4}$ in) of either end. Cut diagonally into each corner (fig. 4).

On small buttonholes turn strip to the wrong side (fig. 5) and fold the sides of the facing to meet in the middle so that there is an equal fold on each side (fig. 6). Overcast opening temporarily (fig. 7) and work two or three overcasting stitches at each end to hold the folds in place. Press on wrong side.

Large buttonholes are made in the same way, but each rolled edge must be worked separately and secured with a small prick stitch along the seamline on the right side (fig. 8).

To finish the buttonhole feel through the facing and mark buttonhole ends with two pins. Cut along the marked buttonhole lines to the width of each buttonhole opening. Fold under the edges and slip-stitch onto the wrong side of the buttonhole (fig. 9). Fig. 10 shows the finished buttonhole from the right side.

Unisex jackets

These blouson jackets in a classic design are ideal for all seasons. The same pattern will fit both young men and women. The sleeves, made in two pieces, are neatly buttoned at the wrist and the jacket is fully lined for extra warmth.

Measurements

The pattern is given in women's sizes 12, 14, 16 and 18 and in men's chest

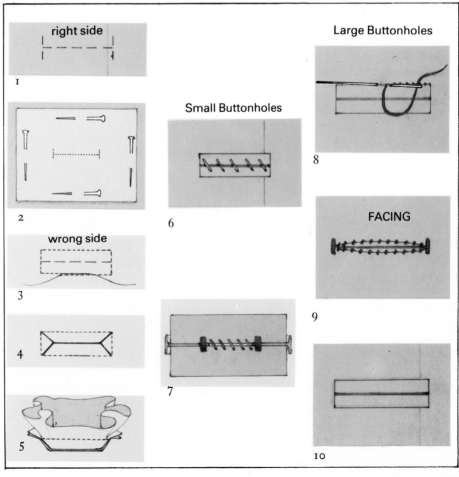

Comfortable unisex jackets.

sizes 81 cm (32 in), 87 cm (34 in) and 92 cm (36 in). Each size is indicated on the graph pattern by a cutting line of a different color.

Note For young men's garments more ease is required, so use size 12 (87 cm) for an 81 cm (32 in) chest and so on.

Making the pattern
Draw up the pattern to scale from the graph pattern given here. One square represents 2·5 cm (1 in) square.

Suggested fabrics
Plaid wool, corduroy, denim, cotton.

You will need:
140 cm (54 in) fabric without nap, all sizes 2·60 m (2¾ yd) or,

90 cm (36 in) wide fabric, with nap, all sizes 3·50 m (3¾ yd).
90 cm (36 in) wide lining, all sizes 1·90 m (2 yd).
90 cm (36 in) wide lightweight woven interfacing, all sizes 1 m (1 yd).
Eight 2 cm (¾ in) buttons.
Sewing thread to match fabric.
Buttonhole twist.
Graph paper for pattern.

Cutting out
No seam allowance is included on the pattern so add 1·5 cm (⅝ in) to all seam edges.

To make the jacket
Front interfacings 1. Baste the interfacing to the wrong side of the jacket fronts.
Pockets 2. Turn under 6 mm (¼ in) on the top edge of the pocket and

finish by machine. Press flat. Placing right sides together, fold the pocket on the fold line. Baste and stitch each side of the pocket from the fold line to the lower edge of the facing. Clip the corners of the seam allowance as shown. Turn the pocket right side out. Turn under the seam allowance on the remainder of the pocket and baste all around. Press flat. Hem the pocket facing edge to the pocket. Baste the pockets in position as indicated on the pattern. Topstitch in place. Slip-stitch outer edge of pocket to garment so it lies flat. Press.
Shoulder and side seams 3. Placing right sides together, baste and stitch the jacket fronts to the jacket back at the shoulder and side seams. Press the seams open. If bound buttonholes are desired work the first stage on outside of garment in positions indicated

on the pattern (right-hand side for women, left side for men).

Front facing and lining 4. Placing right sides together, baste and stitch the front facing to the front lining. Grade the seam and clip on curves where necessary. Press the seam toward the side seam.

5. Placing right sides together, baste and stitch the front facing and lining to the back lining at the shoulder and side seams. Press the seams open.

Collar 6. Baste the interfacing to the wrong side of the under-collar. Placing right sides together, baste and stitch the upper collar to the under-collar around the outer un-notched edge. Trim the interfacing close to the stitching line and grade the seam. Turn the collar right side out and baste close to the stitched edge, easing into shape. Press flat. Topstitch around the outer edge of the collar.

7. With the right side of the under-collar placed on the right side of the jacket, matching center backs and notches, baste the collar to the neck edge.

Joining lining and front facing to jacket 8. Placing right sides together, pin the front facing and lining to the front and neck edges of the jacket, sandwiching the collar between the lining and jacket at the neck edge. Baste and stitch. Grade the seam and clip the curves. Turn the lining to the inside of the jacket and baste around all stitched edges. Complete bound buttonholes. Topstitch the front and lapel edges.

9. Baste the lining to the jacket at the waist seam, matching center backs, side seams and notches.

10. Add two rows of gathering stitches on the lower edge of the jacket fronts and back between the notches.

Waistband 11. Baste the interfacing to the wrong side of the front and back waistband sections. Placing right sides together, baste and stitch the front band sections to the back band at the side seams.

Trim the interfacing close to the stitching and press the seams open. On outside work first stage of bound buttonhole, if desired, in position marked (right-hand side for women, left for men). Placing right sides together, baste and stitch the front and back waistband facing sections at the side seams. Press the seams open.

Placing right sides together, matching center backs and side seams, baste and stitch the waistband facing to the waistband at un-notched and front edges as shown. Grade the seam allowance, trimming the interfacing close to the stitching, and cut across corners. Turn right side out and baste around the stitched edge. Complete bound buttonhole. Press flat.

Joining waistband to jacket 12. Placing right sides together, matching

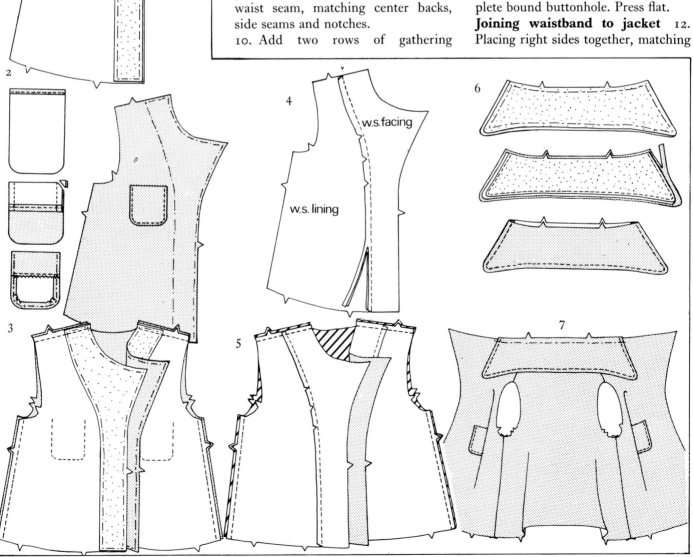

w.s.facing

w.s. lining

center backs, side seams and front edges, pin the waistband to the jacket, pulling up the gathers evenly to fit. Baste and stitch the seam. Grade the seam allowance, trimming the interfacing close to the stitching, Press the seam toward the waistband.

13. Turn under the seam allowance on the raw edge of the waistband facing and baste. Matching center backs and seams, hem the facing to the line of stitching. Press flat.

14. Topstitch around the front and lower edges of the waistband.

Sleeves and sleeve linings 15. Placing right sides together, matching notches, baste and stitch the under sleeve to the upper sleeve, leaving open below the dot on one seam as indicated on the pattern. Press the seams open. Make the sleeve lining in the same way. Add two rows of gathering stitches around the sleeve between the notches.

Placing wrong sides together, matching seams and opening edges, baste the lining to the sleeve at the lower edge. Slip-stitch the lining to the sleeve around the opening. Press flat. Add two rows of gathering stitches at the lower edge of the sleeve through both layers of fabric.

Turn seam allowance to wrong side around the lining sleeve top, baste. Add two rows of gathering stitches close to fold edge between notches.

Cuffs 16. Baste the interfacing to the wrong side of the cuff. On right side work first part of bound buttonhole in position marked if required. Placing right sides together, baste and stitch the cuff facing to the cuff around the outer edge to the dot as shown. Trim the interfacing close to the stitching. Grade the seam allowance and trim the corners. Clip to the dot and turn the cuff right side out. Baste close to the stitched edge, complete bound buttonhole and press flat.

Joining cuff to sleeve 17. Placing right sides together, matching notches, pin the cuff to the sleeve, pulling up the gathers to fit evenly. Baste and stitch. Trim the interfacing close to the stitching and grade the seam allowance. Press the seam toward the cuff. Turn under the seam allowance on the raw edge of the cuff facing and baste. Hem the cuff facing to the line of stitching. Press. Topstitch around cuff and sleeve opening edges as shown. Repeat steps 15-17 for second sleeve.

Setting in sleeves 18. Placing wrong sides together, matching shoulder and underarm seam and notches, baste the jacket lining to the jacket around the armhole edge.

Placing right sides together, matching shoulder seam and notches, pin the sleeve into the armhole, pulling up the gathers evenly to ease in the fullness around the sleeve top. Baste and stitch with the sleeve uppermost. Clip the curves and press seam toward sleeve.

19. Placing wrong sides together, matching seams and notches, pin the sleeve lining around the armhole, covering the raw edges. Using double thread in the needle, hem the sleeve lining firmly to the stitching around the armhole. Repeat steps 18 and 19 for second sleeve.

To finish 20. Make machine or hand-worked buttonholes, if required, on the right hand side of the jacket front and on the cuffs in positions indicated on the pattern. Sew buttons on the left front and on the cuffs to correspond with the buttonholes. Also, sew a button on each pocket as shown.

Note For man's jacket reverse the positioning of the buttons and buttonholes on the front.

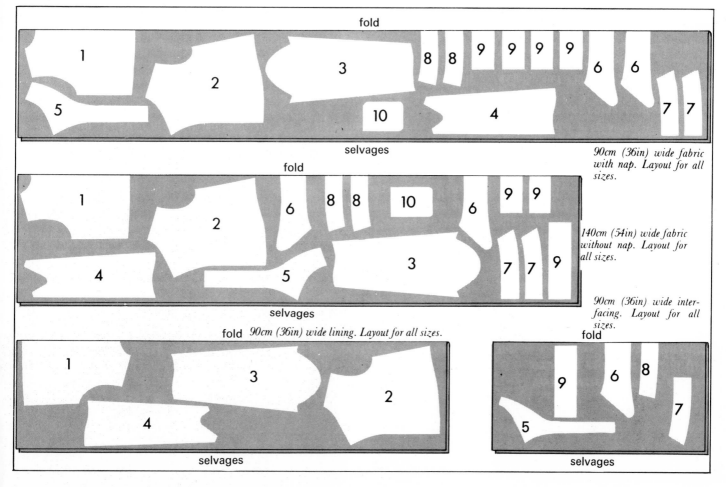

90cm (36in) wide fabric with nap. Layout for all sizes.

140cm (54in) wide fabric without nap. Layout for all sizes.

90cm (36in) wide interfacing. Layout for all sizes.

90cm (36in) wide lining. Layout for all sizes.

Graph pattern for unisex jackets

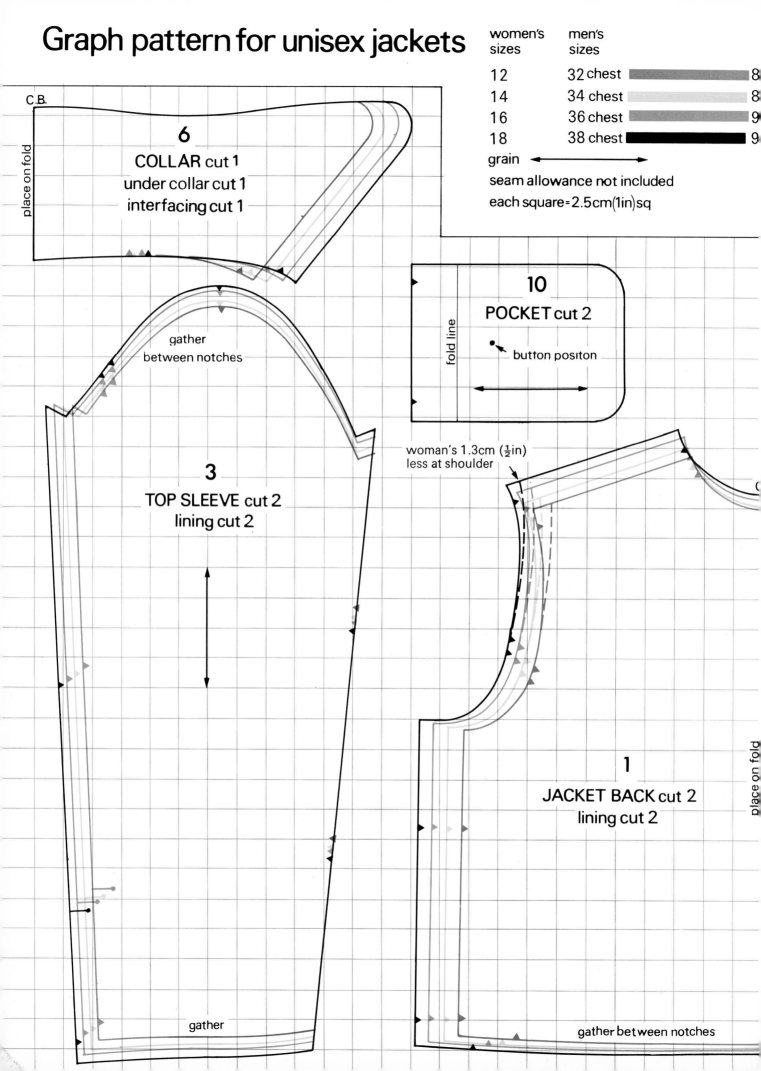

women's sizes	men's sizes	
12	32 chest	8
14	34 chest	8
16	36 chest	9
18	38 chest	9

grain ⟷

seam allowance not included

each square≈2.5cm(1in)sq

C.B.

place on fold

6
COLLAR cut **1**
under collar cut **1**
interfacing cut **1**

10
POCKET cut 2

fold line

button positon

gather
between notches

3
TOP SLEEVE cut 2
lining cut 2

woman's 1.3cm (½in)
less at shoulder

1
JACKET BACK cut 2
lining cut 2

place on fold

gather

gather between notches

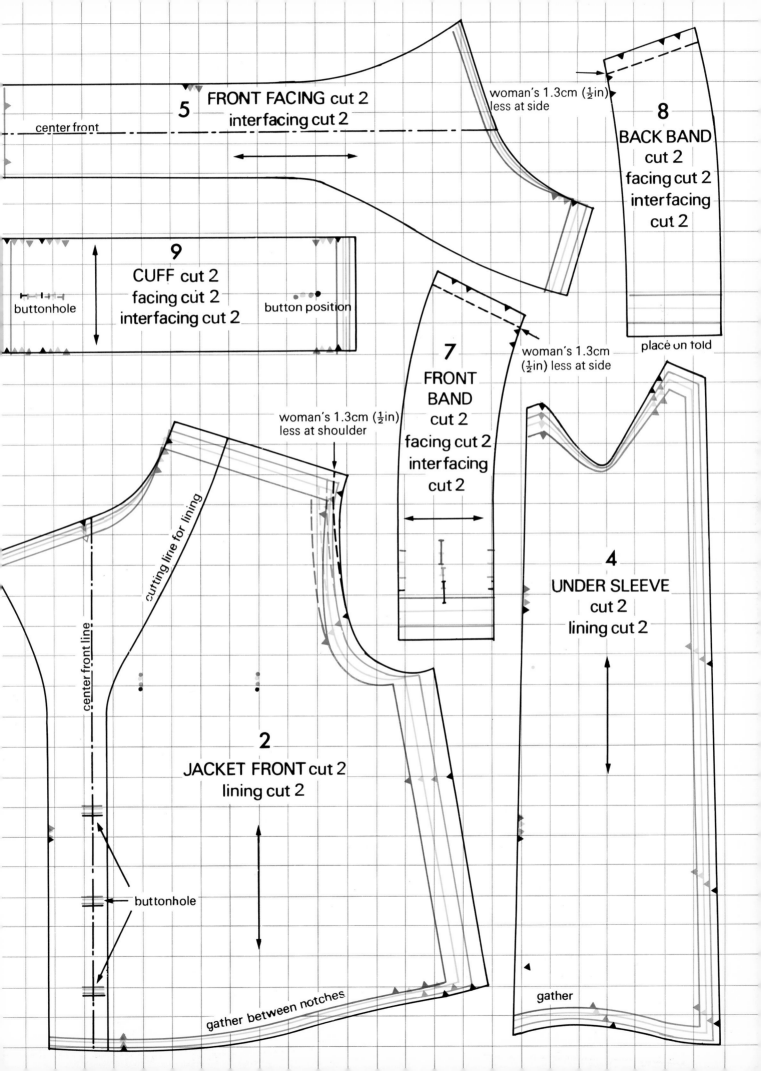

5 FRONT FACING cut 2
interfacing cut 2

center front

woman's 1.3cm (½in) less at side

8 BACK BAND cut 2 facing cut 2 interfacing cut 2

place on fold

9 CUFF cut 2 facing cut 2 interfacing cut 2

buttonhole

button position

woman's 1.3cm (½in) less at side

7 FRONT BAND cut 2 facing cut 2 interfacing cut 2

woman's 1.3cm (½in) less at shoulder

cutting line for lining

center front line

2 JACKET FRONT cut 2 lining cut 2

buttonhole

gather between notches

4 UNDER SLEEVE cut 2 lining cut 2

gather

Slim-fitting Pants

More basic know-how
Adjusting a pants pattern

Patterns generally conform to the measurements of a standard figure and it is often necessary to alter a pattern to accommodate individual figure proportions. Pants create special fitting problems because of the complexity of the proportions involved.

It is important for all major alterations to be made on the pattern, since little can be done once the garment has been cut out of the fabric. If there are several fitting problems, it would be advisable to test the pattern in muslin first. Once a perfect fit has been achieved, use this as a basic pattern which can be adapted for all kinds of pants.

Pants patterns should be chosen according to the hip measurement. To alter the pattern correctly, however, you will need some additional measurements. Before locating the hip line on the pattern, make all the lengthwise adjustments; that is, the crotch length and the leg length. Before cutting the fabric, check the pattern as described in stages below, and then make the alterations necessary for the figure. Although some further minor adjustments may be necessary in the first fitting, you can cut out the parts knowing that the pattern has been proportioned to the individual body measurements.

Adjusting the length of the crotch

To determine the crotch length, sit on a hard chair and measure from the waistline to the seat (fig. 1). To this measurement add 1·3 cm ($\frac{1}{2}$ in) ease if the hips are less than 89 cm (35 in), 2 cm ($\frac{3}{4}$ in) if the hips are 89 cm to 96·5 cm (35 in to 38 in), and 2·5 cm (1 in) if the hips are more than 96·5 cm (38 in). The body measurement plus ease allowance is the total crotch length.

To adjust the crotch length on the pattern, draw a line across the pattern at right angles to the grain line, from the widest part of the crotch to the side seam. The length of the pattern from the waistline to this line should be the same as the crotch length when taken in the sitting position, plus the ease allowance.

If the pattern is too long, then crease along the shortening line and fold a tuck to take up the desired amount. Tape in place. Re-draw the seams and construction markings to retain the original shape of the side seam and the crotch seam (fig. 2).

If the pattern is too short, cut along the lengthening line and open the pattern the desired amount. Insert a piece of paper behind this section and tape in place. Re-draw the seams and construction markings to retain the original shape of the side seam and the crotch seam.

Make the same adjustment to the front and back pattern pieces (fig. 3).

Adjusting the pant leg length

Measure the length of the pattern from the waistline to the lower edge. This should be the same as the measurement from the waist to the ankle. If the pattern is too short or too long, use the same principle as shown in figs. 2 and 3 to correct this. Make sure that there is adequate length for the hem allowance and for cuffs if these are required.

Locating the hip line

For the average figure the hip line is measured 20·5 cm (8 in) below the waistline. Measure down 20·5 cm (8 in) from the waist and draw a horizontal line on the pattern. The hip measurement will be taken at this point.

For the disproportionate figure, it is necessary to take three measurements on the body. First, measure 8 cm (3 in) below the waistline. Secondly, measure 18 cm (7 in) below the waistline and then 23 cm (9 in) below the waistline.

Draw three horizontal lines on the pattern at these points. The widest measurement will be showing at or in-between one of these points. The hip line on the pattern will be the larger measurement.

Adjusting the hip

Take the hip measurement on the pattern at the hip line. There should be 5 cm (2 in) ease allowance. If the pattern does not measure 5 cm (2 in) more than the body measurement, the pattern will need adjusting.

To increase the hip line, determine the amount needed, divide this total by four and increase each side seam by this amount. Measure the amount of adjustment out from the hip line edge at the side seam on both front and back pieces, and mark. Tape a piece of paper underneath each pattern section. Taper from the mark at the hip line into the original cutting line both above the knee and at the waistline, retaining the shape of the leg and the width of the waist (fig. 4).

To decrease the hip line, use the same principle as above but subtract the amount at the side seams (fig. 5).

Adjusting the waistline

The ease allowance at the waistline should be 1·3 cm to 2 cm ($\frac{1}{2}$ in to $\frac{3}{4}$ in). The waistline can be increased or decreased by adjusting the darts. Each dart can be increased or decreased by as much as 6 mm ($\frac{1}{4}$ in) but no more (figs. 6 and 7).

If this adjustment is not sufficient, the side seams can also be altered. Divide the amount of increase or decrease by four, and adjust each side seam edge by this amount. Taper to the hip line, being careful not to change the hip measurement (figs. 8 and 9).

Adjusting width of lower edge

If the lower edge of the pattern is too narrow, determine the amount to be added and divide this by four. Add this amount to the side and inside seam edges at the hemline. Taper from the hemline to the hip line on

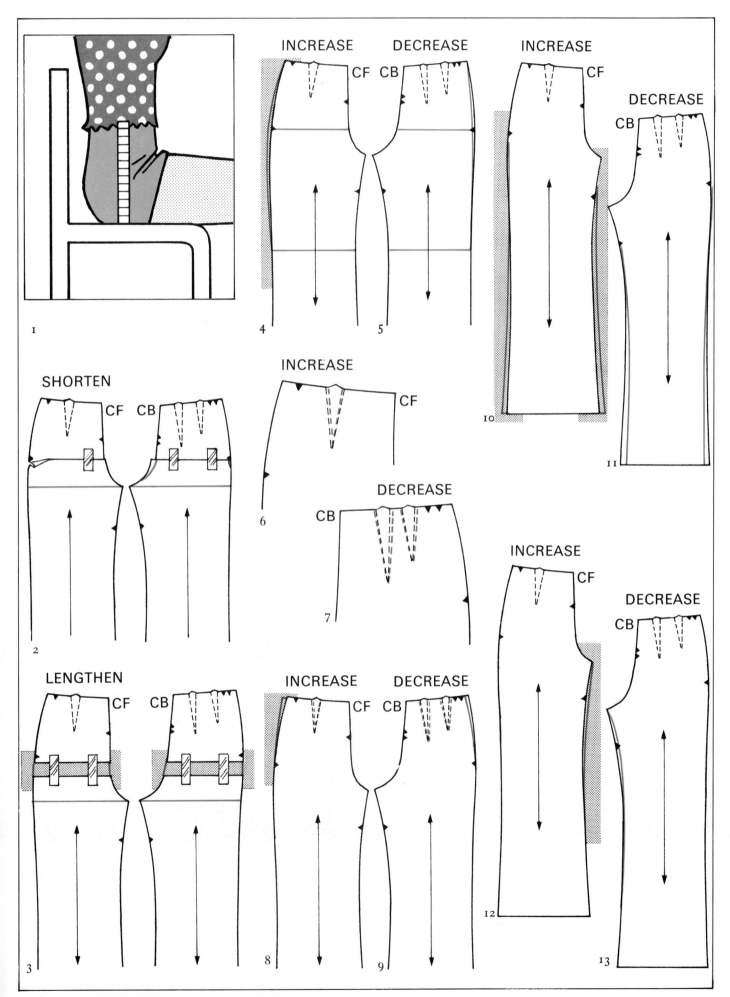

1

INCREASE   DECREASE   INCREASE
CF CB   CF
4   5

DECREASE
CB

10   11

SHORTEN
CF CB

2

INCREASE
CF
6

DECREASE
CB
7

LENGTHEN
CF CB

3

INCREASE   DECREASE
CF CB
8   9

INCREASE
CF

12

DECREASE
CB
13

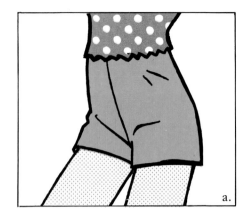 a.

 b.

 c.

the side seams, also from the hemline to the crotch on the inside seams (fig. 10).

If the pattern is too wide at this point, divide the total amount to be subtracted by four, using the same method as above, but subtracting and not adding (fig. 11).

Adjusting the width of the leg

There is no standard amount of ease required for the width of the leg. This is a matter of personal preference and depends upon the size and shape of the leg.

If a leg has large thighs, then add to the front and back inside leg seams at the crotch point, tapering the line to the lower edge of the pattern. Do not add to the side seams. Tightness in the thigh area means that more width is required in the crotch as well as in the leg, and adding at this point will give both (fig. 12).

Altering a pattern to accommodate thin thighs must never be done by decreasing at the side seams. If the thighs are thin, then decrease both the front and back inside leg seams at the crotch point and taper to the lower edge of the pattern (fig. 13).

Alterations for a sway back

If the figure has a sway back this will cause folds in the pants below the back waist. These folds can be eliminated by removing the extra fullness at the center back. Slash straight across the back to the side seam about 9 cm (3½ in) below the waistline.

Overlap the slash line to remove the necessary amount. Re-draw the center back seam, and also the darts if they have been affected. Consequently the back waistline will have been decreased (figs. 14a and 14b).

If the normal waistline width is re-

quired, add the amount trimmed from the center back to the side seam and taper from the waistline to the hip line (fig. 15).

Alterations for a large stomach

A person with a large stomach will need to take great care in altering a pants pattern – particularly if the style is very fitted, which emphasizes the

Illustrations left to right show figure problems to be accommodated:
a. Wide legs, b. Sway back, c. Large stomach, d. Protruding hips and
e. Large and flat seats.

slightest figure fault.

To make this alteration, draw a line through the center of the waistline dart to the knee. This line should be

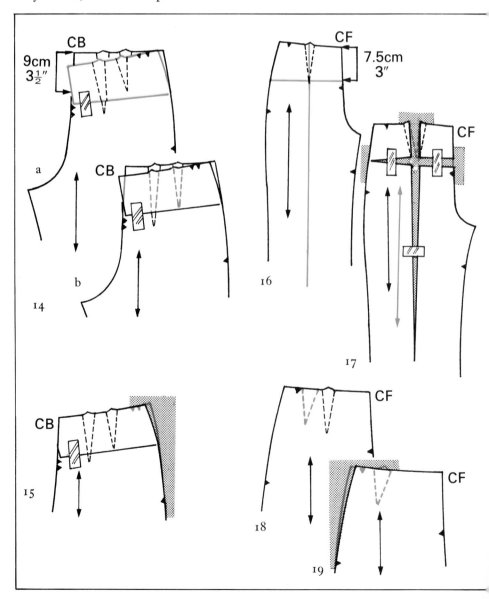

d.

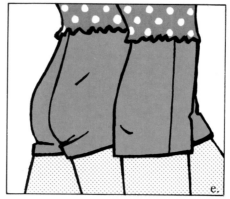

e.

parallel to the grain line. Then draw a horizontal line from the center front to the side seam about 8 cm (3 in) below the waistline (fig. 16).

Slash the horizontal line to the side seam and open the pattern a quarter of the amount required. Slash the vertical line and open the pattern a quarter of the amount required, keeping the center front straight. Insert a piece of

tissue paper under the slashes and tape in position. Adjust the waistline dart in the middle of the slash, returning it to its original position and size (fig. 17).

Alteration for protruding hips Extra dart fullness released at the point of the hip bones will solve this problem. The larger dart releases more fullness. Re-position and increase the

width of the dart so that it is in line with the hip bone – for some figures the dart may need to be shortened as well (fig. 18). As a result, the waistline becomes smaller, so add the difference to the side seam and taper to the hip line (fig. 19).

Alterations for a large seat To make this alteration, the width and length at the fullest part of the seat must be increased.

Determine the amount of increase necessary for the adjustment. Slash the pattern vertically to the knee, between the center back and the back dart, parallel to the grain line. Measure 20·5 cm (8 in) below the waistline and slash the pattern horizontally from the center back to the side seam. Open the vertical and horizontal slashes each to a quarter of the amount required, keeping the center back straight. Insert a piece of paper and tape in place.

Re-draw the cutting lines. If the waistline becomes too large, divide the adjustment equally between the back darts and increase each one (fig. 20).

Alterations for a flat seat In this case proceed as if making the alteration for a large seat, but instead of opening the vertical and horizontal slashes, overlap them each by a quarter of the amount required. If the waistline becomes too small, divide the vertical adjustment equally among all the back darts and decrease them by this amount (fig. 21).

Alteration for one hip higher than natural hip line Measure down 20·5

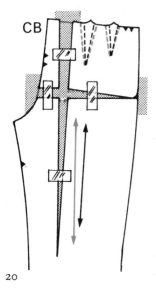

CB

20

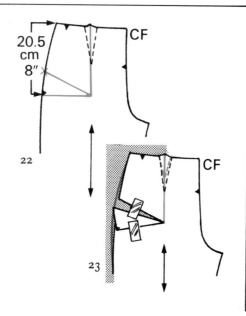

20.5 cm
8"

CF

22

CF

23

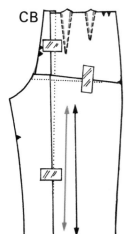

CB

21

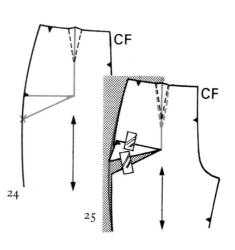

CF

CF

24

25

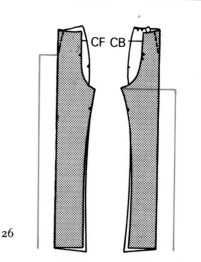

CF CB

26

109

cm (8 in) from the waistline and draw a line through the center of the dart to this position, keeping in line with the straight grain. Draw a horizontal line from the end of this line to the side seam.

At the side seam, where the hip is higher, measure down from the waistline to the hip bone and mark. Draw a line from this mark to the point where the vertical and horizontal lines meet (fig. 22).

Slash along this line and the horizontal line and overlap the pattern. This will open the pattern at the new hip line. Adjust the amount, overlapping to fit the hip, and tape in place. Re-draw the side seam from the waistline, tapering to the new hip line. Make this adjustment to both front and back pattern pieces.

It will be found after making this adjustment, that the dart will have to be shortened to the level of the new hip line (fig. 23).

Alteration for one hip lower than natural hip line For this alteration, the same method is used as above. Having drawn the vertical and horizontal lines, measure down from the horizontal to the new hip line and mark. Draw a line from this mark to the point where the vertical and horizontal lines meet (fig. 24).

Slash along this line and the horizontal line and overlap the pattern. This will open the pattern at the new hip line. Adjust the amount overlapping to fit the hip and tape in place. Re-draw the side seam from the waistline, tapering to the new hip line (fig. 25).

A final tip on fitting pants After the pattern pieces have been cut out in the fabric and marked, fold each piece vertically in half with the wrong sides together. Press in the creases firmly. The front crease points to the first dart or pleat, and the back crease stops at the level of crotch seam (fig. 26).

During the first fitting, make sure that the creases hang straight. If a crease slopes inward, raise the pants at the waistline on the appropriate side until the crease hangs correctly. This occurs because the two hips are not exactly the same.

These casual pants, designed with straight legs, are easy to fit well.

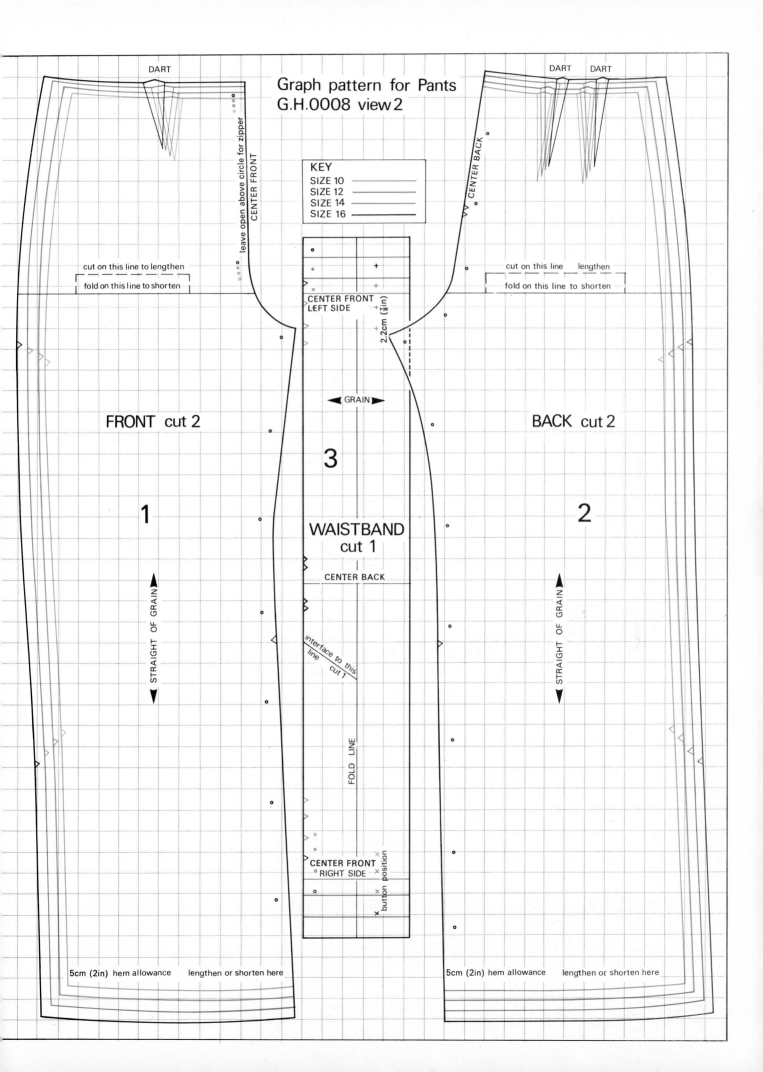

DART

Graph pattern for Pants
G.H.0008 view 2

CENTER FRONT

leave open above circle for zipper

DART   DART

CENTER BACK

KEY
SIZE 10 ————
SIZE 12 ————
SIZE 14 ————
SIZE 16 ————

cut on this line to lengthen

fold on this line to shorten

cut on this line   lengthen

fold on this line to shorten

CENTER FRONT
LEFT SIDE

2.2cm (⅞in)

◄ GRAIN ►

FRONT cut 2

BACK cut 2

3

1

2

WAISTBAND
cut 1

CENTER BACK

STRAIGHT OF GRAIN

STRAIGHT OF GRAIN

interface to this
line
cut 1

FOLD LINE

CENTER FRONT
RIGHT SIDE

button position

5cm (2in) hem allowance   lengthen or shorten here

5cm (2in) hem allowance   lengthen or shorten here

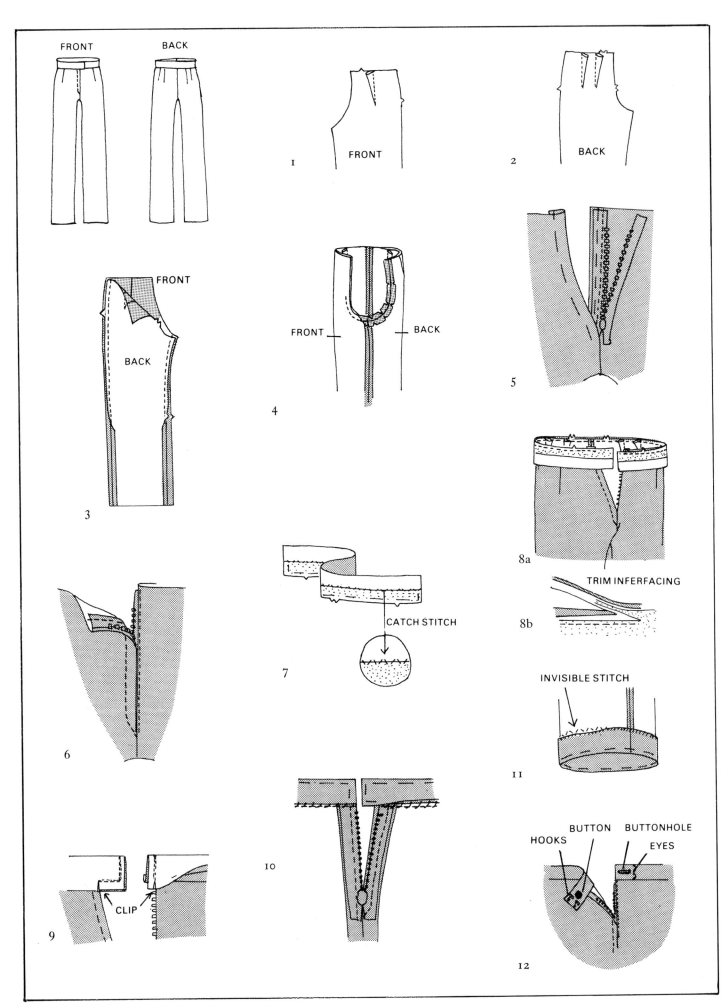

FRONT   BACK

1   FRONT

2   BACK

3   FRONT BACK

4   FRONT   BACK

5

6

7   CATCH STITCH

8a

8b   TRIM INTERFACING

9   CLIP

10

11   INVISIBLE STITCH

12   HOOKS   BUTTON   BUTTONHOLE   EYES

112

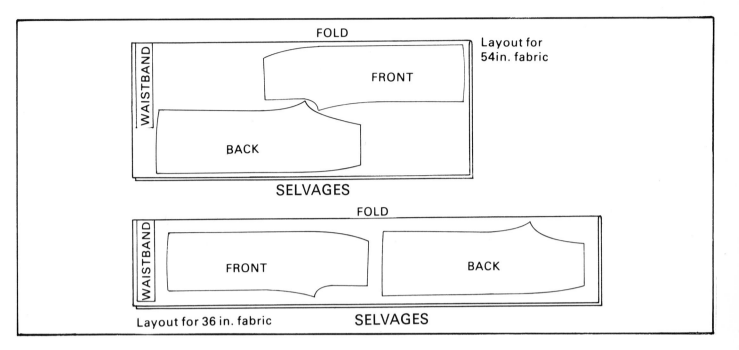

FOLD

WAISTBAND

FRONT

Layout for 54in. fabric

BACK

SELVAGES

FOLD

WAISTBAND

FRONT

BACK

Layout for 36 in. fabric

SELVAGES

Slim-fitting pants

These pants are cut on classic lines with straight legs. They look equally good made in plain fabrics or in bold plaids.

Measurements

The pattern is given in sizes 10, 12, 14 and 16. Each size is indicated on the graph pattern by a cutting line of a different color.

Making the pattern

Draw up the pattern to scale from the graph pattern given here. Each of the squares on the graph represents 2·5 cm (1 in) square.

Suggested fabrics

Wool, tweed, corduroy, linen, denim.

You will need:

140 cm (54 in) fabric without nap, all sizes 2·40 m (2 yd), or
90 cm (36 in) fabric without nap, all sizes 2·75 m (3 yd).
Note Allow extra fabric for matching design if using plaid fabric. (Between 30 to 50 cm ($\frac{1}{4}$ to $\frac{1}{2}$ yd) depending on size of plaid.)
20 cm ($\frac{1}{8}$ yd) interfacing.
20 cm (8 in) zipper.
Two hooks and eyes.
Sewing thread to match fabric.
Graph paper for pattern.

Cutting out

A seam allowance of 1·5 cm ($\frac{5}{8}$ in) has been allowed on all seams and 6 cm (2$\frac{5}{8}$ in) hem allowance.

To make the pants

Darts 1. Placing right sides together, baste and stitch the front waist darts. Press the darts toward the center front.

2. Placing right sides together, baste and stitch the back waist darts. Press the darts toward the center back.

Seams 3. Placing right sides together, matching notches, baste and stitch the inside leg seam and the side seam. Press the seams open.

Crotch 4. Placing right sides together, matching notches and inside leg seams, baste and stitch the crotch seam to small circle. Clip the curved edges and press the seam open.

5. Turn and baste the seam allowance of the right front to the wrong side and press. Place the zipper face down on the left front opening. Baste and stitch in place using the zipper foot on the machine.

6. Baste and stitch the right front to the zipper as shown. If you like, edge stitch the seam close to the zipper teeth on the left-hand side as shown.

Waistband 7. Cut interfacing for waistband as indicated on pattern. Baste the interfacing to the wrong side of the waistband and catch stitch it down to the fold line.

8. Placing right sides together, matching notches, baste and stitch the waistband to the pants waist. Grade the seam allowances, trimming the interfacing close to the stitching. Press the seam up toward the waistband.

9. Placing right sides together, fold the waistband on the fold line and stitch the ends as shown. Clip the seam at center front to the stitching as shown. Trim and grade the seam and clip across the corners.

10. Turn the waistband to the inside. Baste and press. Turn under the seam allowance and hem to the stitching line.

To finish 11. Try on the pants and mark the hem. Baste around the folded edge. Trim the hem to an even width all around. Finish the raw edge of the hem with hand overcasting or machine stitch. Sew the hem with invisible hemming stitch.

12. Make a hand-worked or machine buttonhole in the left front waistband in the position indicated on the pattern. Sew the button onto the right front waistband on the underband. Sew on the hooks and eyes at the waistband opening as shown.

Child's overalls

Measurements

The pattern is given in two sizes to fit a child 4 to 6 years old. Waist sizes, 61 cm (24 in) and 66 cm (26 in).

Making the pattern

Draw up the pattern to scale from the graph pattern given here. One square represents 2·5 cm (1 in) square.

Suggested fabrics

Denim, corduroy.

You will need:

90 cm (36 in) wide fabric, without nap, size 4, 1·90 m (2 yd); size 6,

These tough, practical overalls are straightforward and fun to make. For a special effect, choose bright, boldly decorative patches to contrast with the basic overalls.

2·10 m (2¼ yd).
15 cm (6 in) zipper.
Purchased appliqué motif.
Two 2·5 cm (1 in) buttons.
Sewing thread to match fabric.
Buttonhole twist in matching or contrasting color for topstitching.
Graph paper for pattern.

Cutting out

There are no seam allowances included on the pattern. When cutting out add 1·5 cm (⅝ in) to all seam edges and a generous 6·5 cm (2½ in) hem allowance.

To make the overalls

Seams 1. Placing right sides together, and matching the notches on the pattern, baste and stitch the center front and center back seams, leaving the center back open where indicated on pattern to allow for inserting the zipper.

Insert the zipper. Clip curves and press the seams open.

2. Placing right sides together, baste and stitch the front and back legs together along the side and inside leg seams. Press the seams open.

Bib and facings 3. With right sides together, baste and stitch along three sides of the bib, leaving long edge open. Grade the seams and turn the bib right side out. Baste around the stitched edges and press flat.

4. Placing right sides together, matching center fronts, baste and stitch the raw edge of the bib to the pants front. Grade the seams.

5. Placing right sides together, baste and stitch the facing pieces together at the side seams and center front. Placing right sides together, matching seams, baste and stitch the facing to the waistline. Turn the facing to the inside and baste around the stitched edge. Press flat.

Finish the seam allowance on the raw edge of the facing and hem it to the zipper tape.

6. Starting at the center back, top-stitch along the waistline and bib 1·3 cm (½ in) away from the edge.

Straps 7. Placing right sides together, stitch around the edges of the straps, leaving an opening of 8 cm (3 in) to turn the strap. Turn the strap right side out. Slip-stitch the opening to close. Baste around the stitched edge and press flat. Topstitch 6 mm (¼ in) away from the edge all around the strap.

Buttonholes and buttons 8. Sew buttons at the positions marked on the pattern. Next, make hand-worked or machine-stitched buttonholes at the positions indicated for these on the pattern.

To finish 9. Try overalls on the child, mark the hem and check length of straps. Finish the raw edges of hem, turn up and stitch. Topstitch 1·3 cm (½ in) away from the lower edge of the hem if you wish. Stitch shoulder straps firmly into place at back of pants. Stitch purchased appliqué motif to bib.

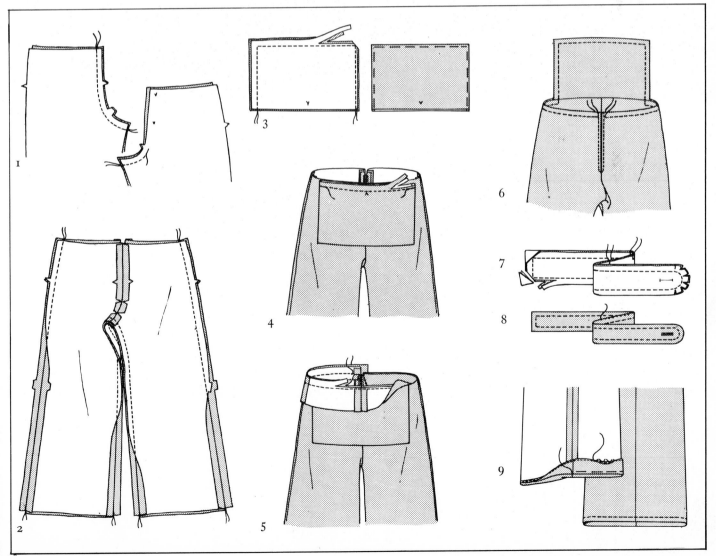

Graph pattern

Each square = 2.5cm sq (1in sq)   Seam allowances not included

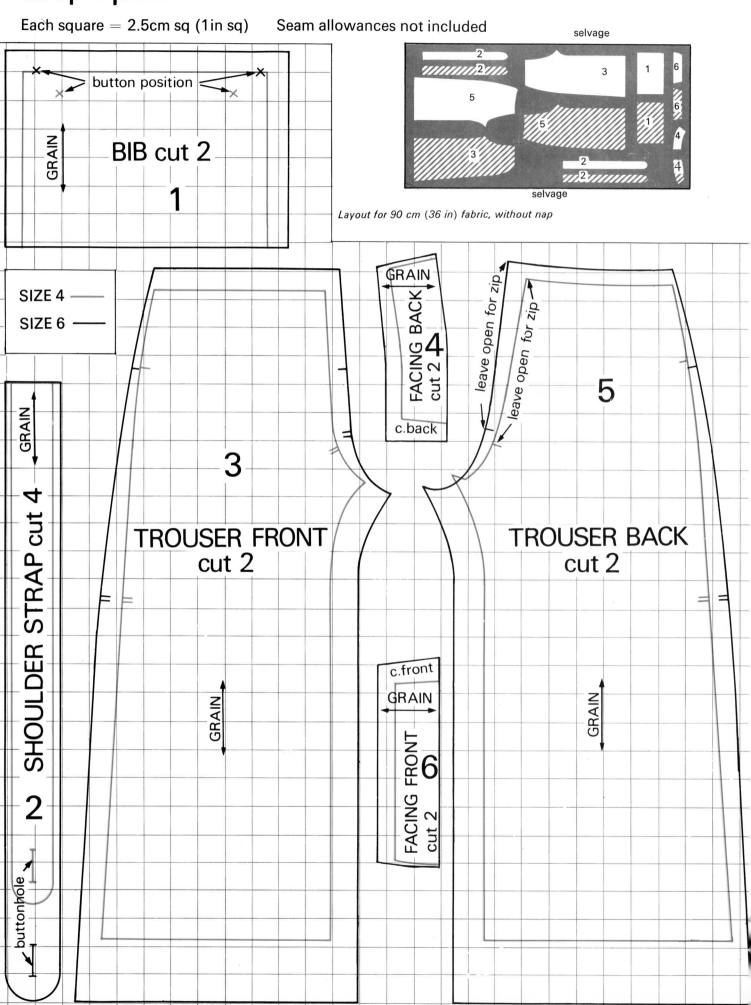

selvage

BIB cut 2

1

button position

GRAIN

2
2
3
1
6
5
6
1
3
4
2
2
4

selvage

Layout for 90 cm (36 in) fabric, without nap

SIZE 4 ——
SIZE 6 ——

GRAIN

SHOULDER STRAP cut 4

2

buttonhole

3

TROUSER FRONT
cut 2

GRAIN

GRAIN

FACING BACK
cut 2

4

c.back

leave open for zip

leave open for zip

5

TROUSER BACK
cut 2

GRAIN

c.front

GRAIN

FACING FRONT
cut 2

6

Home Sewing

Table Linen

Round tablecloths

Round tables – space saving and fashionable – look good in any setting. Here are instructions for making two kinds of elegant round cloth.

*Techniques included: drawing arcs, pin-and-string method.

A round tablecloth can be made in one of two ways.

In the method which is more suitable for patterned fabric, the round cloth is produced from a square of fabric, each side of the square being the same length as the desired diameter of the finished cloth.

It is possible to buy fabrics suitable for tablecloths in wider than usual widths. In most cases, though, the fabric has to be joined at the sides to produce the full width of the square from which the cloth is to be cut.

The second method of making a round tablecloth involves cutting a circular piece of cloth to fit the table top, plus seam allowance, and joining two curved pieces to it, for the overhang. This method uses more fabric, but is more suitable than the first for plain fabrics, for seams crossing the table would be conspicuous on plain fabric.

Choosing fabrics Washable dress or furnishing fabrics, such as cotton, linen, lawn, man-made fiber mixtures and cotton lace, are all suitable for tablecloths. Sheet fabric, available in a variety of patterns and colors, is also suitable, because of its quality and width. For a nursery or kitchen table, Vinyl cloth is a good choice, although it does not hang as well as cotton.

Deciding the size of a round tablecloth The cloth should cover the table and should have a generous overhang all around, ranging from about 25 cm (10 in) to floor level. The actual measurement depends upon personal choice.

To determine the depth of the overhang Lay a tapemeasure across

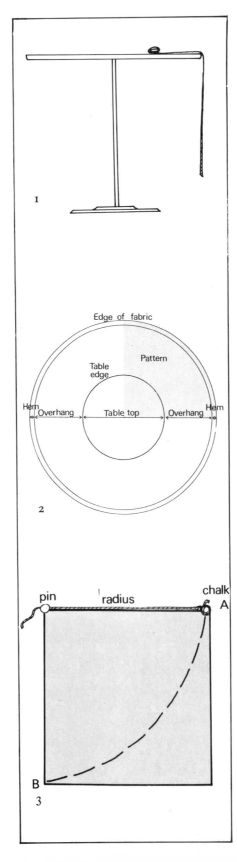

the tabletop and let one end drop down until it reaches the desired depth for the overhang (fig. 1).

To find the diameter of the cloth
Measure the diameter of the tabletop, add this measurement to twice the depth of the overhang, and add 1·5 cm ($\frac{1}{2}$ in) all around, for hem (fig. 2).

If the width of the fabric chosen is less than the diameter of the tablecloth, more fabric will have to be joined to the sides of the main piece, so that the width and the length of the fabric when the pieces are joined are sufficient for the desired diameter of the cloth.

Making a round tablecloth pattern using pin-and-string method
You will need:

A large square of paper, with each side a little longer than the radius (half the diameter) of the proposed tablecloth.

A piece of string 15 cm (6 in) longer than the radius of the cloth.

A stick of chalk.

Several thumbtacks.

*Drawing an arc: pin-and-string method
Work on a flat surface that will not be spoiled if tacks are pushed into it.

Tie one end of the string around the chalk. Starting at the chalk end, measure out the radius of the cloth, including 1·5 cm ($\frac{1}{2}$ in) hem allowance, along the length of the string. Mark this measurement by pushing a thumbtack through the string at this point. Tack the paper down on the flat working surface and push the thumbtack, retaining the string on the point of the pin, into the top left-hand corner of the paper.

Hold the thumbtack firmly with one

1. Determining the depth of the overhang. 2. Finding the diameter for a round cloth. 3. Using a pin, string and chalk to make a circular pattern.

hand and draw an arc with the chalk from A, at the top right-hand corner of the paper, to B, at the bottom left-hand corner (fig. 3).

The pattern thus produced is a quarter of the area of the cloth, plus 1·5 cm (½ in) hem allowance

Making a round tablecloth from a square of fabric
You will need:

Fabric for the cloth.

Trimming, if required, of your own choice (amount required is four times the length of the arc A to B shown in fig. 3, plus 2·5 (1 in) for overlap). Fringe, braid or daisy chain trims are all suitable.

Matching thread.

Matching bias binding (the same amount as for the trimming).

Pins.

Basting thread.

Preparing the fabric If the fabric has to be joined, add pieces to the sides of the main fabric piece; a seam across the middle of the cloth would be very noticeable and could upset the balance of glasses and dishes when the table is set.

Figs. 4 and 5 show how to cut and join 120 cm (48 in) widths to make a round cloth with a diameter of 194 cm (78 in) and a 1·5 cm (½ in) hem. Remember that seam allowances for the joins have to be added.

Join the widths with a machine-stitched flat fell seam, stitched with right sides facing (fig. 6 p. 120). You should now have a square of fabric with each side equal to the diameter of the cloth, plus hem allowance.

Cutting out Matching edges, fold the prepared square of fabric in half, then in half again, and pin the pattern onto the folded fabric, as shown in fig. 7. Cut along the curved pattern edge. Unpin the pattern and unfold the fabric. Snip V-shaped notches into the edge of the cloth 1 cm (⅜ in) deep, at 2·5 cm (1 in) intervals (fig. 8). Turn the edge in 1·5 cm (½ in) to the wrong side, pin and baste it down. The notches will close up, allowing the hem to curve (fig. 9).

Binding the hem Pin and baste the bias binding over the turned hem, to

The trim and the depth of the overhang influences how you use the tablecloth.

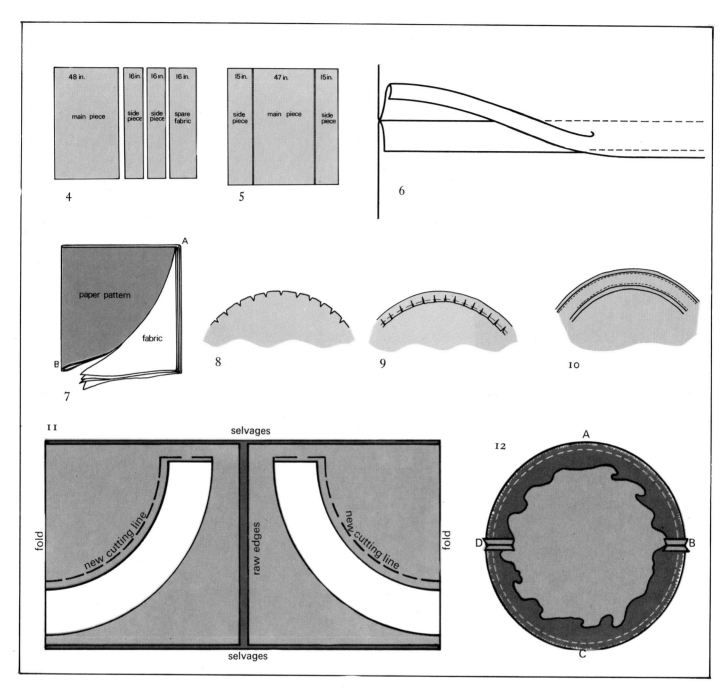

4, 5. *Cutting and joining fabric for a large round cloth. 6. Flat fell seams. 7. Pattern pinned to folded fabric. 8. Snip the hem edge. 9. Turn and tack in the hem allowance. 10. Stitching on the bias binding. 11. Folding the fabric and placing the pattern pieces for cutting the overhang. 12. Stitching the overhang on the center piece of the tablecloth.*

cover the raw edge. Stitch on the bias binding (fig. 10), turning under the ends to finish. Add trimming (optional).

Making a round cloth with curved overhang

This method involves cutting a circular piece of fabric the same size as the tabletop, plus 1·5 cm (½ in) seam allowance all around, and adding two curved overhang pieces. Thus the fabric to be used should be of a width equal to the diameter of the tabletop, plus 1·5 cm (½ in) seam allowance all around, and be of sufficient length to allow the top and overlap pieces to be cut.

Measuring for the pattern Double the overhang of the cloth and add to it the diameter of the tabletop, plus 3 cm (1 in) for seam allowance.

Making the pattern Make a paper pattern of a quarter of the area of the cloth, as for the first method, then draw a smaller arc within the larger arc, the radius the same as the tabletop radius, plus 1·5 cm (½ in) for seams. Cut along this inner line, reserving the outer piece of pattern for the overhang.

Cutting out Cut off a square of fabric from the main length with each side equal to the diameter of the tabletop, plus 1·5 cm (½ in) seam allowance all around. Fold this square in half and in half again, as for the first method, and pin the tabletop pattern piece to the folded fabric, again as before. Cut

out around the curve.

Before unfolding the fabric, mark the straight grain four times at four opposite points on the cloth, by making several basting stitches in from the edge, along the folds. These stitches will act as guidelines when attaching the overhang, ensuring that the grain runs straight on the pieces, so the cloth hangs correctly. Lay the remaining length of fabric flat on the floor and fold over the ends, so they meet in the center (fig. 11).

Pin the pattern piece for the overhang on the fabric, so that one straight edge is on one of the folds. Using chalk, mark on the fabric the cutting line for the inner edge of the overhang, 3 cm (1 in) from the inner curve of the pattern.

Mark another line 1·5 cm ($\frac{1}{2}$ in) from the straight edge of the pattern which is not on the fold of the fabric (fig. 11). Cut along the chalked lines and along the outer edge of the pattern, but do not cut along the fold.

Unpin the pattern and pin the pattern to the fabric at the other fold. Mark the cutting lines as for the first piece. Cut out in the same way.

Clip 1 cm ($\frac{3}{8}$ in) into the inner edge of both overhang pieces, at 2·5 cm (1 in) intervals. Placing right sides together and overhang on top, match the center of the inner edge of one overhanging piece to one of the basting marks on the tabletop piece (fig. 12). Working outward from this point, pin the overhang to the tabletop piece 1·5 cm ($\frac{1}{2}$ in) in from the edge. The clips will open out.

Pin the other overhang piece to the tabletop piece in the same way, matching the center to the opposite basting mark. Where the overhang pieces meet, pin the raw edges together, adjusting the short seamlines so the overhang fits the tabletop exactly. Baste and machine stitch these seams. Press them open and finish the raw edges.

Baste and machine stitch the overhang to the tabletop. Remove the basting and press the seam allowance down on-to the overhang, all around. Overcast the raw edges together. Stitch on the bias binding around the hem, as for the tablecloth made by the first method.

Trimming Trim round tablecloths with bobble braid, fringing, or other decorative trims. To trim a cloth made by the second method, piping in a con-trasting color could be added to the seam joining the overhang to the center piece.

Rectangular tablecloths

Ready-made tablecloths tend to come in a few standard sizes which look all wrong if your table is not a standard size too. Try making your own – then you can decide both size and cost.

*Techniques included: fraying, folded miter, simple stitched miter, mitering bias binding, mitering corner on table-cloth.

Deciding the size of a rectangular tablecloth Measure the length and width of the table and add on 23 cm to 30 cm (9 in to 12 in) for the overhang on each side (about knee level) or the depth to the floor if you prefer a floor length cloth.

The hem allowance depends on the fin-ish you choose – if the cloth is to have a plain hem, add another 5 cm (2 in) to each side; allow only 1·5 cm ($\frac{1}{2}$ in) for a decorative trim or for a floor length cloth. No hem allowance is needed if edges are to be frayed.

If you can buy suitable fabric wide enough – usually from a specialist needlework shop – you will only need one length. If you have to join the fabric to make up the width, you may need twice or three times the length, depending on the width of the fabric and the table, and on where the seams are to fall.

Because a center seam would look ugly, the best method is to join pieces of fabric of equal width to the long sides of the main piece. Ideally the main piece should, when in position on the table, cover the tabletop en-tirely and overhang the sides, as described for a round tablecloth, so that any seams are part of the over-

Small occasional tables often look better with the addition of a simple table cloth, and pillow covers made to match completes the decorative touch.

the edges that they could upset the balance of place settings, it might be better to make the center panel narrower still and make a feature of the seams.

For example, for a table 106 cm (3 ft 6 in) wide the tablecloth – with a 23 cm (9 in) overhang and 5 cm (2 in) hem allowance – would be 157 cm (62 in) wide unfinished. With 120 cm (48 in) fabric, you would need an amount twice the length of the finished cloth plus hems.

The full width of the fabric can be used for the center panel, which is one half of the fabric length, while the side panels are cut from the other half of the fabric.

Work out the width of the panels before buying the fabric. Allow extra fabric for matching a pattern if necessary. You may find that after cutting there will be some fabric left over which can be used for napkins.

Making the panels Cut out the panels, including hems and 1·5 cm (½ in) seam allowance on each side of the center panel and on the inner edge of the side panels. Join them with a plain seam or – if the cloth is to be washed frequently – a machine stitched flat fell seam in which the edges are enclosed, making the seam flat and easy to press (see Round tablecloths). If using patterned fabric, make sure that the pattern matches along the seams.

To make a feature of the seams, cover them with braid or ribbon.

Making the hem For a plain hem on a cloth with 23 cm to 30 cm (9 in to 12 in) overhang, miter the corners to give a flat, neat appearance. Machine stitch the hem near the edge of the inner fold.

Trimming There is a wide variety of trimmings available, including braid and lace, which are suitable for trimming the edges of a tablecloth.

When buying trimming allow about 25 cm (¼ yd) extra for mitering corners and finishing the join.

On adjoining sides of the cloth, fold the raw edge 1·5 cm (½ in) onto the right side and press. Placing wrong sides together, make a mitered corner on this 1·5 cm (½ in) raw hem, so that the finished miter will be on the right side. Pin the trimming around the cloth, over the raw edge, mitering at the corners. Baste and machine stitch along both edges of the trimming.

1. Folds marking the depth of overhang and first rounded corner. 2, 3. Cloth folded to cut remaining corners. 4. Pull threads to fray cloth edges.

hang and do not interrupt the smoothness of the top. If, however, the fabric is narrower than the tabletop, rather than having the joining seams so near

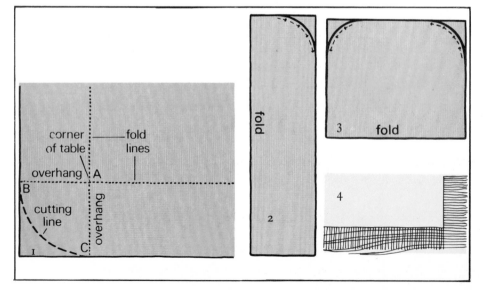

Rounding the corners Before making a hem on a floor length, rectangular cloth it is first necessary to round the corners so that they do not trail on the floor.

On two adjacent sides of the cloth, turn up the depth of the overhang, plus the 1·3 cm ($\frac{1}{2}$ in) allowed for the hem. Press and open out the folds (fig. 1 p. 122). Draw an arc using pin-and-string method (see Round tablecloths) from B to C.

Cut along the curved line.

Fold the cloth in half lengthwise and pin the arc on the first corner onto the second as a pattern. Cut out second arc and remove pins (fig. 2).

Fold the cloth in half widthwise and use the first two corners as a pattern for the third and fourth (fig. 3).

To make a hem on a cloth with rounded corners, snip 1 cm ($\frac{3}{8}$ in) "V" notches into the edge at 2·5 cm (1 in) intervals on the curved sections of the edge. Turn in 1·5 cm ($\frac{1}{2}$ in) all around the edge (including the straight edges). Finish off the hem with binding as for a round cloth.

*To fray the edges of a tablecloth or napkins, pull away the threads parallel to the edges to the depth of the fringe desired (fig. 4). Overcast the edges to prevent further unwanted fraying.

An alternative to overcasting is to run a line of machine stitching around the cloth or napkin, before fraying the edges, at the depth of fringe desired.

Fraying works well on linens and coarse cottons but is not suitable for closely woven cottons.

*Mitering
Folded miter Used mainly on braids (always on woven braid which would make a stitched miter spread). The fullness is simply folded to one side when turning the corner (fig. 1).
Simple stitched miter Used when applying a bulky braid on which the excess must be trimmed (fig. 2).
Mitering corners on a tablecloth
On adjoining sides of the cloth, fold over the raw edges 1·5 cm ($\frac{1}{2}$ in) to the wrong side and press. Make another fold 3·5 cm ($1\frac{1}{2}$ in) from each of the first folded edges and press again. Open out the second folds and turn in the corner on a diagonal line Y-Z going through the point where these fold lines cross, and at an equal distance

from the corner on both sides. Press and then open out the corner fold. Leaving the first 1·5 cm ($\frac{1}{2}$ in) folds turned in, trim off the corner 6 mm ($\frac{1}{4}$ in) outside the diagonal crease, cutting firmly through the folded edges (fig. 3).

Placing right sides together, fold the cloth along A-B and stitch from X-YZ. Press seam open (fig. 4).

Turn the corner right side out, easing out the point gently with a knitting needle. Press (fig. 5).

*Mitering bias binding Unfold one of the creased edges of the binding, and, starting in the middle of one side,

pin it to the cloth, with the raw edges meeting and right sides together. Clip the binding seam allowance at the corners to ease it around. To join the binding, overlap it at the ends, turn-

Napkins to match or contrast with the tablecloth are made from squares of fabric and can be finished with a plain hem, frayed or trimmed with lace as shown here.
1. *Making a folded miter.*
2. *Making a simple stitched miter.*
3. *The corner trimmed away.*
4. *Corner seam stitched and pressed.*
5. *The finished miter.*

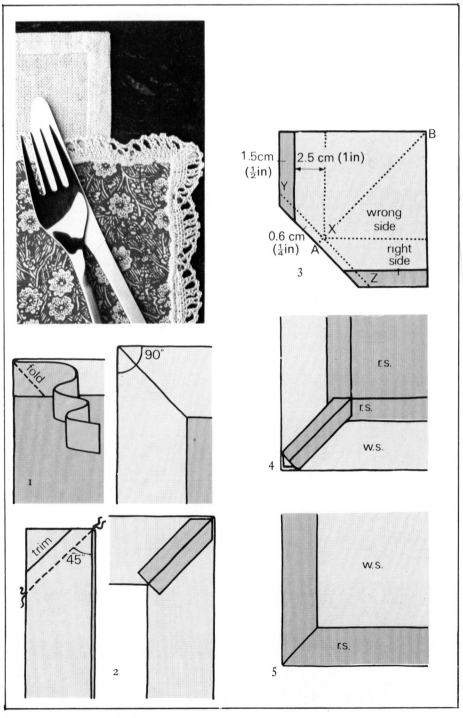

ing under the raw edges to make a neat join. Baste and machine stitch the binding in position, and then press it over completely onto the wrong side of the cloth. Tuck under the excess binding at the four corners, making a diagonal fold. Baste the binding onto the cloth along the inner fold, and machine stitch or hand-hem. Stitch the folds and join with small hem stitching.

Napkins

Dinner napkins traditionally tended to be quite large, not only to protect laps from possible spills but also because they used to be folded into elaborate shapes. Nowadays, when most people fold napkins simply into four, a practical size, and one that makes best use of fabric widths – is 40 to 45 cm (16 to 18 in) square.

Finish napkins with plain hems and mitered corners, as for the tablecloth, but turning over the first fold for 6 mm ($\frac{1}{4}$ in) and the second fold 1·5 cm ($\frac{1}{2}$ in). Stitch by machine, or with small, firm slip-stitching.

Place mats

These tend to be more informal than a tablecloth and are ideal for tables with a surface which you want to show off but protect from scratches. If you also want to protect it from heat, use a cork mat under the fabric. A practical size for rectangular place-mats is 33 by 45 cm (12 by 16$\frac{1}{2}$ in) finished, but this should be adapted according to the width of the fabric. For plain edges, make hems with mitered corners as for napkins (above). For a frayed edge, remove the threads

parallel to the edges to the depth of the fringe desired as described for tablecloths.

Rounded place mats For round tables, mats which are curved at the outer edge and taper toward the center of the table can make more economical use of the space (fig. 1).

In order to make the curve on the mats follow the curve of the table, cut a paper pattern to fit one quarter of the table top using the pin-and-string method previously described. Then measure an equal amount in from the straight sides – judge the amount by eye to get the size mat you want – and draw straight lines parallel to the sides, and to the desired depth. Join the lines at the top and then cut off the excess paper, allowing 6 mm to 1·5 cm ($\frac{1}{4}$ in to $\frac{1}{2}$ in) hem allowance (fig. 2).

Cut out the mats so that the grain on the fabric runs parallel to the sides of the mats (otherwise they may stretch and buckle). Finish the edges with bias binding, so that the binding is completely on the wrong side of the fabric when the mats are finished.

The corners can be mitered following the method above.

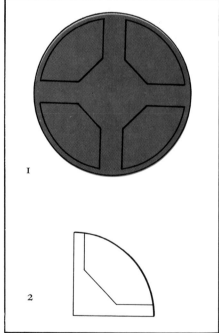

1

2

Left. Matching place mats and table napkins are easy to make and enhance the setting for an informal meal.
Right. If you have a round table and wish to use place mats rather than a cloth, make these mats with a rounded edge. They will make better use of the available space.

Pillows and Slipcovers

Pillows and cushions

Add an individual character to any room with throw pillow covers in your own choice of fabric. Use a variety of shapes, sizes and textures, in colors to blend with your décor.
*Techniques included: piping, cutting bias strips.

The fabric Most fabrics can be used for flat pillow covers (those without welts), although very fine fabrics usually need backing and can be difficult to work on.

How much fabric? For a plain (unpiped) flat pillow take the size of your pillow and then add on at least twice this amount, plus 1·5 cm ($\frac{5}{8}$ in) extra all around for seams. For a well-filled, professional looking finish make the cover 1·5 cm ($\frac{5}{8}$ in) smaller all around than the pillow. For a cover to fit a 30 cm (12 in) flat square or round pillow you will need a piece of fabric 31·5 cm by 63 cm (12$\frac{5}{8}$ in by 25$\frac{1}{4}$ in).

To make a plain flat rectangular pillow
You will need:
A muslin-covered pillow.
Required amount of fabric.
Sewing thread to match fabric.

Making the cover Keeping the fabric on the straight grain, cut two pieces to the calculated size.
Place the two pieces with right sides together, baste and machine stitch around three sides.
On the fourth side fold down the seam allowances onto the wrong side of each section and press. Trim the stitched corners (fig. 1). Finish raw edges and turn right side out. Press. Insert the pillow and slip-stitch the opening neatly by hand. These stitches can be easily removed when the cover is washed.

Making a plain flat round pillow
It is necessary to make a paper pattern to ensure an accurate curve. Use the pin-and-string method (see Table linen) to draw a semicircle on a large sheet of paper. Make the distance between pin and pencil equal to the radius of the finished cover, plus 1·5 cm ($\frac{5}{8}$ in).

You will need:
Paper for pattern.
A muslin-covered pillow.
Required amount of fabric.
Sewing thread to match fabric.

Making the cover Fold the fabric in half lengthwise on the straight grain. Place pattern with the straight edge on the fold. Pin in place and cut along curved line only. Mark the grain line along the fold with basting stitches.

Have fun with fabric and make an array of plain – only in as much as they are easy to sew – pillow covers.

127

Cut another piece of fabric in the same way.

Place the two sections together, with right sides facing and grain lines matching. Baste and machine stitch 1·5 cm ($\frac{5}{8}$ in) from the edge all around the cover, leaving an opening of about one quarter of the circumference for turning right side out.

Clip small V-shapes to within 3 mm ($\frac{1}{8}$ in) from the stitching at 3 cm (1 in) intervals all around (fig. 2).

Finish off as for a square cover.

Muslin-covered pillows Many large stores sell square and oblong muslin pillows in a wide range of sizes. It is, however, quite possible to make your own pillows the size you want.

Filling Down is the most luxurious and most expensive filling and feathers are a good alternative, but many people today prefer to use a synthetic fiber filling which has the advantage of being washable.

Shredded foam rubber and foam rubber chips are inexpensive alternatives.

Covers These can be made from sheets, muslin or any inexpensive, firmly-woven fabric, but if you choose feathers or down for the filling it is essential to buy a down-proof fabric for the cover.

Making the cover Make the cover in the same way as a plain outer cover with a small opening for filling. Remember that it should be 1·5 cm ($\frac{5}{8}$ in) larger all around than the outer pillow cover. Turn out and press.

Stuff the cover with filling so that it is plump but not hard, paying particular attention to the corners.

Pin the folded edges of the opening together. Then baste and machine stitch close to the edge.

*Piping

Piping has several advantages. It gives a stronger seam and a more professional finish to pillows, slipcovers and bedspreads. If you do not feel that you are able to stitch very straight seams piping will hide minor inaccuracies.

Piping will give a neat, well-defined edge and at the same time strengthen the seams of covers to provide greater durability.

It consists of a cord covered with bias-cut strips of fabric and is stitched into a seam.

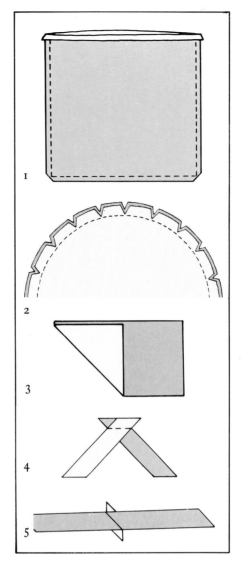

1. *Making a plain pillow cover.*
2. *Clipping seam of a round cover.*
3 to 5. *Making bias strips.*

Piping cord Usually made of three strands of cotton. It comes in a range of thicknesses for use with various fabric weights: use the thinnest for fine fabrics such as silk, the medium weight for cushion covers and the heaviest for slip covers. As the cord is liable to shrink, buy about 25 cm ($\frac{1}{4}$ yd) extra for each cushion. Boil and dry the cord twice before use to ensure that it is fully shrunk.

*Cutting long bias strips

A quick way to cut the long lengths of bias strips needed for piping is as follows:

Take a rectangle of fabric about 23 cm by 46 cm (9 in by 18 in). The length of the fabric should be at least twice the width.

Fold up the bottom right-hand corner to obtain the bias. Press.

Cut off this corner and join to other edge with right sides facing and 6 mm ($\frac{1}{4}$ in) seam.

Press the seam open and trim off any selvages.

Make a cardboard ruler the width of the piping strips. For upholstery the width is usually 4·5 cm ($1\frac{1}{2}$ in) wide.

Using the ruler and tailor's chalk mark lines on the right side of the fabric, parallel to the ends. Then mark a 6 mm ($\frac{1}{4}$ in) seam allowance along each side. Mark points A and B carefully as shown (fig. 6).

Stick a pin through the wrong side of fabric at point A and bring it across through point B. Pin the two sides together very accurately, right sides facing.

Continue pinning along the marked seam to make a cylindrical shape. Baste, and check that the horizontal lines meet exactly.

Stitch, then press seam open using a sleeve board (fig. 7).

Turn to the right side and start cutting along the horizontal lines in a spiral (fig. 8).

Piped square pillow covers

If you intend to pipe the edges of a pillow, do not use a loosely woven fabric, as the cord will show through. Allow another 50 cm ($\frac{1}{2}$ yd) of fabric for making the bias casing strip for the piping cord.

*Techniques included: two ways to insert a zipper.

You will need:

Paper for pattern.

A muslin-covered pillow.

Required amount of fabric.

Matching thread.

Required amount of piping cord.

Zipper, 6 cm (2 in) less than pillow width.

Making the cover The piping should be attached before the cover is made. It is not a good idea to pipe flat round covers as these do not keep a good shape when the pillow is inserted. Cut out cover as previously described. Cut and join enough 4·5 cm ($1\frac{1}{8}$ in) wide bias strips to fit the perimeter of the cover, plus 10 cm (4 in).

Center the piping cord, slightly longer than the strip, along the wrong side of this strip. Fold the edges together, with the cord in the middle. Baste or

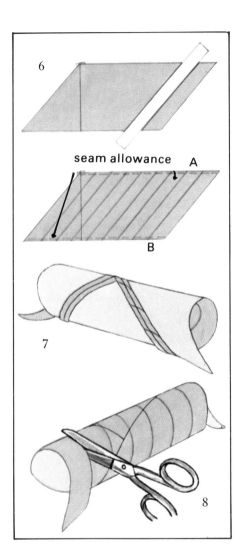

seam allowance

A

B

6, 7, 8. *How to cut long bias strips.*

from one end and one strand from the other. Overlap and twist together the remaining three ends and overcast or bind them firmly (fig. 3).

Fold over the casing and baste around joined cord. Baste the piping to the cushion.

Zipper or piping foot To attach piping successfully by machine it is necessary to use a zipper or piping foot on your sewing machine.

This is made in one piece, instead of split as with the standard foot, enabling you to stitch close to the piping cord.

The pillow cover is usually inserted into the machine with its bulk on the left and the seam allowances under the foot.

The needle should be to the left of the foot, which is pressed up hard against the piping cord.

Keep the foot in this position throughout the sewing. At the corners, leave the needle down, lift the foot and turn the fabric around to the new position. Lower the foot and continue sewing. Place the second cover piece on top of the piped piece, with right sides together and enclosing the piping. Baste and machine stitch the cover together along three sides, stitching as close as possible to the cord.

Finish as for a plain cover.

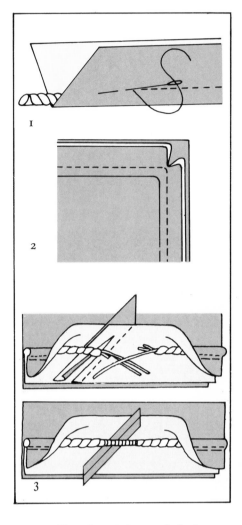

1 to 3. Covering piping cord, fitting to the cover and joining ends.
Below: patchwork pillow with piping.

machine stitch casing firmly around cord to within 3 cm (1 in) of each end, keeping the stitching as close as possible to the piping and using the zipper or piping foot on the machine (fig. 1 p. 129).

Starting in the middle of a side, pin the casing all around the edge on the right side of one cover piece. The raw edges of the folded casing must be even with the raw edges of the cover. At each corner, clip into the casing seam allowance to within 3 mm ($\frac{1}{8}$ in) of the basting stitches of the casing. This will make the piping lie flat (fig. 2).

To make a neat join in the piping, unfold the unbasted portion of the casing at each end and overlap ends by 1·5 cm ($\frac{5}{8}$ in). Adjust the overlap to fit the pillow cover exactly. Join the ends as for bias strips, trimming to 6 mm ($\frac{1}{4}$ in).

Overlap the cord for 3 cm (1 in) and trim off the excess. Unravel 3 cm (1 in) at each end and cut away two strands

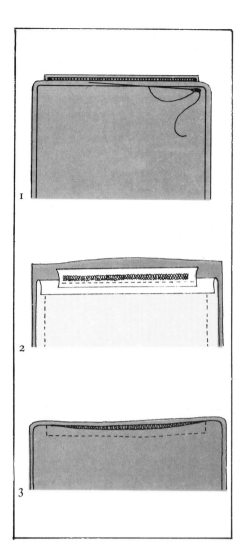

If a pillow cover has to be removed for laundering, it is a practical idea to make the cover with a zipper fastening. Do not use zippers on round pillows as they will distort the seams.
1. Zipper sewn in by hand.
2, 3. Zipper stitched in by machine.

Two ways to insert a zipper

When a cover needs to be removed frequently for washing you may prefer to insert an easy-opening type of fastening, such as a zipper.

Zippers are most suited for use on pillows with straight sides, as a zipper is inclined to distort the shape of a round pillow.

The methods given here are for plain or piped pillow covers.

Inserting a zipper by hand This is a very neat way of putting in a zipper. Make the cover in the usual way, but stitch along the fourth side for 3 cm (1 in) at each end. Fasten off the stitching securely. Turn the cover right side out.

Press under the seam allowance along the piped edge if piping has been used.

Place the piped edge over the right side of the closed zipper so that the folded edge of the seam allowance is centered along the zipper teeth.

On the right side of the cover baste along the gulley between the piping and cover (fig. 1).

Fold under the unpiped edge of the opening and put it onto the zipper so that it meets the piped edge. Baste in position close to the edge of the zipper teeth, curving the stitching into the fold at the top and bottom.

Using double sewing thread, prick stitch the zipper to the cover along the basting line.

Zipper stitched by machine With the cover inside out, place the zipper face downward on the piped edge of the opening, with the teeth as close as possible to the piping cord.

Baste and machine stitch the zipper to the seam allowance and piping only, close to the teeth, using a zipper foot (fig. 2).

Turn the cover right side out and place the other folded edge over the zipper to meet the piped edge.

Baste and machine stitch the cover to the zipper 1 cm ($\frac{3}{8}$ in) from the fold; take the stitching across to the fold at each end (fig. 3).

Turn the cover inside out and snip into the stitched-down seam allowance at each end.

If you prefer, the zipper can be inserted before the other three sides are stitched.

Box cushions

Box cushions are block-shaped cushions with squared-off edges. They are usually made from foam rubber shapes and are often used on the seats and backs of chairs. They also make good floor cushions. Covers are made with a strip of fabric (the welt) separating the top piece from the bottom. Box cushions are sometimes used with conventional armchairs and sofas. They can be re-covered to match the slipcovers.

The shape If you are buying your own foam shape to make box cushions, check that it is of the correct quality foam for your purpose. To give the best wear, seat cushions should be of a higher density foam than back cushions and for comfort they should be 7.5 to 10 cm (3 to 4 in) thick. Back cushions can be slightly thinner.

The fabric If the cushions are to be used regularly, buy the type of fabric recommended for slipcovers. It is also advisable to make an inner cover which protects the foam and prevents the main cover from sticking to it. This inner cover can be of muslin, drapery lining or any lightweight cotton.

Making a cutting chart The simplest way of estimating the amount of fabric you need is to draw a cutting chart to scale. Take one small square on the graph paper to represent 2 cm (1 in). To do this, draw a straight line to represent the width of your fabric. Draw two more lines at right angles to each end of this. Then draw on the cover pieces; a top and bottom and four welt pieces (or one long strip to go right around the cushion). The outer cover for a box cushion should be exactly the same size as the shape.

A zipper can be inserted into the center of one of the shorter welt pieces. In this case this section is made in two halves and seam allowances must be added for the zipper.

Add 1.5 cm ($\frac{5}{8}$ in) seam allowances for each cover piece. Complete the rectangle after the last piece. Measure the length of the rectangle to give the amount of fabric required. If the cushion is to be piped, add about 50 cm ($\frac{1}{2}$ yd) to pipe the top and bottom of each cushion.

To make a box cushion cover
You will need:
A cushion shape.
Required amount of fabric and matching thread.
Pre-shrunk piping cord (twice perimeter of shape plus 30 cm (12 in).
Zipper, 1.3 cm ($\frac{1}{2}$ in) shorter than width of shape.

Cutting out Pieces should be cut on the straight grain of the fabric. If the fabric has a pile or one-way design this should run from back to front on the top and bottom pieces and from top to bottom on the welt. Cut out one top, one bottom and strips for welt of cushion to sizes marked in cutting chart.

Join the side strips to each side of the front strip along the short edges, taking 1.5 cm ($\frac{5}{8}$ in) seams. Taper the stitching into the corners 1.3 cm ($\frac{1}{2}$ in) from the begining and end of each seam (fig. 1 p. 131).

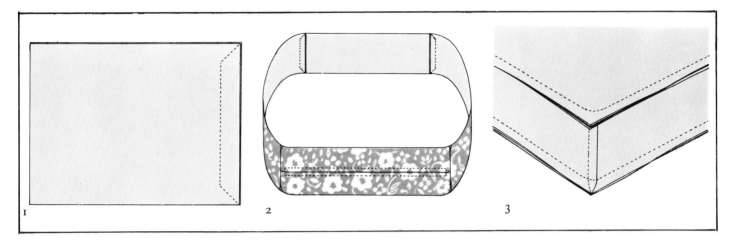

1   2   3

If putting in a zipper, join the halves of the remaining welt strip for 2 cm (¾ in) at each end, taking 1·5 cm (⅝ in) seams. Insert zipper into the opening. Attach to the ends of welt strip, taking 1·5 cm (⅝ in) seams and tapering stitching as before (fig. 2). Press the seam allowances to one side.

(If the welt has been cut in one piece, insert the zipper in the center of the bottom section.)

Piping A box cushion looks better if it is piped. Make the piping as previously described and attach it to the top and bottom sections before joining them to the welt.

Placing right sides together, pin top of cover onto welt, matching the seams of the welt to the corners. Baste and machine stitch as close to the piping as possible.

Stitch the bottom section of the cover in the same way (fig. 3). Press and turn the finished cover right side out.

Round cushion with welt

This type of cushion is ideal for bedrooms, bathrooms and kitchens. It can be made with ties and used to transform a plain wooden stool into something really practical and attractive.

1. Stitching side strips to front piece.
2. Zipper stitched into welt strips.
3. Finishing the box cushion.
Below: A day bed is transformed into a sofa by matching pillows and cover.

You will need:

Paper for pattern.
Required amount of fabric and matching thread.
A round cushion shape.
Pre-shrunk piping cord, twice the cushion circumference plus 1 m (1 yd).

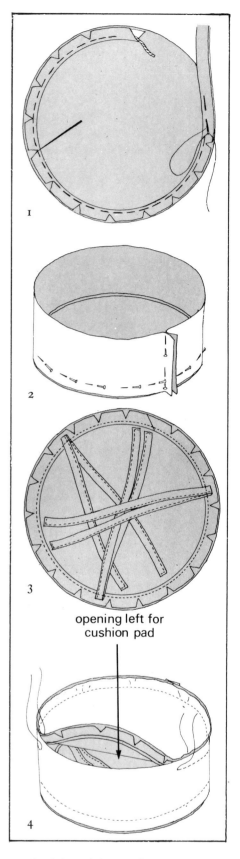

1. Applying piping to the edge of a round cushion with welt.
2. Pinning the welt to the top cover piece.
3. Placing ties on cushion cover.
4. Stitching bottom cushion piece.
A round cushion with welt is ideal for a kitchen stool.

opening left for cushion pad

Cutting out First make a circular paper pattern to the size of the cushion. For top and bottom cut two circles of fabric, adding 1·5 cm ($\frac{5}{8}$ in) seam allowances all around. Remember to center any design when cutting out.

For the welt, cut a piece of fabric on the straight grain of the fabric to the required depth of the welt plus 1·5 cm ($\frac{5}{8}$ in) seam allowance each side and to the circumference of the circle plus 10 cm (4 in) for seams and easing. Cut 4 cm (1$\frac{1}{2}$ in) wide bias strips using the quick spiral method previously described. You will need enough for twice the circumference of the cushion plus 20 cm (8 in) for ease.

Applying the piping Make and apply the piping as described for piping square cushion covers. Clip into the seam allowance at frequent intervals so that the piping will mold to the shape (fig. 1).

Piping should be stitched to both top and bottom cover pieces.

Finishing the cushion Pin the welt to the top cover piece, wrong sides together, and mark the exact position for the join on the welt (fig. 2).

Baste and machine stitch the welt seam and press seam open.

Placing right sides together stitch the welt to the cushion top using a zipper or piping foot to stitch as close as possible to the piping.

If you want ties to attach the cushion to a stool, cut three or four 4 cm (1$\frac{1}{2}$ in) wide straight strips of fabric each about 60 cm (24 in) long.

Fold in half lengthwise, wrong sides together, and press. Turn in all edges for 6 mm ($\frac{1}{4}$ in) and press again. Machine stitch folded edges together. Mark positions for the ties on the bottom of the cushion. Position them on the right side as shown (fig. 3).

Baste the welt to the bottom of the cover in the same way as the top, leaving an opening large enough to insert the cushion (fig. 4). Stitch. Turn to right side.

Insert the cushion and slip-stitch opening to close.

Tie-on cushions

Individually-shaped cushions are an easy way to add color to the plainest

Pretty tie-on cushions add comfort to dinner table seating arrangements.

Top. *Measuring for tie-on cushions.*
Middle. *Position for ties on cushion.*
1. *Deep-buttoning a cushion.*

kitchen chair—and style to your kitchen. Fabrics for these cushions should be firmly woven. Depending on the purpose of the cushion, linen, cotton or canvas are all suitable washable fabrics, while more elegant versions could be made in velvet or corduroy.
*Technique included: deep buttoning.

You will need:
Paper for pattern.
Required amount of fabric.
Sewing thread to match fabric.
A thin foam cushion shape, 2 to 2·5 cm ($\frac{3}{4}$ to 1 in) deep and a little larger then the size of the chair seat.
Required number of button molds and bottom buttons; also carpet thread for deep buttoning (optional).

Making the pattern Lay a sheet of newspaper across the chair seat and mark around front and side edges of the seat. Mark the shape around any struts at the back of the chair so that the cushion will fit snugly. Check the fit before cutting out a final pattern (fold this in half lengthwise to ensure that sides are uniform). Mark the position of the back chair legs on the pattern.

Cutting out Lay the pattern onto the cushion shape and draw around it with a ballpoint pen. Cut out the shape with scissors. Using the pattern, cut out top and bottom cushion pieces on the straight grain of the fabric, adding 1·5 cm ($\frac{5}{8}$ in) seam allowances.

To make the cushion cover Cut and make two fabric ties as described for round pillow with welt. Position the ties to correspond with back legs of chair as marked on pattern. Placing right sides together baste and machine stitch the two cover pieces, leaving an opening in the back to insert the cushion. Turn right side out. Insert cushion and slip-stitch opening to close.

*Deep buttoning
To button the cushions first cover button molds with cushion cover fabric, following manufacturer's instructions. With long needle and carpet thread sew through the shank of the bottom button, up through the cushion, through the shank of the top button, down through the cushion and back to the button on the underside. Pull the threads tightly so that the top button sinks into the cushion slightly. Knot the threads firmly (fig. 1).

Slipcovers
It is quite simple to make your own slipcovers and it is considerably less expensive than having them made. Complicated patterns are not required. The fabric is cut directly on the chair or sofa and "molded" to fit the con-

A bedroom chair slipcovered in a brightly colored fabric, and with the deep skirt box pleated at the corners.

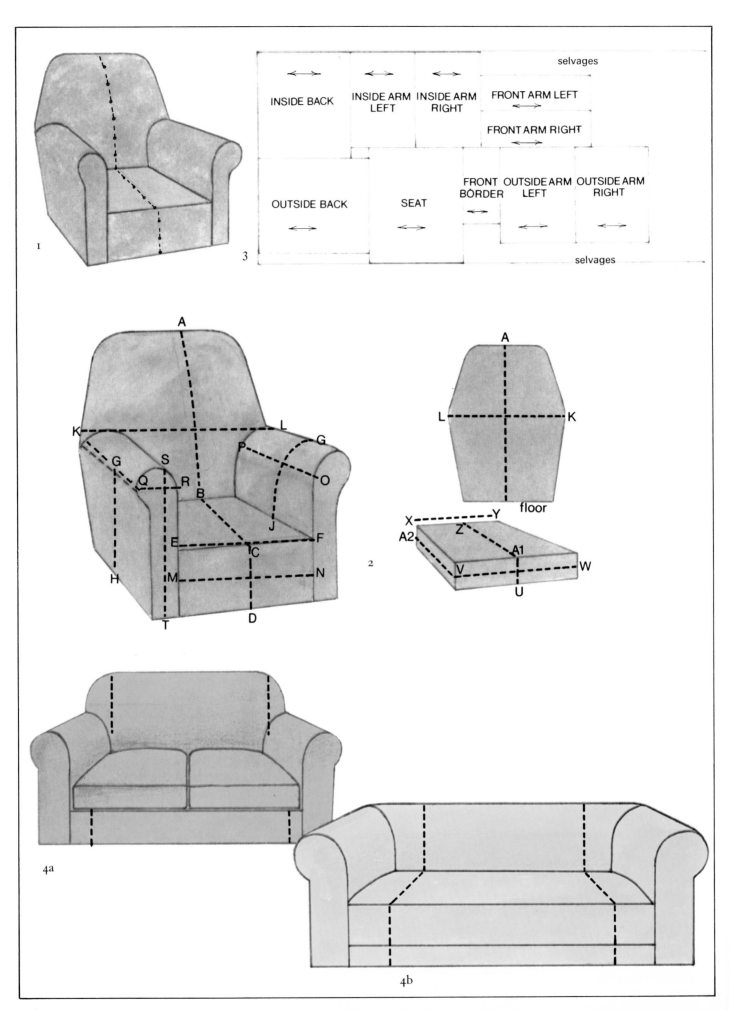

			selvages
INSIDE BACK	INSIDE ARM LEFT	INSIDE ARM RIGHT	FRONT ARM LEFT
			FRONT ARM RIGHT
OUTSIDE BACK	SEAT	FRONT BORDER	OUTSIDE ARM LEFT / OUTSIDE ARM RIGHT
			selvages

1

3

2

4a

4b

tours of the upholstery by pinning. It is a satisfying experience to see the shape emerging as you work.

Although the shapes and sizes of upholstered furniture vary, the same basic techniques are used for all styles – both to estimate the fabric required and to cut and fit covers.

One particular chair shape has been used here of the purpose of illustration. Different shapes or additional insets are treated in the same way, but it is important to follow the seamlines of the original upholstery as closely as possible.

What can be covered With the exception of velvet and leather, almost any upholstered chair or sofa can be fitted with slipcovers.

Before you start always clean the chair or sofa with dry upholstery shampoo.

Choosing the fabric Choose furnishing fabrics which are tough and hard-wearing, firmly woven, color fast and pre-shrunk. Avoid very thick fabrics as these will be difficult to work with, especially if you are piping the seams. Medium-weight cottons and linens treated for crease resistance are

1. Pins placed down the center front.

2. Take measurements across the widest and deepest sections of the chair.

3. A sample chart. Use measurements taken to work out your own chart.

4a. Position of seams on a small sofa using 120 cm (48 in) wide fabric.

4b. Position of seams on a large sofa using 120 cm (48 in) wide fabric.

5. Outside back pinned in place.

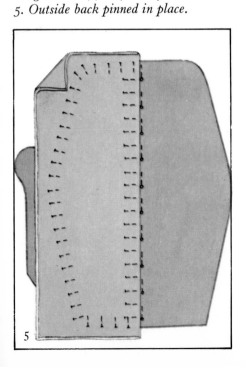

ideal, but do not attempt to use dress fabrics as they are not strong enough.

Taking the measurements
Before buying the fabric and cutting out, the separate sections must be measured.

Write all measurements down, as they will be needed for calculating the amount of fabric needed and also when cutting out the individual sections of fabric.

Remove the cushion or cushions, if there are any, and mark a line with glass headed pins up the center of the outside back of the chair, down the inside back and along the seat from the back to the front border (fig. 1).

Using a fabric tapemeasure, measure each section, including cushions, at its widest point (fig. 2). If your particular chair or sofa sections are not pictured here, these should be measured following the same principle.

Outside back From A to floor; from K to L.

Inside back From A to B plus 15 cm (6 in) for tuck-in; from K to L.

Inside arm From G to J plus 15 cm (6 in) for tuck-in; from P to O plus 15 cm (6 in) for tuck-in.

Outside arm From G to H; from K to Q.

Seat From B to C plus 15 cm (6 in) for tuck-in; from E to F plus 30 cm (12 in) for tuck-in.

Border From C to D; from M to N.

Front arm From Q to R; from S to T.

Cushion top From X to Y; from Z to A1.

Cushion front inset V to W; from A1 to U.

Cushion side inset From A2 to V.

Fabric requirements
Most upholstery fabrics are 120 cm (48 in) wide. To cover a chair you will require about five times as much fabric as the height of the back. However, a more precise estimate is needed for each individual piece and this can be accomplished using the measurements just described.

Draw a small chart to scale on a sheet of paper or graph paper. (Large quantities of fabric will be involved.) Draw two parallel lines to scale to represent the width of the fabric. Use a simple scale such as 1 mm for every centimeter (or $\frac{1}{10}$ in for every inch).

Using the measurements you have taken draw out rectangles to scale to represent each section needed for the cover, adding 3 cm (1¼ in) to each measurement for seam allowances (fig. 3). Label each piece and mark the dimensions as you progress. Remember that some sections, such as sides, arms and cushion parts, have to be cut twice.

Extra allowances Should the fabric you choose have a repeated pattern this will have to be taken into consideration and extra fabric bought. The quantity depends on the size of the repeat.

Piping Allow an extra 1·40 m (1½ yd) for cutting bias strips if you intend to pipe a chair. Increase this estimate proportionally for a sofa.

Sofa Special allowances must be made for joins in the fabric if necessary to obtain the correct width (figs. 4a and 4b). A repeated pattern must always match at the seams.

Skirt Extra fabric will also be needed should you want a ruffle or pleated finish to the bottom.

For a ruffle, you will need twice the circumference of the bottom of the chair by the depth of ruffle plus seam and hem allowances.

For a plain tailored skirt with a pleat at each corner you will need the circumference of chair or sofa plus 88 cm (32 in) by the depth of trim plus seam and hem allowance.

Having drawn all the pieces out to scale on paper, measure the total length and convert to full scale to find out the amount of fabric required.

Making slipcovers
You will need:
Calculated quantity of fabric.
Sewing thread to match.
Calculated length of heavy piping cord.
Desired fastening.

Cutting the fabric Following the chart you have made, mark out with chalk and cut a rectangle of fabric for each area to be covered. Make sure that the lengthwise grain of each piece runs with the grain of the fabric, and that the pattern, if any, matches. Be sure to add 3 cm (1 in) seams allowance around each piece.

Fitting the cover The method of fitting the fabric to the chair is to fold the rectangles of fabric in half with right sides together and, working from the center marked with pins, fit, pin and trim closely. The fabric is then opened out and the pieces are stitched together, with piping inserted in the appropriate seams.

Starting with the outside back pieces, fold in half and place the folded edge level with the pins down the back of the chair; the allowances made for seams and hems should project at the top, side and bottom. Pin down the fold, then smooth the fabric out to the side of the chair and pin it to the padding, placing the pins at right angles to the edge of the fabric. Keep the fabric smooth and taut with the grain of the fabric straight in both directions (fig. 5).

Pin the seat piece to center of seat in the same way, so that the allowance for the tuck-in lies at the back and side and a seam allowance in the front. Pin the fabric all around and fold back the tuck-in allowance onto the seat for the time being (fig. 6).

Fold the inside back piece, pin it to the center line, smooth it out and pin it to the padding as before. Then pin to the outside back piece at the top of the chair, following the shape of the chair exactly.

With some fabrics you may be able to ease in the fullness. With others, such as linen on a curved back, you may have to make small darts at the corners. Pin the pieces together down the sides, working from the top down. As you reach the arm, cut into the fabric from the sides so that the inside back can be wrapped around smoothly to join the back. Carefully cut the fabric over the arm to fit the curve and then extend gradually outward to the full 15 cm (6 in) tuck-in allowance at the bottom of the section (fig. 7). Clip into the seam allowance on the curve.

Fitting the arms Place the two inside arm pieces together with wrong sides facing, then place them onto the inside arm. Pin the front edge to the padding first and the top to the "sight line". This is an imaginary line (fig. 8a) where a seam must be made in slip-

6. Seat piece in position. 7. Inside back pinned to outside back. 8. Inside arm pinned and trimmed. 8a. Dotted line in sight line. 9. Outside arm pinned at top and back. 10. Arm front pinned in place. 11. Seams trimmed.

138

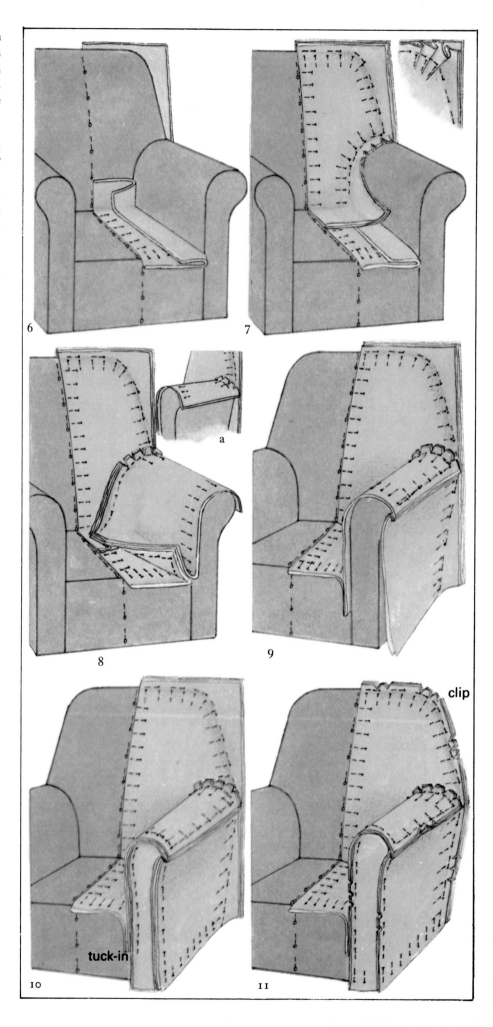

covers and does not already exist in the upholstery. The seam allowance should overlap the front and the "sight line". Smooth to back of arm, with grain parallel to side of chair. Pin the bottom edge to the tuck-in edge of the seat and cut the back edge of the arm to correspond with the inside back tuck-in. Clip the seam allowance over the top curve of the arm where necessary (fig. 8).

Place the outside arm pieces together with wrong sides facing; keep the straight crosswise grain of the fabric parallel to the floor. Pin the top edge to the inside arm on the "sight line". At the very back of the arm where the padding is less rounded, more fabric may have to be pinned into the seam.

12. Piping basted to outside back, top of outside arm and front arm.
13. Inside back, inside arm, outside arm and seat stitched together.

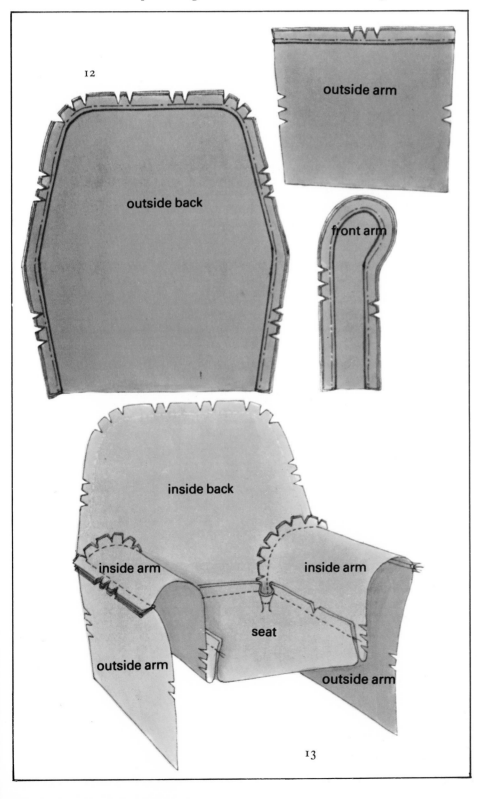

12

outside arm

outside back

front arm

inside back

inside arm

inside arm

seat

outside arm

outside arm

13

Pin the back edge of the outside arm piece to the outside back and to padding; leave front edge free (fig. 9).

Fitting the arm fronts Position both front arm pieces together, wrong sides facing, to the widest part of the arm front, and pin carefully to the outside arm piece following the shape of the chair as closely as possible. Continue pinning to the inside arm as far as the end of the tuck-in (fig. 10).

The front panel or border This cannot be cut until after the other pieces have been cut and all the main seams have been stitched and tuck-ins positioned correctly.

Trimming the seam allowance If you are satisfied with the fit of the cover so far, trim all the seams exactly to within 1.5 cm ($\frac{5}{8}$ in) of the pinned fitting lines. Cut notches in the corresponding seams in groups of two and three, so that you will be able to fit the pieces together again (fig. 11). Remove all the pins, take the sections off the chair and open them out.

Make lengths of piping by enclosing the piping cord in the bias strips as previously described. (See Piped square pillow covers.)

Attaching piping Pin and baste the piping on the right side of the fabric sections shown (fig. 12). Make sure raw edges are together. These include the top and sides of the outside back, the front arms and the top edges or "slight line" of the outside arms. The front border will be cut and piped later.

Box cushions (See Pillows and cushions for details of cutting, fitting and making up.)

Stitching and pressing You will find that a neat and crisp finish will be easier to achieve if you press seams as you work.

Remember to take 1.5 cm ($\frac{5}{8}$ in) seams throughout; before stitching the sections together always pin and baste them first.

Stitch all seams with right sides facing and finish the raw edges by stitching them together with a zigzag stitch, or overcast by hand. Press all seams away from the front of the chair. Baste and stitch the tuck-in seam at the back of the seat and the bottom of the inside back. This is an unpiped seam.

Next stitch the outside arms of the slipcover to the inside arms, stitching

139

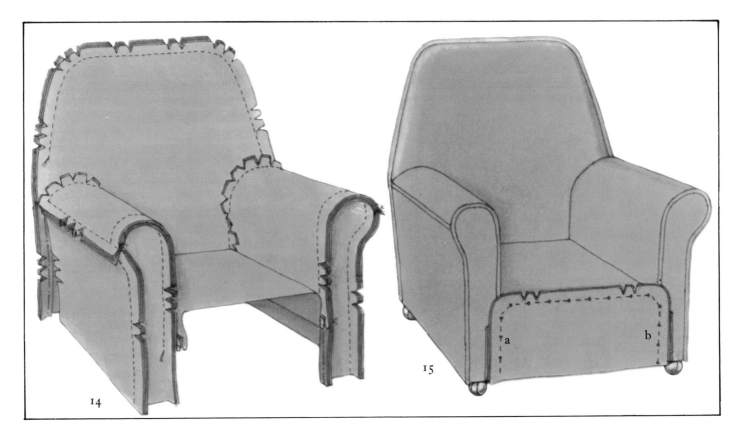

14

15

a   b

the piping neatly into the seam.

Stitch the bottom of the inside arms to the sides of the seat tuck-in, then stitch the arm to the inside back. (This seam is not piped.) Fig. 13 shows seams stitched together so far.

Stitch the outside and inside back together along the top and down one side, continuing down to the bottom of the chair. Then stitch the other side to about 10 cm (4 in) above the top of the arm, leaving an opening so that the cover can be fitted onto the chair. The length of the opening depends on the shape of the chair, as you must be able to slip the cover on easily. This is a piped seam.

Stitch the front arm pieces in place. Stitch from the outside arm inward and finish at the tuck-in on the inside arm (fig. 14).

Fitting the front border Put the cover onto the chair right side out. Tuck in the sides and back tuck-in pieces, and leave the seam allowance protruding at the front edge. It is at this stage that you will be able to decide how long the back opening should be.

Place the front border in position (fig. 15). Pin it to the front of the seat cover and to the seam allowance of the tuck-in at both sides and to the lower front arms, wrong sides facing. Trim the seam allowance to 1·5 cm

14. Stitching pieces together.

15. Stitching front border in place.

($\frac{5}{8}$ in), mark position with notches and remove the cover from the chair.

Unpin the front border and insert piping along the seamline of the top edge from tuck-in to tuck-in (A to B in fig. 15). Pin together, right sides facing. Baste and stitch the front border into position. The piping will run from A to B along the front of the seat and below A and B on the front arms.

Back opening The opening down the back of the cover can be finished with a zipper, hooks and eyes or snap fasteners – they are all equally suitable.

Strong upholstery zippers are available and furnishing tape with large snaps or hooks and eyes already inserted can be bought by the meter (or yard). If the chair or sofa has a very curved back, separate hooks sewn on by hand with hand-worked bars will give a neater finish. The length of the zipper or snap tape will depend on the finish used at the bottom. Take the zipper or snap tape to the planned bottom seam line.

Fitting a zipper Measure the length required. The zipper should not come to the bottom corner, as the tongue may protrude.

Clip the front seam allowance at the top of the opening. Press the seam allowance on both edges to the wrong side and baste on the folds.

Place the closed zipper on the cover with the right side of the zipper to the inside of the cover, and the open end down. On the right side baste the zipper in place close to the teeth. The piping cord will be over the teeth.

Using a zipper or piping foot, machine-stitch close to the teeth and again near the outside of the tape which will both add strength and keep the zipper tape from catching in the zipper (fig. 16).

Tape with snaps or hooks Clip the front seam allowance at the top of the opening.

With the two pieces of tape fastened together, pin the tape into the opening making sure there is a snap or hook just above the bottom of the chair cover. One edge of each tape should be on the seamline. Now open the tape and baste and stitch each tape in place. The back tape is stitched on both sides flat against the back but the tape attached to the side bends around to the back of the chair. Stitch side tape close to the seamline. Work another row of stitching on the tape 6 mm ($\frac{1}{4}$ in) from the first (fig. 17 and 18).

With the tape fastened finish top raw

ends of tape and stitch together.

Hooks and hand-worked bars Sewn on plain tape. If back of cover is very curved it will be neater to use this method. The tape is attached to the cover in the same way as tape with hooks and eyes or snaps. Hooks are then sewn on at about 5 cm (2 in) intervals and bars worked by hand in strong thread to correspond with the hooks. On some curves it will be necessary to place the hooks and bars closer together so that the opening does not gape (fig. 19).

Finishing the bottom There are several ways to finish the bottom of a slipcover, depending upon the style of the chair or sofa and your own personal taste.

A plain finish This type of finish can be piped or left plain. It consists of strips of fabric fitted under the chair between the legs, with a narrow hem forming a channel (fig. 20 p. 142).

If the bottom is to be piped attach the piping to the slipcover with raw edges together and baste into place before proceeding.

Cut four strips of fabric about 10 cm (4 in) wide and the correct length to fit between the legs.

Make a narrow hem at the ends of each piece and a channel 1·5 cm ($\frac{5}{8}$ in) wide along one long side to take the tape.

Stitch the raw edges of the strips to the bottom of the cover, sandwiching any piping in between. Finish the raw edges and press up onto the cover.

Insert a long piece of tape through the channel. Place the cover on the chair and tie the tape in one corner.

Ruffle finish (fig. 21) Decide upon depth of ruffle required and add 1·5 cm ($\frac{5}{8}$ in) for seam allowances at the top and 2·5 cm (1 in) for a small hem.

Measure around the bottom of the chair and double this measurement. This will be the ruffle length. Cut fabric into strips the required depth and join the strips to obtain the right length, taking 1·5 cm ($\frac{5}{8}$ in) seams. Clip the selvages and press the seam open.

Make a small hem along the bottom of the ruffle by turning up 2·5 cm (1 in). Make a small hem on the short ends for the opening in the same way, mitering the corners.

Divide the ruffle into four equal sec-

tions and mark with pins. Run a gathering thread between the pins. The open end will go to the back opening.

With the cover on the chair mark the position of the stitching line for the ruffle with pins, measuring from the floor. Trim the cover to 1·5 cm ($\frac{5}{8}$ in) below the pins and pipe the bottom of the cover.

Divide the measurement around the piped edge of the cover by four and mark with pins.

Take the cover off the chair. Draw up the gathers on the ruffle. Placing right sides and raw edges together and matching the pins, pin and baste the ruffle to the cover, distributing the

gathers evenly. Stitch and press up; overcast the raw edges together.

Plain tailored finish To make skirting for a plain tailored finish, a border of fabric is placed around the chair or sofa with a pleat at each corner (fig. 22). Measure the bottom front, back and sides of the chair or sofa and add 10 cm (4 in) to each measurement.

Cut strips of fabric to these lengths and to the depth of border required, plus seam and hem allowance; mark

16. Back opening closed with a zipper.
17. Using tape fitted with snaps.
18. Alternatively, use tape fitted with hooks and eyes.
19. Hook and straight eye closing.

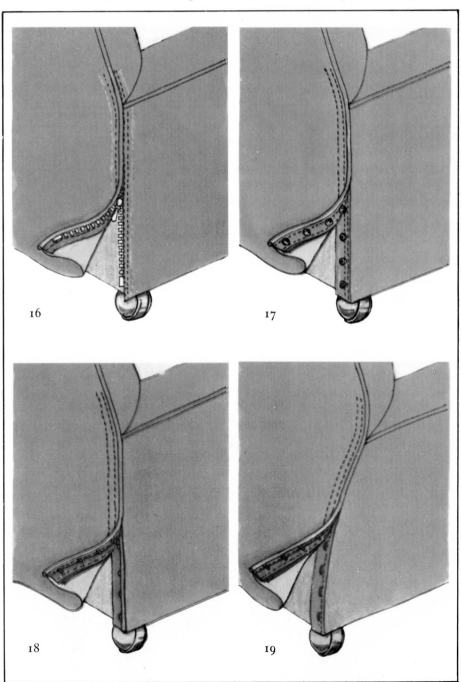

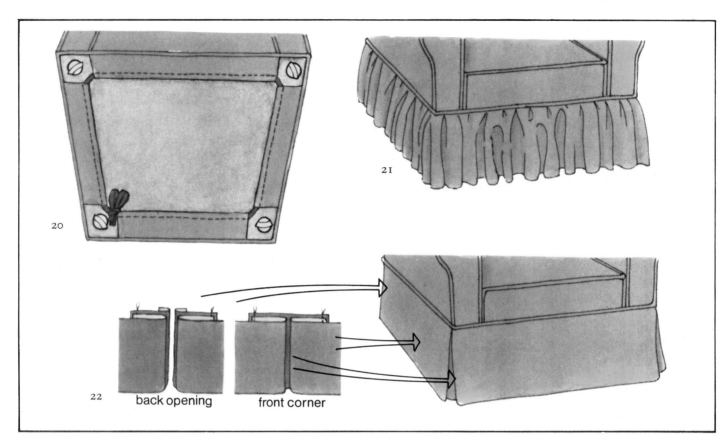

20. *A piped plain finish, with tape threaded through channel.*
21. *A ruffled finish.*
22. *Plain tailored finish with box pleats. On a back corner the pleat is left open to extend back opening.*

A printed linen slipcover is removable, washable and thus practical.

each piece. Cut three strips 10 cm (4 in) by the depth of the border and two strips 6·5 cm (2½ in) by the depth of the border. These are for the corners. With the cover on the chair mark the depth of border required with pins and trim the cover to 1·5 cm (⅝ in) below the pin line. Pipe the edge all around the bottom of the cover.

Join the border pieces together, placing a short piece at each corner and the two very short pieces at the back opening. Take 1·5 cm (⅝ in) seams. Make a small hem along the bottom and turn in 1·5 cm (⅝ in) at the ends. Finish and press.

On the right side make a 4 cm (1½ in) inverted pleat at each corner and baste. The seams will sit inside each pleat.

Baste and stitch the border to the cover with right sides together, sandwiching the piping. Finally finish and press.

Curtains and Draperies

The sheer curtains match the unlined draperies and the slipcovered chair.

Unlined draperies

The first thing to be said for unlined draperies – as against the lined variety – is, obviously, that they're easier to make. But they also have another advantage: they let in more light. Sunlight filtering through the fabric can create a lovely warm glow in a room. And if you choose one of the many interesting sheer fabrics available, you will be delighted with the play of light and texture at your windows. Sheer fabrics require special handling techniques, which are explained on page 149. Below are the basic techniques you will need to know to make unlined draperies from either sheer or closely woven fabrics.

Choosing the fabric   Unless you are planning to use a sheer fabric, you should select one that has plenty of body. Ask the salesperson to help you by holding up a length of the cloth and gathering it in folds so that you can see whether it hangs well. Compare several different fabrics in this way before making up your mind.

Measuring the width   Before you go to buy your fabric, you must make a number of careful measurements to determine exactly how much fabric you will need. First decide on the width the finished draperies must cover. Add to this width the amount of the return (the distance on either side from the rod to the wall). This distance will vary slightly depending on whether you are adding glass curtains or a separate pair of sheer draperies underneath, but usually it is about 9 cm ($3\frac{1}{2}$ in). Remember to allow *twice* this figure – the return on each side. Add another 10 cm (4 in) for the overlap at the center, if you are making draw draperies. (Omit this extra width for stationary panels or for a one-way draw drapery.)

Now divide the total figure you've obtained by two to get the finished, pleated width of each drapery panel. Then add 10 cm (4 in) for each side hem, 2·5 cm (1 in) for each seam (if any), and the allowance for pleats. The simplest way to make pleats in draperies is to use the special pleater tape, which is widely available. One kind of pleater tape requires double the finished width; in other words, the pleats take up the same amount of

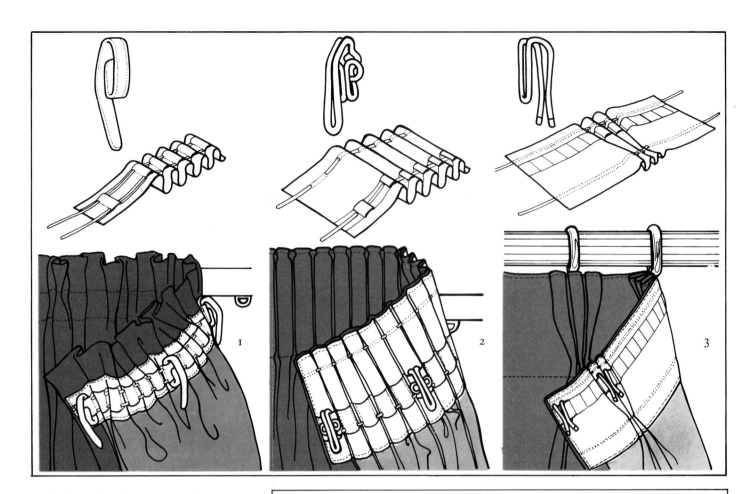

1. *Gathered heading: 2.5 cm (1 in) wide tape. Width of drapery required, one and a half to double length of rod.*
2. *Pencil pleats: 7.5 cm (3 in) wide tape. Width of drapery required, two and a half to three times rod length.*
3. *Pinch pleats: 9 cm (3½ in) wide tape. Width of drapery required, two and a half to three times rod length.*

fabric as is needed to go across the rod. Some other tape gives you more flexibility in the number, fullness and positioning of the pleats. Remember, however, that you will need at least twice the finished width (plus seams and side hems) to achieve a pleasing effect. If you are making your own pleats (see page 155), you should first decide how deep you want each pleat to be; multiply by the number of pleats and add this measurement to the finished width figure already obtained through previous calculation. To make the most economical use of your fabric you can figure the pleat fullness another way: first select your fabric and make a note of its width. Next, figure how many fabric widths you will need to make an unpleated panel at least twice the finished width. Then divide the surplus (the amount

Widths of fabric required

Width of drapery area	Number of 120 cm (48 in) widths per window (for simple gathered heading)
120 cm (4 ft) and under	2
130 cm to 170 cm (4 ft 6 in to 5 ft 6 in)	3
180 cm to 230 cm (6 ft to 7 ft 6 in)	4
240 cm to 300 cm (8 ft to 10 ft)	5

4 **Measurements to take for planning fabric quantity**

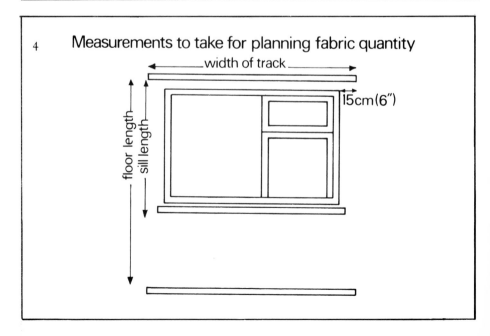

remaining when the finished width is subtracted) by the number of pleats desired to get the amount of fabric taken up in each pleat. For example, suppose your fabric is 120 cm (48 in) wide, and the finished width of each drapery panel will be 95 cm (37½ in). Two widths of fabric seamed together and hemmed will make a piece approximately 217 cm (85½ in) wide – more than twice the finished width. Rather than trimming away the excess to make the fullness exactly double, you can make fuller pleats and thus achieve a more luxurious look. If using whole widths of fabric in this way will result in a drapery that is too full, you can divide one width in two and add one half width in each of the two panels.

Measuring the length Decide on the placement of the rod. If you are using a conventional traverse rod, the top of the draperies will be just above the upper edge of the rod. If you are using a decorative rod, the top of the draperies will be just below the rings. Measure from this point on the wall to the place where the finished lower edge of the draperies will be. If the draperies are floor length add 20·5 cm (8 in) for clearance at the bottom. To this finished length subtract 2·5 cm (1 in) for a double hem at the bottom, plus 1·5 cm (⅝ in) seam allowance at the top if you are using pleater tape. If you are making your own pleats add, instead, 11·5 cm (4 in) for a top hem.

Multiply the total length of a single panel (including bottom hem and top hem and/or seam allowance) by the number of fabric widths required for a single panel, and then multiply this figure by two (assuming you are using two panels on the window) to get the total amount of fabric you must buy. If you are making draperies for different-sized windows, you must, of course, calculate the fabric amount separately for each window. If all the windows are the same size, simply multiply the amount required for one window by the number of windows.

If your fabric has a pattern, you will need to buy extra to allow for matching. The pattern must match at the seams, and if it is a large one with noticeable repeats, the two panels must match not only each other but

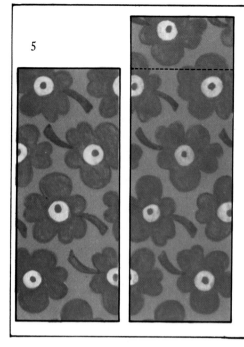

5

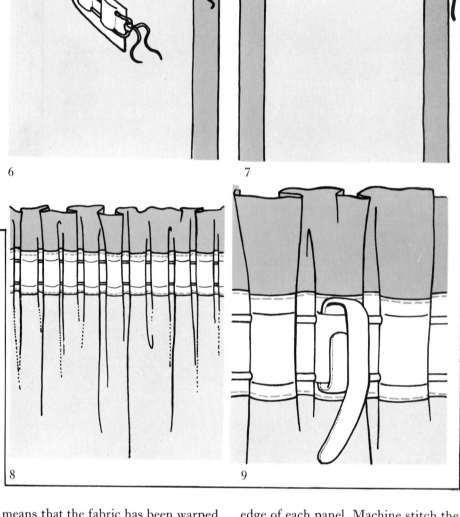

6

7

8

9

5. *Matching patterned fabric.*
6. *Tape in place over the raw edge.*
7. *Top of tape basted to drapery.*
8. *Drapery evenly gathered.*
9. *Inserting hooks into heading tape.*

also the other draperies in the room. The salesperson will help you calculate the extra amount needed.

Making the draperies
You will need:

The required amount of fabric (as calculated above).
Sewing thread to match fabric.
Pleater tape, the same length as the total drapery width for each panel, and hooks.
Drapery rod(s) and rings.
Weighted tape.
Tapemeasure and ruler.
Scissors.
Needles and pins.

Lay the fabric on a large flat surface for cutting out – you must be able to see the complete drapery length at once. Use the floor if you don't have a large enough table. Straighten the top edge of the fabric by drawing a thread at right angles to the selvage and then cutting along the line. Measure the drapery length from this point, draw another thread, and cut along it. Cut the next length in the same way, matching the pattern if necessary (fig. 5).
Note if the corners of the fabric lengths do not make right angles, this

means that the fabric has been warped on the bolt. Before making the draperies, you must straighten each length. Take one of the corners that is less than 90° and grasp the selvage and the crosswise edge in your two hands. Give the fabric a little tug. Move your hands a little farther from the corner and tug again. Continue in this way along the whole length of the fabric (you will need to get someone to help you if the fabric is wide), making sure that you stretch the fabric on the bias – at roughly a 45° angle to the selvage – each time. Repeat if necessary until the fabric is straight.

Seaming plain fabrics Use a 1·5 cm ($\frac{5}{8}$ in) plain seam to join the pieces for each drapery panel, placing the right sides of the fabric together, selvage to selvage. If you are using half widths, place them on the outer

edge of each panel. Machine stitch the lengths together, using a loose tension and a fairly long stitch. Press the seams open and clip into the selvages if they are tight, or cut them off so that the drapery does not pucker.

Seaming patterned fabric Joining two pieces of fabric so that the pattern matches exactly requires a slightly different technique from that usually used on plain fabric.
Begin by finding the same point in the pattern on both pieces of the fabric. Place the two pieces together, right sides facing, and pin them together at that point, with the pin at right angles to the edge. (Normally pins are placed on the seamline, parallel to the edge.) Continue pinning the pieces together at about 5 cm (2 in) intervals. At about 30 cm (12 in) intervals turn the fabric right side up to check that

146

the pattern still matches. If it has started to slip, take out the pins and re-pin the pieces, making sure you are not stretching either of the lengths.

Baste the pieces together along the seamline in the usual way, but leave the pins in place. (If your basting stitches are usually large, make them smaller for this.) Still leaving the pins in, machine stitch, following the basting line and removing the pins as you stitch. Remove the basting and press the seam open.

Attaching pleater tape Lay the tape along the upper edge of the drapery panel, right side of tape (the side with the openings) to right side of fabric. Position the tape so that the first pleat at the outer edge will fall just at the corner. To do this, measure in from the outer edge a distance equal to the side hem – 5 cm (2 in) – plus the return. Place the first slot for the first pleat at that point. Trim away both ends of the tape 5 cm (2 in) in from the side edges. Pin, baste and stitch the tape to the fabric, stitching just above the slots in the tape. Fold the tape to the wrong side of the fabric, and press the seam and the upper edge of the drapery. Stitch the tape in place along its lower edge, making sure to clear the open ends of the slots.

Side hems Fold about 1 cm ($\frac{3}{8}$ in) to the wrong side along the side edge of the drapery; baste. Then fold over the remaining hem allowance, pin and baste and hem. If your machine will do blindstitch, you can hem the side edges by machine.

Hanging the draperies Insert the hooks in the slots to pleat the draperies. Sew a single drapery hook at each outside edge to attach the draperies to the rod return and one at each inside edge as well.

Hang the draperies on the rod and let them hang, unhemmed, for several days to allow the fabric to sag, if it is going to.

Making the hem When you are

A wall of draperies with a pinch pleated heading.

ready to do the hems, mark the line for the length at each side of the drapery while it is still hanging. Full-length draperies should end 2·5 cm, (1 in) above the floor so that they will hang properly and not become worn at the lower edge. Sill-length draperies should either just clear the sill, or hang about 2·5 cm (1 in) below it.

Insert pins at short intervals along the hemline. Check the length by turning up the hem allowance and pinning it in place, then measuring the distance from hemline to floor. Remove these extra pins to release the hem allowance, if necessary, to make it even. Fold up half the hem allowance and pin along the fold. Then fold again along the hemline. Baste along hemline and along turned-under edge. Hem by hand. Insert a length of weighted tape in each hem. Catch in place at each end with a few stitches. Close the side openings in the hem with slip-stitching.

Sheer draperies and curtains

Sheer fabrics give a lovely soft look to a window, diffusing light and – in the case of textured sheer fabrics – casting interesting patterns on walls and floors.

The most commonly-used kind of sheer fabrics are the fine sheers, such as marquisette, which are used for glass curtains. Glass curtains are hung against the window to give privacy to a room which can be seen into. The fabric used for glass curtains used to be cotton, but these days it is more often a man-made fabric such as polyester, which is strong and resistant to the sun. Glass curtains are normally white and are often combined with draw draperies, which give complete screening at night.

Textured sheers are heavier than the fabrics used for glass curtains, but because they are open weave most of them permit more light to enter.

They are more often used as draw draperies (unlined) than as curtains, and they are ideal for large picture windows, where the idea is to admit plenty of light and show off the window itself, even when the draperies are closed. They also make good room dividers. Here again, it is better to

Rings are once again becoming a popular way of hanging various drapery styles.

make them draw draperies.

Because they are so transparent, textured sheers are often paired with opaque draw draperies to give privacy at night. Or, you can hang a separate lining drapery underneath your sheers on a traverse rod. In this way you can enjoy the beauty of the sheers at night without having their color dulled by the darkness behind them.

Handling sheer fabrics Sheer fabrics are not difficult to sew, provided you use a fine, sharp needle and set your machine with a loose tension to prevent puckering. It is usually advisable to baste all folds, hems and seams, as fine sheer fabric – and some of the very open sheers – tend to slip while being machine stitched. You should use synthetic thread, unless fabric is made from natural fibers.

If you have difficulty in feeding the fabric through the machine, or if it still slips in spite of being basted, it may help to put strips of tissue paper under the fabric as it is being fed into the machine.

Textured sheer draperies These are made in essentially the same way as plain unlined draperies, but there are one or two special techniques required. First, you should plan the depth of the hems so that any spaces in the weave of the fabric fall on top of each other and the stitching can be made on a solid section of the weave.

If you do not like the effect of the curtain tape showing through the mesh you can disguise it by inserting a strip of plain fabric in a color matching the drapery fabric, between the drapery and the tape. If the draperies are washable, the strip should be of a similar type of fabric so that it will react in the same way when washed.

Making glass curtains

Ready-made glass curtains are relatively inexpensive and available in a wide range of sizes, so you may not find it worthwhile to make your own. However, if you are curtaining odd-sized windows, or want a special kind of fabric or a color other than white, you may find it necessary to make the curtains yourself.

Calculating fabric requirements

Glass curtains should be two and a half to three times the gathered width. Allow 5 cm (2 in) for each side hem and 3 cm (1¼ in) for each seam.

To calculate the length: measure the distance from the bottom of the curtain rod to the place where the lower edge of the curtain will be – for floor length curtains, 2·5 cm (1 in) above the floor. To this measurement add 13 cm (5 in) for the casing and heading and 13 cm (7 in) for the lower hem. Multiply this total unfinished length by the number of fabric widths required to make curtains of the desired fullness.

To make the curtains
You will need:
The required amount of fabric.
Sewing thread to match fabric.
A conventional curtain rod.
Tapemeasure and ruler.
Scissors.
Needles and pins.

Measure and cut the fabric lengths on the straight of the grain as described under Making unlined draperies.

Join the fabric widths for each curtain with French seams or flat fell seams. Make double side hems by turning under half the hem allowance, then the other half, then pinning, basting and machine-stitching.

Make the casing and heading as follows:

First turn under 1 cm (⅜ in) at upper edge and baste. Then fold half the remaining heading allowance to the wrong side. Baste and machine stitch close to the folded-under edge.

Insert the curtain rod in the heading, close to the stitching line and place a pin above the upper edge of the rod, through both thicknesses of the heading. Allow enough space between the stitching and the pin to accomodate the rod easily. Remove the rod. Continue pinning along the whole width of the curtain, measuring the distance with a ruler as you go. Now machine stitch along the line of pins, removing the pins as you stitch, to complete the casing. The narrow heading above the casing gives the effect of a small, neat ruffle once the curtains are gathered onto the rod.

Hang up the curtains and allow them to sag for a few days. Then turn up a double hem; pin, baste and machine stitch along the turned under edge.

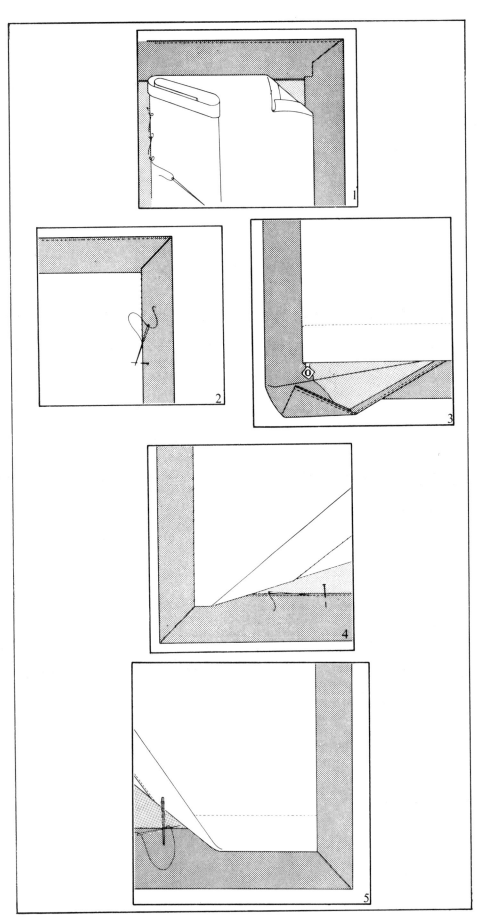

Lined draperies

Techniques included: mitered corners, locking.

Lining improves the appearance of most draperies, making them seem fuller and hang better. A lining also protects the drapery fabric from fading and soiling on the window side. It makes the fabric more opaque and gives an extra barrier against heat loss. In the following pages you will find instructions for sewing in a lining by hand and by machine, for making a detachable lining using the European-style pleater tape (which uses cords instead of pronged hooks) and for making hand-sewn pleats.

Calculating the fabric required

The instructions that follow are for lined draperies with a stiffened heading in which you make pleats by hand (see page 155). If you are using pleater tape, you will need to make slight adjustments in the measurements, as explained on page 144. First measure the area to be covered with the draperies as described in Unlined draperies. The width measurement will be the same, but you will need to adjust the length measurement by adding 11 cm ($4\frac{1}{2}$ in) for the top hem. Calculate the required amount of lining fabric in the same way as for the drapery fabric, but subtract 21·5 cm ($8\frac{1}{2}$ in) on each length.

Choosing lining fabric Use a conventional lining fabric, such as cotton sateen. This is available in white, beige and a few colors in the normal furnishing width of 120 cm (48 in). If you want to have lining in a color to match your drapery fabric, and cotton sateen is not available in that color, choose a fabric that is closely woven and lightweight, or dye white cotton sateen to the desired color.

You will need:

The calculated amount of drapery fabric (see Unlined draperies).
The calculated amount of lining fabric. If the lining fabric is a different width, you will need to make separate calculations. If it is the same width, only the length must be altered.
Belting or crinoline – enough to make a strip 10 cm (4 in) deep, running across the entire width of each drapery panel.

1. Locking in the lining, starting at the upper edge. 2. Hemming the lining to the side hem. 3. Turning up the lower edge (weight has been sewn at corner). 4. Hemming the lower edge of the drapery under the lining. 5. Making a bar tack to hold the lining in place.

151

Pale blue lace curtains lined with fabric in a dark shade to accentuate the design of the lace.

Weights, two for each drapery panel.
Sewing thread for fabric and lining.
Drapery rod.
Tapemeasure and ruler.
Scissors.
Needles and pins.

Hand-sewn method Cut out the drapery fabric and join the widths if necessary. Cut out the lining lengths, making them 21·5 cm (8½ in) shorter than the drapery lengths, and join the widths, adjusting the seams, if necessary, to match those on the drapery. Press all seams open.

Join the strips of crinoline to make a strip of the required length by overlapping the short ends slightly and machine stitching them together. Trim away 10 cm (4 in) from one end, and place the strip along the upper edge of the drapery on the wrong side of the fabric, leaving a margin of 5 cm (2 in) at each end. Pin, baste and machine stitch the crinoline in place along its lower edge. Fold heading to wrong side, enclosing crinoline. Press.

Turn under 5 cm (2 in) for each side hem. Press. Miter the two upper corners: first, make a diagonal fold in the hem allowance; press. Then open out the hem allowance and trim away the rectangle of heading hem allowance taken up in the side hem. This is done to reduce bulk. Then re-fold the side hem on the diagonal. Make a small clip in the raw edge of

the side hem, level with the lower edge of the heading. Turn under raw edge from this point to the diagonal. Pin, baste and slip-stitch side hem to heading hem at both upper corners.

On the lining, fold under the top edge 1·5 cm (⅝ in); press. Turn under 1·5 cm (⅝ in) along the lower edge; press. Turn under another 5 cm (2 in), pin and machine stitch in place. Lay the drapery, wrong side up, on a large flat surface (the floor is ideal if you don't have a large enough table). Lay the lining, wrong side down, on top of the drapery, matching the seams – top folded edge of lining, just covering lower edge of heading.

Now lock in the lining. First fold back half of the lining to one side. Now hand-sew the lining to the drapery along the center as shown on page 150, making a series of looped stitches and taking care not to draw the thread too tight. Anchor the thread to the lining – not to the drapery – and begin and end the stitching several centimeters (inches) from the upper and lower edges of the lining.

When you have finished the first, center line of locking, work outward to one side, then to the other. The lines of locking should be approximately 50 cm (20 in) apart. If the drapery has any vertical seams, adjust the intervals of locking as necessary to lock the lining and drapery along the seams.

Tack seam allowances together.

When the locking is complete, trim the side edges of the lining so that they overlap the drapery side hem allowances by about 2·5 cm (1 in). Turn under 1·5 cm (⅝ in) along the lining and baste and slip-stitch it to the drapery on each side.

In the same way, hand-sew the upper edge of the lining to the heading hem. Make hand-sewn pleats (see p. 155).

Hang the draperies from the rod for several days before hemming.

Turn up the lower edge of each drapery so that it clears the floor by 2·5 cm (1 in). Insert pins along the hemline. Take down the draperies. Trim the hem allowance, if necessary, to make an even depth of about 10 to 11 cm (4 to 4½ in).

Turn under 1·5 cm (⅝ in) along the raw edge and machine stitch.

Sew a weight to the side hem allowance just below the lining.

Turn up the remaining hem allowance along the line of pins. Miter the corners as for the upper side hems, so that lower hem allowance is folded diagonally over the side hem allowance. Slip the stitched edge under the lining. Pin, baste and hand-hem the lining to drapery.

Machine-stitched method
This is a quicker method than the one described above, and it does not include locking in the lining. For this reason, it is less satisfactory for very wide draperies, on which it is important that the drapery and lining be joined so that they hang well together. First stitch the strip of crinoline to the upper edge of the drapery as for the hand-sewn method, but do not fold the heading to the wrong side.

Trim the lining so that it is exactly 5 cm (2 in) narrower than the drapery. Hem the lower edge by machine, as in the hand-sewn method and turn under 1·5 cm (⅝ in) along the upper edge. Press.

Place the drapery on a large flat surface, right side up. Lay the lining on top of it, wrong side up, so that the pieces are aligned along one side edge. The upper, folded edge of the lining should be 19 cm (7½ in) down from the upper, raw edge of the drapery. Pin the two side edges together carefully and machine stitch, taking a 1 cm (½ in) seam. Press the seam allowances toward the lining. Now lay the drapery and lining out flat again, right sides together, and pull the free side edge of the lining over to meet the free edge of the drapery. Pin and stitch them together as described, and press the seam open.

Turn the lined drapery right side out. Adjust the side edges so that the drapery margins are equal.

Turn the heading hem to the underside and press it. Cut off the corner of the heading where it overlaps the side hem and miter the corner as described in the hand-sewn method. (The side hem seam allowance has already been pressed under after stitching in the lining.) Hand-sew the upper edge of the lining to the heading.

Make pleats as instructed on page 156. Hang the draperies and leave them unhemmed for several days. Then turn up hems as instructed in the Hand-sewn method.

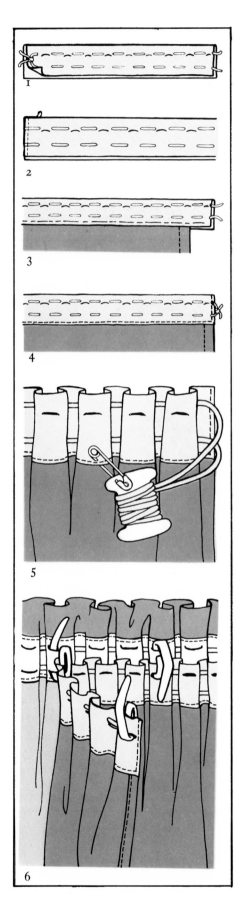

1. The cord pulled free and knotted.
2. End folded under and stitched.
3. Raw edges of lining sewn into tape.
4. Cord ends knotted.
5. Lining gathered, cord put onto tidy.
6. Hooks through drapery and lining.

Lined draperies using pleater tape

In the calculating the fabric required for the drapery, subtract 10 cm (4 in) from the length of each panel. The lining fabric requirement is the same as for draperies with hand-sewn pleats. Cut and join lengths for both drapery and lining, remembering to omit the 10 cm (4 in) heading allowance when cutting the drapery fabric.

Before attaching the lining, by hand or by machine, stitch the tape to the upper edge of the drapery as instructed in Unlined draperies, page 147. If you are attaching the lining by machine, do not turn the tape to the wrong side. Proceed as instructed in Machine method, above. Position the lining so that its upper folded edge will just clear the tape when the tape is folded down in place. When you have stitched the lining to the drapery at the sides, turn the tape to the wrong side and stitch its lower edge to the drapery. Hand sew the side hems over the tape, then hand sew the upper edge of the lining to the drapery, just below the tape.

If you are attaching the lining by hand, first turn the tape to the wrong side and stitch the lower edge in place. Hand sew the side hems over the tape. Then lock in the lining as instructed above.

Detachable linings

If you prefer, you can make detachable linings for your draperies, using the European style tape which is now available. This kind of tape uses cords, rather than pronged hooks, to draw up the draperies. The advantage of a detachable lining is that it can be removed for cleaning when necessary – which is often before the drapery itself needs cleaning. First measure, cut and make the draperies as for Unlinined draperies, using corded tape and attaching it following the manufacturer's instructions.

Making the detachable lining

Finished linings should be 2·5 cm (1 in) smaller on either side and 2·5 cm (1 in) shorter than the draperies when the lining is in position.

Measure and cut out the linings.

Join the widths or half widths where necessary, with 1·5 cm ($\frac{5}{8}$ in) plain seams and press open. Snip the selvages every 10 cm (4 in).

Make side hems by folding over 2·5 cm

(1 in) and then another 2·5 cm (1 in). Baste and machine stitch. Do not sew the bottom hems.

Attaching the lining tape To prepare the tape, pull free 4 cm (1½ in) of the draw cords at one end and knot cords together. Trim surplus tape to within 6 mm ($\frac{1}{4}$ in) of cord (fig. 1). Fold under 1·5 cm ($\frac{5}{8}$ in) of the knotted raw end and machine stitch across the fold, stitching through the tape to secure the knotted cords (fig. 2).

With the right side of the lining fabric and the corded side of the lining tape facing you, slip the top raw edge of the lining between the two sides of the tape, leaving 2·5 cm (1 in) of tape free at the unprepared end (fig. 3).

Pin and baste the lining in position on the tape. The underside of the tape is slightly wider than the top, so that in stitching from right side both sides of tape will be caught in stitches.

1 and 2 below show the main steps in using the quick machine method.

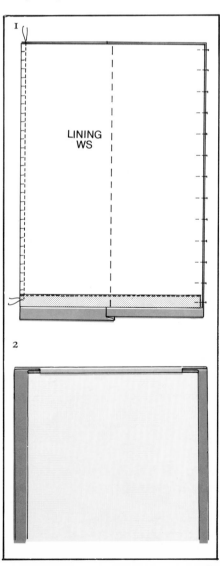

These reversible draperies make an attractive room divider.

Fold under the surplus tape at the unprepared end, even with the side hem edge of the lining, so the edge is neat. Machine stitch the tape to the lining, finishing the unprepared end in the same way as before but leaving the cords free for gathering. Knot the loose ends to keep them from disappearing back into the tape (fig. 4).

Gather up the lining to match the gathered or pleated draperies and wind the surplus cord onto the cord tidy. Attach the cord tidy to the lining tape with a safety pin (fig. 5).

Attaching the linings to the draperies With the wrong side of drapery and lining together, insert the hooks through the "buttonholes" at the top of the lining tape, then through the pockets in the standard heading tape on the drapery before turning the

hooks into their final position. Both the draperies and their linings will hang from the same hooks (fig. 6).

Finishing the lined draperies
Note For a perfectly finished straight hem you must be very careful. On some long draperies it is possible to finish the hem without detaching the lining and taking the gathers out, but the hem may not hang well.

Hang the lined draperies from the rod and mark the correct length of the linings with a row of pins. The linings should be 2·5 cm (1 in) shorter than the draperies. Take down the draperies and detach the linings.

On each lining, unwind the cord from the cord tidy and pull out the gathers. Lay the lining on a large flat surface and turn up the hem to the line of pins. Slip-stitch the hem by hand. Check linings are the correct length. Attached the finished linings to the draperies again and re-hang.

Reversible draperies

If you want to use draperies as a room divider, you should make them double (unless you are using sheer fabric), so that they look equally good from both sides. You can choose the same fabric for both sides, or contrasting fabrics. You must make hand-sewn pleats, as the pleater tape would look conspicuous – although you could use the tape if the draperies are to be hung so that the upper edge is over a beam or archway, so that the heading is concealed on one side.

Calculate the amount of fabric required as for Unlined draperies, then double this amount.

Cut and join the fabric for each layer, making each the same size.

Baste a strip of crinoline 10 cm (4 in) wide along the top of the wrong side of one layer. The crinoline should extend to the raw edges at the sides. Now lay the other layer on the first layer, right sides together. Pin and

1. Attaching tape to top of curtain
2. Fixing curtain hooks along length.

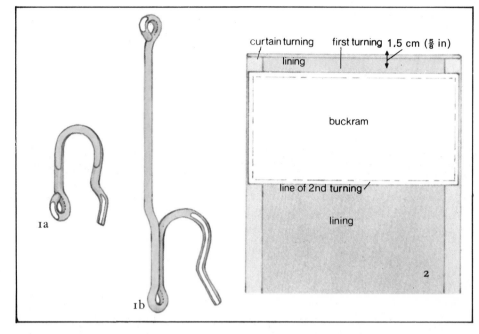

1a. *Sewn-on hooks for plain draperies.*
1b. *Hook used for deep-headed draperies.*
2. *Placing buckram on top edge.*

stitch along both sides and across the top, taking 1·5 cm ($\frac{5}{8}$ in) seam allowances. Trim edges of crinoline close to the stitching and clip corners. Turn the drapery right side out. Baste and press side and top edges. Make pleats in the stiffened heading. (Inevitably, the drapery will have a "right" and a "wrong" side, so you must decide which way you want pleats to face.)

Sew small drapery hooks to the pleats and hang the draperies from a ceiling-fixed rod. Allow them to hang for a few days. Mark the hemline with a line of basting on each side. Take the draperies down and trim the hem allowance to about 5 cm (2 in). Turn under the lower edge of both drapery and lining and baste, then slip-stitch the folded edges together.

Hand made pinch pleats

To give your draperies a professional look, you should make the pleats by hand. This is the way to get really crisp pleats. Also, by making hand-sewn pleats you can often use the fabric more economically, as already explained under Unlined draperies.

One rule you should observe, however, is to have an even number of pleats at the window. If you are making draw draperies, each panel can have either an odd or an even number of pleats. For stationary panels, you should make an odd number of pleats on each panel – though a single, wide stationary panel should have an even number. The amount of material available for pleating is the amount left over when you have subtracted the distance the finished drapery must cover (including return and overlap).

When the drapery has been seamed and hemmed (and lined, if required) measure and mark the pleats on the stiffened heading. Divide the amount of fabric to be taken up in pleats by the number of pleats you are making. Mark the position of the outer pleat: measure the distance of the return and place a line of pins at this point. Then measure off the amount to be taken up by the pleat and insert another line of pins. In the same way, measure and mark the position of the first pleat at the inner edge. This pleat should be

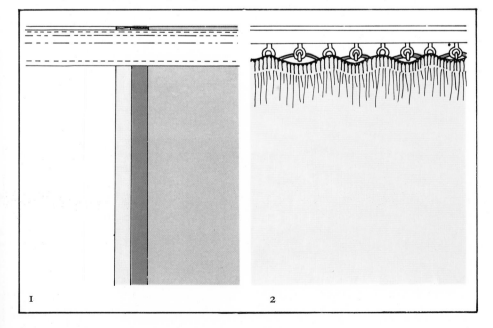

positioned about 5 cm (2 in) from the hemmed edge. Measure the amount of fabric between the outer and inner pleats. Subtract the amount to be taken up by the remaining pleats. Now take the remaining figure (the total amount for the spaces between the pleats) and divide it by the number of spaces (one more than the number of remaining pleats) to get the distance between each pleat. Starting at the inner edge of either of the two marked pleats, measure off a space, then make a line of pins then measure off the amount for a pleat and make another line of pins. Continue in this way across the drapery.

Forming the pleats First bring together the pin-marked lines for each pleat, and re-pin them along the same line. Machine stitch just inside this line (that is, on the side toward the fold of the pleat), starting at the top edge and finishing about 1·5 cm ($\frac{5}{8}$ in) below the heading hem. Fasten the thread at ends with backstitching. Finger-crease the fold thus formed into three equal sections. Baste these folds in place across the lower part of the pleat (where machine stitching ends) and across the upper edge. Then machine stitch the pleat folds together along the lower line of basting. Or sew them together by hand, using buttonhole twist and backstitch. At the upper edge of each pleat sew the folds together with a few overcasting stitches.

The stiff heading on these draperies made with hand-sewn pinch pleats holds the top of the drapery neatly along the ceiling, concealing the drapery rod and giving a neat finish.

3. Depth of pleat marked with pins and then stitched. 4. Pleat folded evenly into three and stitch. 5. Overcast the top edge of each pleat section. 6. Sew hooks in place at top and bottom holes, and then along length of hook.

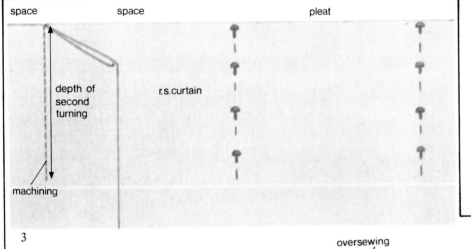

3

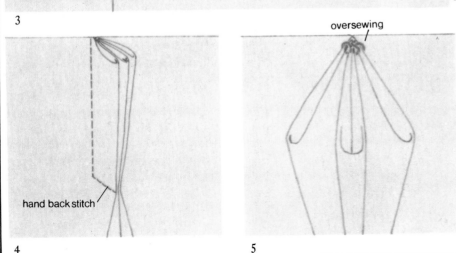

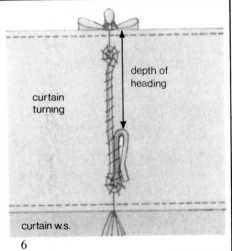

4　　　　　　　　　5　　　　　　　　　6

Sewing on hooks Place each hook in turn on the wrong side of the curtain in line with the seamline of the pleat. For long-stemmed hooks, leave the required depth for the heading between the top of the hook and the top of the curtain.

Using buttonhole twist double, overcast the hooks to the curtain through the holes at the bottom and then, on long-stemmed hooks, up the stems and around the holes at the top. Fasten off securely.

Position the hooks for the two edges to correspond with the appropriate places on the traverse rod. They should be the same distance from the top of the drapery as the other hooks.

A final touch

To make sure that your draperies hang in straight, even folds, you should train the folds for a few days after you have hemmed the draperies.

Open the draperies. Run your hands down each fold for about 30 cm (12 in), sharpening the pleats. When you have done this for the whole width of the drapery, loosely tie some woven tape around it at that level. Continue smoothing the folds down from the tape a short way, then tie again at the lower point. Repeat at regular intervals down the drapery. Leave the draperies tied for a few days, then remove the ties.

Café curtains

One way to solve the problem of combining large windows and privacy is to add glass curtains under your draperies. Café curtains, used on their own or with draperies, make a decorative and informal alternative.

These curtains originated in France in the old coffee houses and are still to be seen in restaurant windows in many parts of Europe. Café curtains

Classic café curtains have a scalloped heading and are suspended from rings.

are really short curtains, hung from a rod which is placed halfway down the window; they may be kept permanently closed, thus hiding an unattractive outlook. Café curtains are made and hung in various ways. They can be trimmed with braid and combined with window shades or valances.

Choosing the heading The simplest type of heading for café curtains having a lower tier only is a plain casing, through which a dowel rod or length of curtain wire can be inserted for hanging them in the same way as for ordinary lightweight curtains. It is not very easy to draw the curtains with this type of heading, so it is suitable only if they are to be kept closed.

Alternatively – and this is more attractive but more complicated in the initial calculations and cutting out – the heading can be scalloped. By this method the curtains can be hung from a decorative curtain rod with rings which are stitched to the top of the straps between the scallops; or these

straps can be made to loop around the rod. As an extra decoration on curtains to be hung with hooks, the straps can be pinch pleated.

Measuring for café curtains
First decide where the rod or wire should be placed – usually about halfway down the window and preferably in line with a glazing bar. Fix the rod or wire in position.

To measure for café curtains you must determine the "drop" required. This is the finished length of the curtain. It will probably be influenced by the amount of privacy desired. Although café curtains conventionally cover half the window, sometimes two curtains are used, one for the top half of the window and one for the bottom half. These are called "tiered cafés" and are both made in exactly the same way.

Café curtains usually hang either to the sill or 5 to 10 cm (2 to 4 in) below the sill.

Measure the rod with a meter/yardstick or steel ruler, not a tapemeasure

These double-tiered café curtains can be used to cover the window completely.

as these may stretch so an accurate measurement cannot be obtained. Allow one and a half times the length of the rod if you are lining the curtains. The width needed depends on the weight and texture of the fabric – lighter more delicate fabrics look better with extra fullness. In the case of a scalloped heading less fullness is required to show the shaped top to advantage.

To the required length add 15 cm (6 in) for both top and bottom hems if using a heading tape or hem casing. For scalloped headings add the depth of the scallop, usually 7.5 to 10 cm (3 to 4 in) plus 12.5 cm (5 in) for the hem. Allow extra length if using a patterned fabric, and work out the repeats to see if the curtain lengths can be cut economically. Remember when choosing the fabric to ask the size of the pattern repeat, as large repeats can be expensive. (See Unlined curtains and draperies for table of

widths required and sewing methods.)
Suitable fabrics In order to let the maximum amount of daylight filter through, café curtains are best if made in cotton and left unlined. However, some fabrics may look more effective used with a light cotton lining and less fullness, particularly where a pattern can be shown to advantage.

To make the café curtain with plain heading
You will need:
Calculated amount of fabric.
Sewing thread to match fabric.
Curtain rod or wire.

Measure and cut out curtains as previously described, joining fabric with plain seams if necessary.
Side hems First cut off the selvages to avoid pulling, and fold and baste 1·3 cm ($\frac{1}{2}$ in) double hems at both sides of the curtain. Stitch by hand or machine (fig. 1).
Turn under 1·5 cm ($\frac{5}{8}$ in) at the top of the curtain and press down. Turn under the edge of the allowances again for 4 cm ($1\frac{1}{2}$ in) and baste and stitch down. Press.
Insert the rod or wire through the hem at the top of the curtain, arranging the gathers evenly along its length, and try the curtain in position. Leave it for a couple of days in case the fabric stretches and then mark the exact position of the lower edge of the hemline with pins while it is still hanging. Take down the curtain and mark hemline with basting.
Bottom hem Turn up 5 cm (2 in) along marked hemline, trimming if necessary, and make a 2·5 cm (1 in) double hem. Hand-stitched hems look better and hang well, and really are worth the extra trouble (fig. 1). Press the finished curtain completely and re-hang it.
Ruffled heading As a variation to the plain top casing, you could make a casing with a ruffle above it. Add an extra 5 cm (2 in) to the allowance at the top of the curtain and turn over 2·5 cm (1 in) of this with the main allowance. Stitch as before and make a second line of stitching 2·5 cm (1 in) below the top fold, Insert the rod or wire in the casing between the rows of stitching. When the curtain is gathered up to fit the rod, the fabric above it will form a ruffle (fig. 2).

Strap heading If you are using straps to hang the curtains, add on an amount equal to the circumference of the rod plus about 2·5 cm (1 in) for ease. If you are making curtains in two tiers, the top tier should be long enough to cover the scallops of the lower tier when closed, so add the depth of the scallops plus 10 cm (4 in) for the hem to the bottom of the curtain.

Scalloped café curtains
***Working out scallops** To make a paper pattern for the scallops, cut a piece of paper as wide as the curtain fabric and about 30 cm (12 in) deep. A piece of wallpaper or shelf paper is ideal for this.
Draw a line across the paper about 7·5 cm (3 in) down from the upper

1. Sewing side and bottom hems.
2. A ruffled heading is made by stitching along the center of the top hem edge.
3. Working out pattern for scallops.
4. Stitching scalloped heading.
5. Hemming the scalloped edge.
6. Sew a ring to each strap.

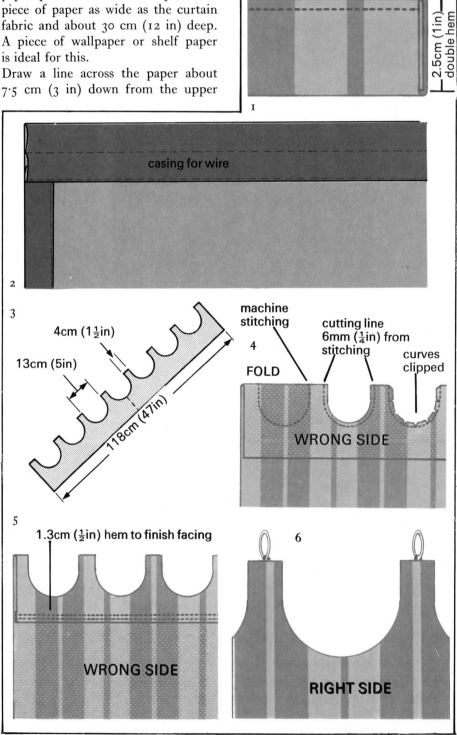

Allowance is made for pinch pleats in the width of each scallop.

edge. Decide at this point how deep you want the scallops to be. Draw another line the depth of the scallop below the first line. Now mark the paper vertically down the middle because it is easier to plan scallops on a narrower width. Plan one half of the width first and then trace another half for accurate placing.

Use a compass and a pencil for drawing the first scallop. You may have to try several times until you can fit a complete row of scallops into your planned width of fabric.

Make a cardboard template when you have finalized the size and shape of the scallops. If you draw around the template the scallops will be of uni-

form size. Leave no less than 4 cm (1½ in) between each scallop and approximately 4 cm (1½ in) each end of the curtain. When all the scallops have been drawn in, cut the scallops out for a pattern (fig. 3).

To make the scalloped café curtain
You will need:
Prepared paper pattern.
Calculated amount of fabric.
Sewing thread to match fabric.
Button thread.
Iron-on interfacing.
Curtain rings.

Measure and cut out curtains. Make side hems as for the café curtain with a plain heading.

With right side of fabric up, fold over

top of the curtain to the depth of the scallops plus 7·5 cm (3 in) (fig. 4). Baste. If the fabric is flimsy, cut a piece of iron-on interfacing to fit the width of the curtain and slightly deeper than the scallops. Iron it inside the heading allowance so that its edge comes even with the fold.

Place the prepared paper pattern on the fold, pin, and mark around the scallops with tailor's chalk. Remove the pattern and machine stitch on the marked line. Cut out scallops 6 mm (¼ in) outside the stitching line. Clip into curves and trim corners diagonally.

Turn the heading right side out. Poke out the corners of the straps carefully, then baste along the seamline so that none of the facing shows on the right side of the curtain. Press. Turn under

the lower edge of the facing for 1·3 cm (½ in) and machine-stitch or slip-stitch to the curtain (fig. 5).

If you are making the straps into pinch pleats form these by hand or stitch on tape (see Headings and Hand-stitched pinch pleats).

Sew brass or plastic curtain rings to the top of the straps using button thread (fig. 6). Stitch fairly loosely, to allow the ring to twist around when it is fitted on the rod.

If you are using the straps to hang the curtains, turn over the amount allowed for fitting it around the pole and stitch firmly in position.

Finally, hang the curtains in position and turn up the hems as for café

curtains with a plain heading.

Tie-backs

Tie-backs were very common in Regency and Victorian times when windows were tall and narrow, and the draperies would simply be looped back to the sides without actually being drawn back along the rod. It is still a good style for these windows because it relieves their bare outline. Tie-backs are also used with light-weight, sheer curtains to create a graceful, draped effect that is particularly suitable for bedrooms.

Tie-backs may be made from fabric to match draperies, in which case they can be shaped, or from a commercial

Shaped tie-backs can add a touch of glamour to floor-length draperies.

braid, in which case they are usually straight. Rings are sewn to each end of the tie-back and these are slotted onto a hook on the wall at the side of the window.

To calculate the length of the tie-back Loop a tapemeasure around the drapery, adjusting it so that the drapery is not crushed; 5 to 6·5 cm (2 to 2½ in) is usually the best width. Decide on the position of the tie-back and height of the hooks and attach a hook firmly to the wall on the window frame on each side. If you are using braid, cut a piece of the right length and turn under the ends to make a V-shaped point. Hem in position and sew a curtain ring to each end.

If you are making a shaped fabric tie-back, cut a paper pattern first and hold it in position to see the effect. You may want to try out several different shapes, such as curves or scallops, before you finally choose.

To calculate the amount of fabric

For a curved tie-back, cut a piece of paper just wider than the length required, fold in half and draw the shape from the center fold to one side. Cut around the shape, open it out and you will have a pattern (fig. 1). Add 7·5 cm (3 in) all around; measure the width and depth to give you the amount of fabric needed. Double this for two tie-backs.

To make a pair of shaped fabric tie-backs
You will need:

The calculated quantity of fabric.
The same quantity of interlining, belting and lining fabric.
Sewing thread to match fabric and strong button thread.
Four 2·5 cm (1 in) diameter brass curtain rings.
Two cup hooks or decorative hooks.
Prepared paper pattern. Fabric adhesive.

Preparing the tie-backs Fold the tie-back fabric in half lengthwise along the grain and place the paper pattern on it with the center line on the fold. Cut out, adding 1·3 cm (½ in) seam allowance all around. Cut out the lining in the same way. Cut the interlining and belting without seam allowances. Repeat for second tie-back. Lay fabric flat with its right side facing down. Place the interlining on top, then the belting, leaving an equal seam allowance all around. Baste through all layers. Turn the edges of the fabric over onto the belting and press down with your fingers, keeping the fold of the fabric exactly even with the edge of the belting. Snip the fabric where necessary around the shaping. Using a little fabric adhesive, carefully glue the edges of the fabric over the belting. Do not pull the fabric too tightly, as it should "give" a little when the tie-back is bent into the shape it will finally assume. Turn under 1·5 cm (⅝ in) all around the edge of the lining, snipping where necessary, and press down. Center the lining on the back of the tie-back and pin it to the seam allowances only (so that the pins do not go through to the right side). Slip-stitch the lining to the seam allowances all around.

To finish off, sew a brass curtain ring to each end of tie-back using strong thread and buttonhole stitch. Make second tie-back in the same way.

Quick and easy window shades

By making your own shades in a fabric to harmonize with your draperies or upholstery, or to match the wallpaper, you will achieve a co-ordinated look in a room.

Window shades are very easy to make and the parts are readily available. Roller lengths vary from 61 cm (2 ft) to 2·75 m (9 ft).

The shade can be hung either inside or outside the window recess. If the recess is deep, hang the shade inside it; if the recess is shallow or the window narrow, hang the shade outside. Make the shade as wide as the window frame will allow – because if it is only fractionally wider, it will be sucked in and out by the breeze when the window is open and the edges of the shade will be spoiled. Before buying your parts check that the brackets are suitable for hanging from the desired position.

Fixing a shade is simple. The only tools needed are those normally needed for everyday domestic repairs.

To make a window shade
You will need:

A window shade with a wooden roller the required length or longer, and fitted at one end with a spring; metal cap and special lipped nail which fits onto the other end; two metal wall brackets, one slotted and one with a round hole; wooden lath for bottom of shade; plastic cord holder and cord; shade pull and several tiny screws and tacks.
Fabric and matching thread.
Fabric stiffening spray.
Saw, hammer, small tacks.
Screws, wall-plugs, screwdriver.
Scissors and tapemeasure.
Bias binding if required.
Pins.

Prepare a pattern for the tie-backs, and place center front on fabric fold.

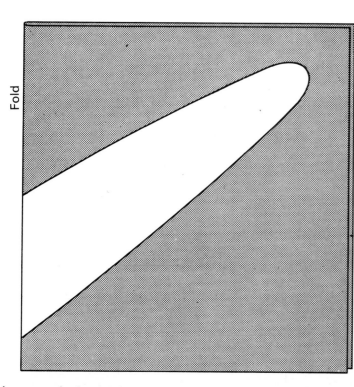

Fold

To make a pattern for shaped tie-backs

Calculating fabric requirements

For a shade inside the recess (fig. 1)
Measure the width of the recess. Use a wooden meter/yard stick or steel ruler, rather than a fabric tapemeasure, so that the measurements are absolutely accurate. The roller should be cut 2·5 cm (1 in) smaller than this measurement to allow for the pins and brackets to be fitted at each end of the roller.

The width of the fabric should be the same as the roller before the pins are attached plus 5 cm (2 in) if seam allowance is required at the sides.

For the length of fabric required measure the height of the recess from the window sill to the top. Add 30·5 cm (12 in) to allow for the fabric to be attached to the roller at the top and for the lath casing at the bottom; this also allows the fabric to cover the wooden roller when the shade is down.

For a shade outside the recess (fig. 2) Measure the width of the recess and add 15 cm (6 in). Cut the roller to this length. The roller will extend beyond the recess at either side by 7·5 cm (3 in). The width of the fabric should be the same as the roller plus 5 cm (2 in) for side hems if required. The finished shade should be placed 7·5 cm (3 in) above the recess and have 7·5 cm (3 in) below the recess.

For the length of fabric required, measure the length of the shade desired and add 30·5 cm (12 in). This allows for the fabric to be attached to the roller at the top and for the lath casing at the bottom; it also allows the fabric to cover the wooden roller when the shade is down.

Choosing the fabric Fabric for a window shade should be firm and closely woven. Holland (a stiff linen) is widely used and available in many widths and colors. The main advantage of using holland is that it can be trimmed to the correct width and does not fray, so you need not hem. Closely woven fabrics such as cotton and canvas can also be used, although you will need to make side hems. Fabrics with large pictorial scenes or very large designs are very good for shades. If you use a special fabric stiffening spray hems may not be necessary. Vinyl fabric in strong colors and patterns is ideal for the kitchen or bathroom.

Cutting the fabric The fabric must be cut accurately and the grain of the fabric must be straight so that the shade hangs well and rolls up smoothly without puckering. To straighten fabric pull out a thread and cut along this line or measure accurately from the selvage, mark with pins and cut out.

If you have to use more than one width of fabric to get the size required, add extra fabric to each side of the full width so that a center seam is avoided. Should the pattern go into the selvages, join each half section to the sides of the main piece by overlapping the selvages for 1·3 cm (½ in) and machine-stitching once down each edge (fig. 3, p. 166).

If the pattern does not extend across the selvage, or the selvages do not match each other, trim them and then join the pieces with a flat fell seam (fig. 4). Press well on both sides.

Making the shade
Cut out the fabric to the correct size. If the edges need finishing either bind them with bias binding or hem the sides. To bind the edges place the edge of the shade on the center of the binding and then fold over the sides of the

This original way of using a window shade gives privacy during the day, and the matching lined draperies can be pulled over the door in the evening for extra warmth and luxury.

1. A window shade fitted inside the window recess.

2. A window shade fitted outside the window recess.

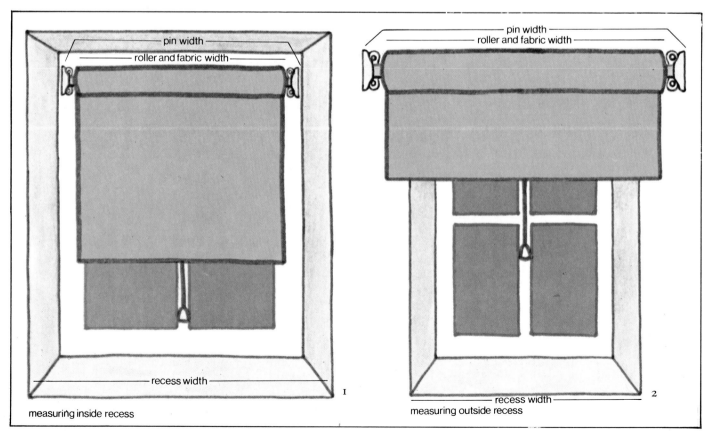

measuring inside recess

measuring outside recess

binding equally, baste and machine stitch through all thicknesses (fig. 5). To hem the sides fold over 2·5 cm (1 in) onto the wrong side along both edges, press and baste. (For vinyl fabric crease the fold and hold in place with masking tape, as the holes made by the needle when basting will not close up when the thread is removed). Machine stitch, using a large zigzag stitch and positioning the raw edges in the center of the stitch (fig. 6).

Alternatively, raw edges can be finished by hand and then straight-stitched by machine.

To make the lath casing along the bottom edge, turn under 1·3 cm (½ in) on the wrong side. Turn under another 4 cm (1½ in) and machine stitch close to the first fold.

Cut the lath 1·3 cm (½ in) shorter than the fabric width and insert it into the hem. Stitch up the openings at the sides (fig. 7).

Thread the cord through the holder, knot to secure and screw the holder to the center of the lath so that the cord hangs down (fig. 8).

Stiffening Before attaching the fabric to the roller, iron and then spray with the fabric stiffening spray. Spray fabric on both sides, working in a well ventilated room. Hang fabric up to dry completely.

Assembly Following the manufacturer's instructions, assemble the roller

3

5

7

wrong side of fabric

8

4

6

9

3. *Overlap and stitch the selvages.*
4. *On raw edges stitch a flat fell seam.*
5. *The side edges can be finished with a binding.*
6. *To hem the sides, fold over the raw edge and zig-zag stitch.*
7. *Insert the lath into the bottom hem.*
8. *Fix card holder on the wrong side.*
9. *Tack the fabric to the roller with the spring on the left.*
10. *The right way (top) and wrong way (bottom) of hanging the blind.*

right

wrong

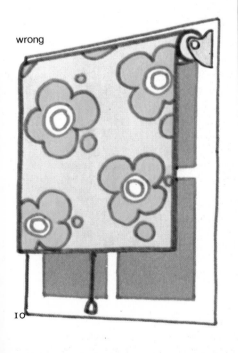

A dormer window can be a problem to cover. A fabric shade, such as this tie-dyed one, is the perfect solution.

and the end pins. Screw the brackets in place. If the shade is to go inside the recess allow enough room above the brackets to give clearance for the fabric when it is rolled up.

Place the prepared fabric right side up on the floor. Lay the roller across the top with the spring mechanism on the left-hand side.

Attach the fabric to the roller with small tacks, working from the center toward the edges (fig. 9).

Roll up the shade by hand; place in the brackets. Pull the shade down and make sure it hangs properly and rolls up smoothly; if not, take it down and roll it up again by hand. Be careful not to over-tension the spring, because if it snaps up too quickly the mechanism may be damaged. The shade should hang with the fabric nearer to the window and the roller toward the room (fig. 9).

Thread the loose end of the cord into the shade pull.

Note If your window is wider than 2·75 m (9 ft) it would be possible and effective to divide the window into two, three or even four sections and place several shades side by side. The brackets should then be placed close together on the window frame.

167

*Window shades are an inexpensive way
to insure privacy and can be used
successfully to cover both windows and
doors as shown.*

Bed Linen

Throw-over bedspreads

The focal point of a bedroom should be the bed – and the bedspread is the finishing touch. A throw-over bedspread is one of the quickest and easiest kinds of fabric furnishing to make, and if you team the fabric with your wall covering and curtains, it will give the room a beautifully coordinated effect.

*Technique included: fitting around bedposts.

Calculating fabric requirements

Measure the bed with its bedclothes and pillows as shown (p. 171). For the width, measure from the floor on one side, up and across the bed to the floor on the other side. For the length, measure from the top of the pillow to the floor at the foot of the bed (fig. 1). If you wish to tuck the bedspread around the pillows, add an extra 30 cm (12 in) to the length.

As furnishing fabrics are usually 120 cm (48 in) wide, you will need to join two fabric widths for either a twin or a small double bed, so double the length measurement to calculate how many meters (or yards) you should buy. Very large beds may need three lengths; 5·50 to 7·50 m (6 to 8 yd) is usually ample for an average twin or double bed.

If your fabric has a large design or motif, add extra to the over-all length in order to match it at the seams or to position it to best advantage on the bed – the additional amount could vary from an extra half pattern to as much as two pattern repeats. Ask your retailer for advice if in doubt, because so much will depend on where the first measurement is taken on the fabric roll. Choose a time for buying the fabric when the store is quiet and take a note of the bed measurements with

you. Ask to have the fabric unrolled so you can examine the design fully and decide how you would like it positioned on the bed.

Making the bedspread

If you are using two lengths, avoid having an ugly seam down the center of the bedspread by cutting the fabric across into two equal lengths and then cutting one of these pieces in half lengthwise, thus making one full width of fabric for the center panel and two half widths for the sides. Allowing a total of 11 cm (4½ in) for seams and side hems, with 120 cm (48 in) wide fabric, the bedspread will have a maximum finished width of 229 cm (7 ft 7½ in).

For a twin bed, however, this would mean that the seams run along the side of the bed, rather than the top, and the paneled effect is lost. To avoid this,

cut off the excess from the full width, rather than the halves (the leftover piece could be used for pillow covers).

Joining the panels To join the side pieces to each side of the center panel pin and baste with right sides together, raw edges even, taking 1·5 cm (⅝ in) seams. Make sure the pattern is matched and the fabric runs the same way on each panel. Place the bedspread on the bed and check the size. Cut off any excess fabric at top and bottom, leaving 2·5 cm (1 in) for hems. Measure and cut the sides in the same way.

Machine stitch the seams, using a medium length stitch, following the basting line. Remove the basting. Clip the selvages at intervals if they are tight (this helps the seam to lie flat), and press the seams open. Finish the raw edges by overcasting by hand or by machine.

The centerpiece of a bedroom is the bed. Throw-over spreads accentuate this, especially if they are made to measure, and, for twin beds, in matching fabric.

Square corners To make 2 cm ($\frac{3}{4}$ in) double hems down the long sides of the bedspread, fold over the raw edge 6 mm ($\frac{1}{4}$ in) to the wrong side of the fabric. Make a second fold 2 cm ($\frac{3}{4}$ in) deep, so the raw edge is now enclosed. Baste and machine stitch through the three thicknesses, along the first fold. Remove the basting and press the hems. Turn under 2 cm ($\frac{3}{4}$ in) hems at the top and bottom, making the corners square (alternatively the corners can be mitered). Baste, machine stitch and press (fig. 2). Trim with braid or fringing if you wish.

Rounded corners Join the panels as above. Position the bedspread carefully on the bed. Place a row of pins along the top edges on one side and along the foot to mark the depth of the overhang, plus 2·5 cm (1 in) for hems.

Remove the bedspread, spread it flat and continue the line of pins to the edges. Draw an arc on this corner, using the pin and string method (see Table linen). Cut along the curved line, including the seam allowance (fig. 3).

Fold the bedspread in half lengthwise; pin and cut the other corner to match. Turn under the hem at the foot and along the sides of the bedspread, easing the fabric at the corners. Baste and machine stitch the hem, remove the basting and press the hem. Make a hem the same depth at the top of the bedspread, leaving the corners square. Press. Trim with braid or fringing if you wish.

*Fitting around bedposts
Join the panels as above. Place the bedspread on the bed and fold back the side panels from the edge of the bed with the fold lying just inside the posts (fig. 4). Pin a line along the fold from the corner of the bed (point A)

Left. This double bedspread has the bottom corners rounded.

Top right. Joining seams can be concealed with decorative braid.

1. Measure the bed with the covers and pillow in place.
2. Finishing square corners.
3. Making rounded corners.
4, 5. Fitting around bedposts.

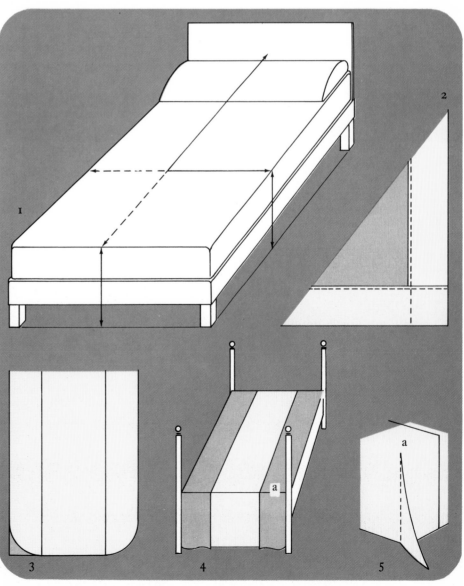

down to the floor. Unfold the sides and fold up the foot of the bedspread in the same way. Pin along this fold from point A to the floor (the pin lines should meet at point A).

Remove the bedspread and, using the pin lines as a guide, pin the corner as shown in fig. 5. Check fit, then cut off the corner 1·5 cm ($\frac{5}{8}$ in) from the line of pins. Using this as a guide, cut out a similar corner from the other side of the bedspread. Clip into the angle and make a narrow hem; press. Make 2 cm ($\frac{3}{4}$ in) hems all around the bedspread, leaving the corners square. Press.

Flounced bedspreads

*Techniques included: drawing a cutting plan, making a flounce.

A bedspread with a gathered flounce gives a softer look to a room. A throw-over flap is attached to keep your pillows neatly covered.

Suitable fabrics Light or medium-weight fabrics, including dress fabrics and lace fabrics, can be used, but do not use a heavy fabric for this type of bedspread, as it will not gather easily. Avoid very large patterns, because you will have wastage in matching it at seams, particularly on the flounce.

Calculating fabric requirements

Measure the bed with its bedclothes but without the pillows. For the width, measure from edge to edge across the bed and add 3 cm (1$\frac{1}{4}$ in) for the seam allowances. For the length, measure from the top of the bed to the foot and add 3 cm (1$\frac{1}{4}$ in) seam allowances. If the bed has a foot-board, add 45 cm (18 in) to the length measurement so that the bedspread can be tucked in at the bottom. For the depth of the flounce, measure from the edge of the bed to the floor and add 4 cm (1$\frac{5}{8}$ in) hem and seam allowance. To determine the length of the flounce, multiply the bed's length by three – (i.e. a length and a half for each side, excluding any extra length allowed for the tuck-in extension).

For Hollywood beds, the flounce should also go around the foot, so add on one and a half times the bed's width.

The addition of a flounced skirt to a bedspread gives a softer, more decorative look to a bed.

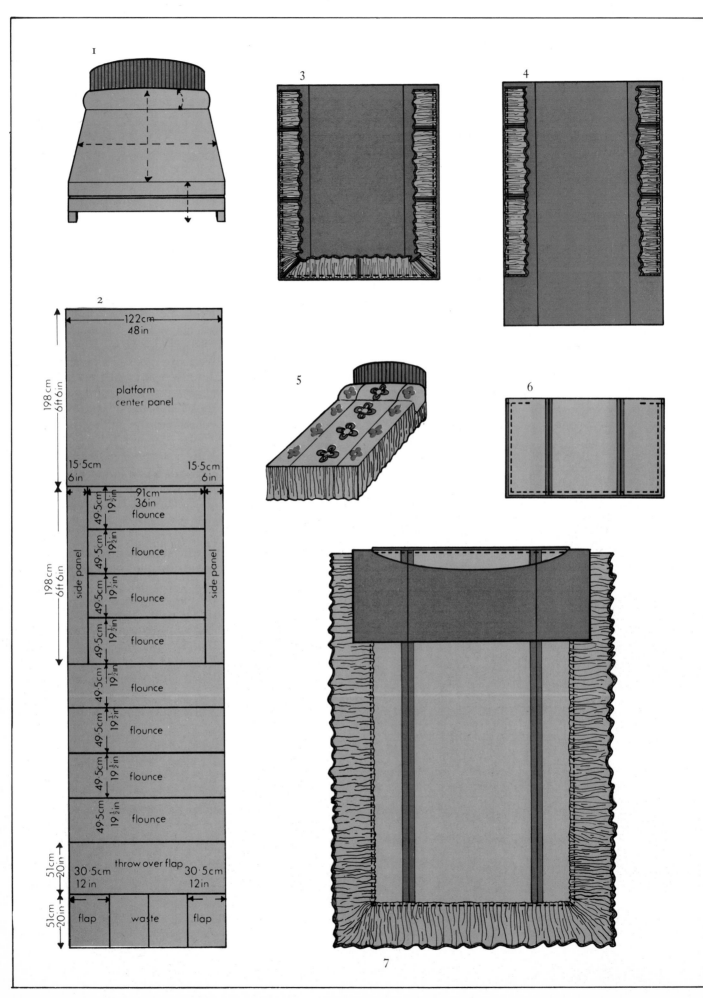

1

3

4

2

122cm
48in

198cm
6ft 6in

platform
center panel

15·5cm
6in   15·5cm
                       6in

91cm
36in

49·5cm
19½in   flounce

49·5cm
19½in   flounce

198cm   side panel   49·5cm   side panel
6ft 6in   19½in   flounce

49·5cm
19½in   flounce

49·5cm
19½in   flounce

49·5cm
19½in   flounce

49·5cm
19½in   flounce

49·5cm
19½in   flounce

51cm
20in   throw over flap
           30·5cm   30·5cm
           12in   12in

51cm
20in   flap   waste   flap

5

6

7

174

Next, put the pillows on the bed and measure for the throw-over flap from the bottom of the pile of pillows at the top of the bed, up and over the pillows to the other side (fig. 1). Add 15 cm (6 in) for seam allowances and so that the flap can be tucked in. For the width of the flap, add 30 cm (12 in) to the width of the bed, so that the flap will cover the pillows easily. To calculate the quantity of fabric required, draw a cutting plan. Fig. 2 shows a layout for an average double bed. The simplest scale to use is 1 cm to 10 cm (1 in to 10in). Draw the main section first. If the bed is wider than the fabric, measure the remaining section on either side, adding 3 cm (1¼ in) to the width of each section for seam allowances.

Draw these panels along the selvages so that the pattern can be more easily matched with the main piece.

For the flounce, cut strips across the width of the fabric, so that the pattern will run down toward the floor.

To calculate the number of strips needed for the flounce, draw the strips to the required depth. Work out how many strips would be needed to make up the required length. Allow 3 cm (1¼ in) on each width for seams.

Draw the pieces for the throw-over flap, working out the width as for the main section.

Cutting out and sewing

Cut out the center and side panels (if any) as calculated above, matching the pattern. Join the pieces with a 1·5 cm (⅝ in) plain seam, clip the selvages or finish raw edges; press seams open.

*Making a flounce Cut out and join all the strips for the flounce with 1·5 cm (⅝ in) plain seams. Clip the selvages or finish any raw edges and press the seams open. Make 1·5 cm (⅝ in) hems on the short sides of the flounce, and press. Make a 2·5 (1 in) hem along the foot of the flounce, stitch and press.

Divide the flounce into eight sections for the sides and foot of the bed, marking the divisions with pins. Then divide the side sections and foot of the main section into eight similarly. Gather the flounce, using a long machine stitch or running stitches, 6 mm (¼ in) down from the top edge and again 1 cm (⅜ in) from the edge. (It is advisable to stitch each division

separately, as such a long length of gathering is likely to break when the thread is pulled up.)

Match the divisions on the flounce to those on the top. With the right sides of the fabric facing, pin the pieces together at the division marks with the pins at right-angles to the edge. Pin the ends of the flounce to the top section 1·5 cm (⅝ in) in from the edge.

Lay the top section out flat (use the floor if necessary), with the flounce on top of it. Secure one end of each gathering thread, and, leaving the divisional pins in position, draw up the other end until the flounce fits the top. Secure the threads by winding them around the divisional pins.

Space out the gathers evenly, pin the flounce to the top (putting the pins at right-angles to the edge at 2·5 cm [1 in] intervals), and baste, using small stitches (fig. 3). Remove the pins and, taking 1·5 cm (⅝ in) seams, machine stitch the pieces together, with the flounce uppermost (this helps to keep the gathers from puckering as you stitch). Remove the basting and gathering threads, and press the seam toward the top section. Finish the raw edges with bias binding, or by overcasting them together.

Footboard beds Make the flounce for each side separately, and attach them to the top section, leaving the 45 cm (18 in) extension free (fig. 4). Make a narrow hem on the sides and foot of the extension.

Throw-over flap Join the pieces of the flap as for the main section. With right sides facing, stitch the lining to the flap with a 1·5 cm (⅝ in) seam, leaving an opening the width of the main section along the top edge (fig. 5). With the right side of the flap facing the wrong side of the main section, fit the top edge of the main section into the opening, and pin it to the flap only, leaving the lining free. Stitch the pieces with a 1·5 cm (⅝ in) seam (fig. 6). Press the seam toward the flap. Fold lining over seam and hem, enclosing raw edges. Press. Fig 7 shows the finished bedspread.

Eiderdown set

A snug eiderdown ensures a good night's sleep and a loose cover is simple to make, as it is simply two rectangles of fabric stitched together

and fastened at one end with a zipper or touch and close tape. Complete the set with pillowcases, a fitted sheet and a dust ruffle to conceal the base of the bed. Make them to match or in complementary fabrics.

The quantities and instructions are for either twin or small double beds. The set can be made in polyester and cotton sheeting or plain cotton sheeting which is made in especially wide widths for the purpose.

Note Individual quantities have been given for each piece of the set. If you are making the set for a twin bed it is worthwhile making a cutting layout before buying your fabric (see Flounced bedspreads), as you will be able to cut either pillowcases or the dust ruffle pieces from the extra width of fabric.

Eiderdown cover

Measurements The average size of an eiderdown is 137 by 198 cm (54 by 78 in) for a twin bed and 198 cm (78 in) square for a small double bed. The quilt cover should be about 5 cm (2 in) larger all around than the quilt. This enables the quilt to move freely inside the cover.

You will need: (for either size of bed)
228 cm (90 in) wide fabric: 4·30 m (4⅝ yd).
1 m (40 in) touch and close fastening or 75 cm (30 in) zipper.
Sewing thread to match fabric.

Cutting out For a twin-size cover: cut two rectangles, each 150 by 211 cm (59 by 83 in). For a double cover: cut two rectangles, each 211 cm (83 in) square.

To make the cover

Finish the raw edges at one end of each piece of fabric with zigzag stitch. Turn 2·5 cm (1 in) to the wrong side and press.

Placing right sides together, stitch the edges along creased line, leaving an opening in the center of the seam for inserting touch and close fastening or a zipper.

Insert the zipper or stitch fastening tape to both sides of the opening. Stitch the remaining three sides together with French seams. Turn cover right side out and press lightly.

Fitted sheet

A fitted bottom sheet with elastic corners to fit neatly over the mattress.

You will need: (for either size of bed)
228 cm (90 in) wide fabric: 2·70 m (3 yd).
1 m (40 in) narrow elastic.
Sewing thread to match fabric.

Cutting out   Cut a rectangle of fabric to cover the top and sides of the mattress plus 38 cm (15 in) all around.

To make the fitted sheet
Center the sheet on the bed and mark the position of each corner with a pin. Mark two lines from the corner point to the two edges, thus forming a square (fig. 1). These two lines then form the seamline for the corner. Placing right sides together, stitch the seam at each corner, trim, overcast and press (fig. 1).

Measure 25·5 cm (10 in) along each side of each corner and mark these points. Work a small hem around the outside edge of the sheet. First turn under 6 mm ($\frac{1}{4}$ in) and then 2 cm ($\frac{3}{4}$ in). Machine stitch close to the fold. The hems between points marked at corners will be channels for the elastic. Unpick a few stitches at each end, thread a 25 cm (10 in) length of elastic through channel. Secure ends by topstitching firmly by machine (fig. 2). Repeat at the remaining corners.

If you do not look forward to the daily chore of making up the bed – tucking in sheets, folding blankets, straightening bedspreads – why not use an eiderdown and a fitted bottom sheet? An eiderdown cover, fitted sheets and pillowcases, are easy to make.
1. Preparing the corners for a fitted sheet. 2. Inserting elastic in corners. 3. Folding the fabric for a pillowcase. 4. Pin the layers together. 5. Stitch down each long side.

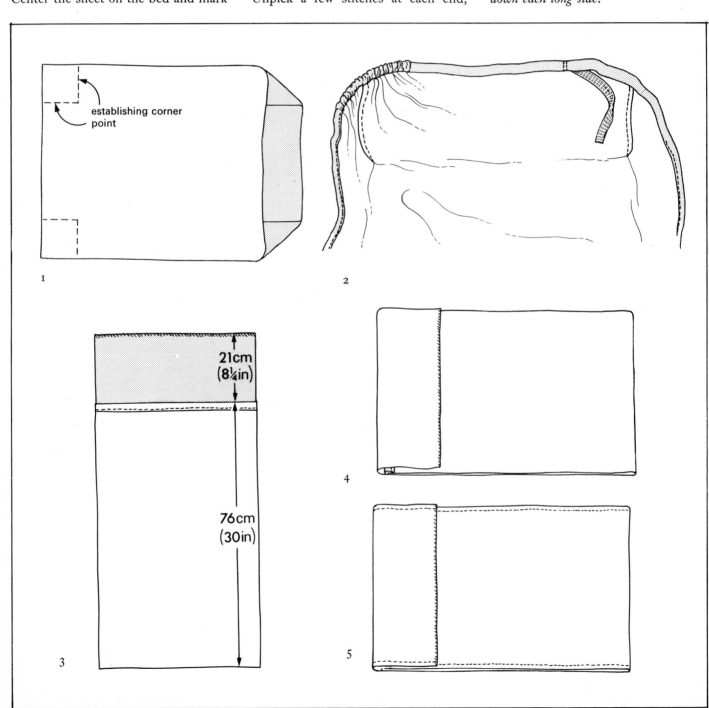

establishing corner point

1

2

21cm (8¼in)

76cm (30in)

3

4

5

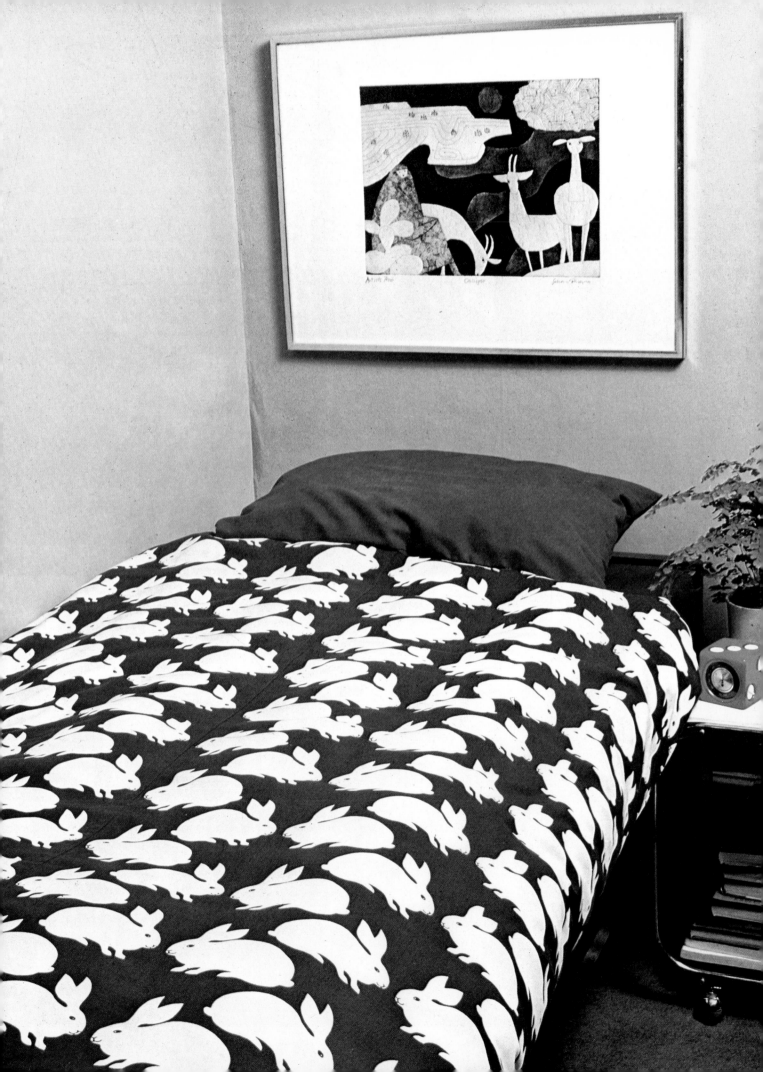

Dust Ruffle

A dust ruffle is a flounce of fabric attached to a rectangle of matching fabric or muslin and placed under the mattress so that the flounce hangs to the floor, covering the base of the bed.

You will need: (for either size of bed)
228 cm (90 in) wide fabric: 4·10 m (4½ yd).
3 m (3 yd) tape for ties.
Sewing thread to match fabric.

Cutting out Cut a rectangle of fabric to fit the top of the bed, plus 1·5 cm (⅝ in) allowance all around.
For the flounce, cut four strips of fabric each from the full width of the fabric, 33·5 cm (13½ in) deep.

To make the dust ruffle

Stitch the pieces into one long strip. Make a 1·5 cm (⅝ in) double hem along one long edge and across short ends. Attach to the top section (see Flounced bedspreads).
Cut the tape into four equal lengths and stitch the center of each piece to a corner of the flounce on the wrong side. Press.
Place the completed dust ruffle on the base under the mattress and tie the tapes around the legs of the bed under the flounce.

Pillowcase

An English-style pillowcase has a flap, which encloses the pillow neatly. It's easy to make, too.

Measurements The finished pillowcase measures 47 by 76 cm (18½ by 30 in).

You will need:
For two pillowcases:
228 cm (90 in) wide fabric: 1 m (1 yd).
Sewing thread to match fabric.

Cutting out For each pillowcase, cut a rectangle of fabric 50 by 175·5 cm (19½ by 69 in).

To make the pillowcase

At one short end turn under 5 mm (¼ in), then 1·5 cm (⅝ in) to make a 1·5 cm (⅝ in) double hem.
Overcast the other short edge of the panel to finish, or make a small double hem.
Fold the fabric 76 cm (30 in) from the hemmed end with the hem on the outside. The finished end then extends 21·5 cm (8¼ in) beyond the hemmed end (fig. 3, p. 176). Fold flap over the top of the hemmed end and pin the three layers together (fig. 4).
Pin and stitch down each side of the pillowcase, taking 1·5 cm (⅝ in) seams (fig. 5). Finish the seams. Press.

A beautifully made bed with matching pillowcases, eiderdown cover and dust ruffle, which conceals the box spring.

Lampshades

Lampshades

One way to perk up a room is to give a lamp a new shade. You needn't necessarily go out and buy a new shade; you can easily re-cover the original frame with the material of your choice. You might find an old shade in a junk shop. Give it a new cover and you have a bargain.

Fabric lampshades can be made in many shapes and sizes but in most cases the basic techniques involved are the same and once you have learned how to make one shade you can easily go on to make others.

The frame This is the basis of every type of lampshade. Frames come in several different styles and sizes with various fittings for attaching them to the lamp. They are made from tinned or copper wire and joined by spot welding or by soldering.

Each frame consists of two rings, one of which contains the fitting for at-taching the lampshade to the base. The rings are joined by struts or staves, which may be curved or straight. The relative diameters of the rings and the length of the struts determine the size of the lampshade, and the shape of the rings and the struts governs its shape.

Lampshade frames vary considerably, and different frames lend themselves to different treatments. The curved, Tiffany-style shape is generally used for hanging lamps. It can be covered with a simple, elasticized removable cover or with a cover that is stitched to the lower ring of the frame. Straight-sided types, such as the drum shape and the panelled, rectangular type, are relatively easy to cover, as the fabric is stretched along the straight of grain. Waisted frames are trickier, as the fabric must be cut and stretched on the bias to fit the frame exactly. It's best not to attempt this kind of shade until you have had a bit of prac-tice with the simpler kinds of shades.

The drawings on this page show some of the various kinds of fittings used on lampshade frames for hanging lamps, table lamps and floor lamps. Hanging lamps have a ring at the top which fits around the lampholder (the part that holds the bulb). Frames for table lamps and floor lamps are usually of the harp-and-finial type. The harp, a curved piece of wire with a detachable knob on the top, fits onto the base of the lamp. The shade rests on the upper part of the harp and is held in place by the knob – called a finial.

Another kind of fitting consists of two metal "arms" which attach the shade to the base of the lampholder, below the bulb. The arms are hinged so that the shade can be tilted.

Large shades are sometimes made with a large ring at the top, which rests on a three-pronged harp.

The clip-on fitting consists of two wire loops which clamp directly onto the light-bulb. This type .of shade comes in small sizes and is used mainly on bedroom lamps, wall fixtures and some multiple ceiling lamps.

The fabric Medium to light natural fabrics can be used to make lamp-shades, although for those styles which are fitted on the bias or cross of the fabric some printed fabrics with a definite design – such as flowers with stems – may not be suitable.

You should choose the fabric to suit the decorative scheme of your room, but bear in mind the fact that some colors change when seen under arti-

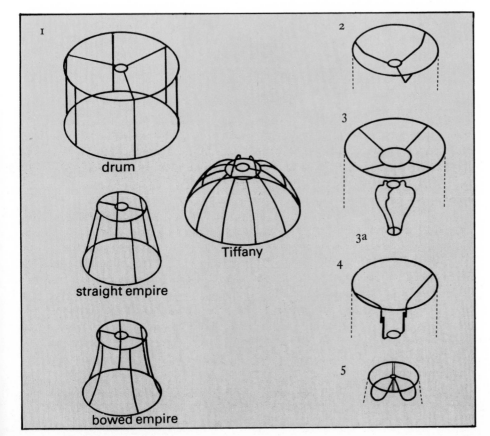

The three frames at the far left are used with the harp and finial type of fitting. The Tiffany frame is generally used for hanging lamps. The kind shown at upper right has a dropped fitting to conceal the lampholder. A three-pronged finial is used to support large shades. The hinged type of fitting allows the shade to direct the light as required. At bottom, a clip-on fitting.

1

drum

straight empire

Tiffany

bowed empire

2

3

3a

4

5

ficial light and they may affect the type of light which the shade will give. Dark colors, for example, tend to absorb the light, whereas pale colors reflect it and allow the light to pass through. Lining a dark color with a white, pink or beige fabric will help to give more light. If possible hold your chosen fabric with the lining over a lighted bulb to get an idea of the effect before you buy it.

Silk This is the traditional fabric for lampshades and although it is the most expensive of the fabrics you might choose, it is worth the extra cost because it is pliable and easy to fit, it does not sag or split easily, it cleans well and does not shrink. Most kinds of pure silk can be used and there are some imitation silks which are also suitable.

You are more likely to find suitable silk or imitation silk fabrics among the dress fabrics than among furnishing fabrics, which tend to be too firmly woven to give easily when they are fitted to the frame.

Cottons Many kinds of cotton can be used for lampshades. However, if your frame has curved struts and you want to make a fitted cover you should choose a solid color, rather than a print, because you will need to fit it on the bias.

Linens These are normally too firmly woven to be good for lampshades, and they are difficult to fit smoothly. Also, they may not allow much light to pass through. Some of the finer embroidery linens, however, may be used for drum or panelled shades, which are relatively easy to cover. Linen which has been embellished with drawn thread work makes a pretty shade cover.

Man–made fabrics such as nylon or polyester are not usually suitable to use because they tend to sag and some weights split.

Fabric requirements

For a tailored cover On frames with straight struts, such as the drum or the straight empire, the fabric is fitted on the straight of the grain. Measure half the circumference of the bottom ring of the frame (or its widest measurement) between two struts on opposite sides and then measure the height of the frame (fig. 6). Allow enough fabric to cut two rectangles to

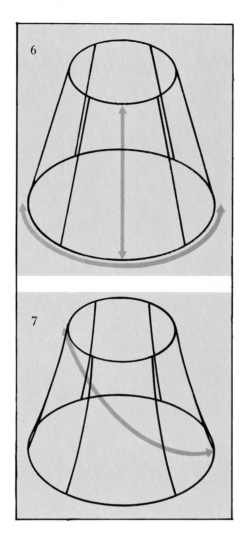

6. *Measuring for a tailored cover.*
7. *Measuring for bias-cut cover.*

these measurements plus about 7·5 cm (3 in) all around for fitting.

For frames with curved or bowed struts On a bowed empire frame, the fabric is fitted on the bias. Measure the frame diagonally over the struts on opposite sides of the frame from the top ring to the bottom ring (fig. 7). Allow enough fabric to cut two squares of the fabric along the grain to this measurement plus about 7·5 cm (3 in) for fitting.

Covering methods

There are two main methods of making the cover for a fabric shade.

Semi-fitted This is the simplest fitted cover and also the quickest. The cover is made to fit the widest part of the frame and is gathered or pleated to reduce the fullness on either or both rings if they are narrower than the widest part.

Use this method for Tiffanys and balloon shades (like a Tiffany, but spherical). You can also use it on any type of frame with straight struts.

Fully fitted or tailored This is the method requiring most skill and time. The cover is made to fit the frame tightly all over so that the finished lampshade is smooth and taut. Except on the drum shape, this is normally achieved by using the fabric on the bias, although some pliable fabrics can be used on the straight grain. The cover is usually made in two halves, one for each side of the frame. The seams joining the halves should be placed exactly over the struts of the frame. This method can be used for all styles of shade with circular rings.

The trimming

The trimming is the finished touch for the shade and is fitted around the rings to hide the stitching and raw edges of the fabric.

Naturally, it should harmonize with the color and style of the shade. On a Tiffany style shade a deep fringe is appropriate, and on a bedroom shade you can add a pretty, frivolous touch in the form of gathered eyelet lace or perhaps some ball fringe, if it is in keeping with the decor. For most shades, however, trimmings should be simple. Velvet ribbon to match the shade fabric is a good choice for a formal shade. Woven braid makes another suitable trimming.

You can find what you need in the notions department or furnishing fabric department of a good-sized department store. For a trimming that matches the shade exactly, make bias strips of the shade fabric. To calculate how much trimming to buy, measure the circumference of each ring and add on 2·5 cm (1 in).

Tools

You probably already have all the tools you need, including:
Scissors with sharp blades for cutting the fabric and trimming the edges.
Pins. Use rustless steel dressmaker's pins of the glass-headed type for fitting the cover. The very short fine type of pins are particularly useful, as they are less likely to scratch you while you are stitching the fabric.

Bowed empire lampshades such as these are usually lined and finished with a simple binding around the rings.

Sewing thread to match your cover fabric. Needles. "Between" needles are ideal because they are short and stiff and unlikely to bend or break when they touch the frame. Clear, non-staining adhesive for finishing seams and attaching the trimming.

Preparing the frames

If a frame is not a plastic-coated one, paint it first, using a metal primer and a fast-drying enamel or cellulose paint to match the color of the cover. Paint will prevent the frame from rusting and make it less conspicuous if the shade is unlined. Stand the frame on a newspaper and paint it. You may have to do this in two or more stages so that you can reach all sides of the rings without smudging. The paint is usually touch dry quite quickly but leave the frame for 24 hours to harden before you bind it. Next, when the paint is completely dry, bind those rings and struts of the

frame to which the fabric is to be fitted and stitched. (The traditional method, in which all the struts and rings were bound, is considered unnecessary these days because it can spoil the smooth finish of the shade.) Use 1·3 cm ($\frac{1}{2}$ in) cotton tape sold for the purpose. Allow twice the circumference for the rings and one and a half times the length for each strut. The binding is the most important stage of the preparation. It must be very tight or it will slip and the fabric will not be tautly stretched over the frame, however much time you spend on the fitting. For most styles of lampshade the rings and two struts, on opposite sides of the frame, are bound so fabric can be pinned and fitted. The binding on the struts is then removed because it is no longer needed, but it is kept on the rings so that the cover can be stitched in place. To bind the top ring, place the end of the tape under the ring at the top of

A detachable shade is a quick way of covering a Tiffany frame, and best suited to an informal setting.

a strut (fig. 1a, p. 183). Bring tape over the joint of the ring and strut and bind over the end of the tape (fig. 1b). Continue binding as tightly as possible, keeping the tape at an acute angle and overlapping it slightly. At each strut, wrap the binding around the ring an extra time and then go onto the next section (fig. 1c, d, d, f). To finish, stitch down the end of the tape on the outside of the ring. Turn frame upside down and bind bottom ring.

To bind the struts, start at the top of one strut and loop the end of the tape round the T-joint (fig. 2a). Bind over the end and continue tightly down the strut (fig. 2b, c). Finish by winding around the ring on both sides of the strut (fig. 2d). Pull the end through a previous loop. Bind opposite strut.

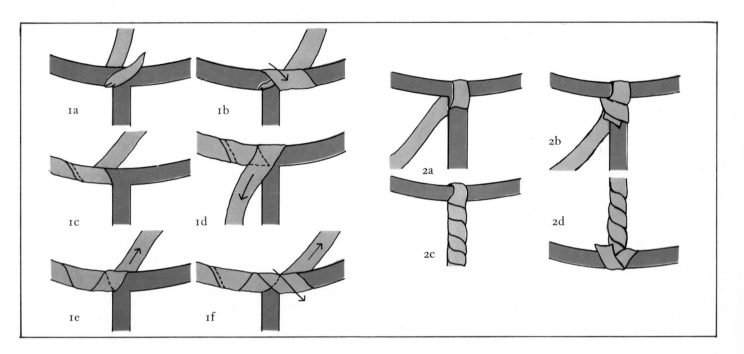

Detachable Tiffany cover

One of the easiest and quickest ways of covering a Tiffany frame is to make a detachable cover. This method has the extra advantage in that the cover can easily be removed for washing, and you do not need to bind the frame because the cover is not fitted or stitched directly to it. It is, however, advisable to paint the frame.

You will need:

Fabric (see below).
Painted frame.
Matching thread.
Elastic, 6 mm ($\frac{1}{4}$ in) wide by the circumference of the bottom ring.
Cotton tape, 6 mm ($\frac{1}{4}$ in) wide by the circumference of the top ring, plus about 10 cm (4 in).
Bodkin, needle, sewing thread, pins.
Washable trimming (optional) to widest circumference of fabric plus 2·5 cm (1 in) for joining.

Making the cover Measure the frame at its widest part (this is not necessarily the bottom ring). If the measurement is less than the width of the fabric, the cover can be made in one piece. If it is more, the cover should be made in two halves.
Measure the length of the struts and add 9 cm ($3\frac{1}{2}$ in). If you are making the cover from one piece of fabric, allow enough to cut one piece along the grain to the length of the struts plus 9 cm ($3\frac{1}{2}$ in) by the measurement of the circumference of the widest part plus 2·5 cm (1 in). If you are

making it in two halves, allow enough to cut two pieces along the grain to the length of the struts plus 9 cm ($3\frac{1}{2}$ in) by the measurement of half the circumference plus 2·5 cm (1 in).
First join the fabric so that it fits the widest part of the frame. Use a plain seam and trim the seam allowances to 3 mm ($\frac{1}{8}$ in). Finish the edges with overcasting or with a machine zigzag stitch. Alternatively, you could use a French seam.
Fold over 6 mm ($\frac{1}{4}$ in) onto the wrong side along both long edges of the fabric and press. Fold over 1·3 cm ($\frac{1}{2}$ in) again to make casings, baste and machine stitch, leaving openings in the stitching of about 1·3 cm ($\frac{1}{2}$ in).
Pin and machine stitch the trimming (if used) 2·5 cm (1 in) above the lower edge of the cover.
Thread the elastic through the casing along the lower edge of the cover, draw up elastic, pin ends together.
Thread the tape through the casing along the upper edge of the cover.
Place the cover on the frame so that the trimming is positioned on the lower ring. Draw up the elastic tightly to draw the margin of fabric under the frame. Pin and stitch the elastic at the required place and trim off the excess. Arrange the gathers of fabric neatly.
Arrange the fabric neatly on the frame at the top and draw up the tape so that the cover is firmly held over the frame, making sure the trimming is still correctly positioned. Tie the tape neatly and trim off the excess length. Stitch up the openings in the casings.

1a-1f. Binding top ring.
2a-2d. Binding the struts.

Semi-fitted Tiffany shade

The cover fits the bottom tightly but is gathered to fit the much narrower top, and it looks prettiest in a light cotton or eyelet embroidery fabric. A scalloped or lace trimming can be added.

You will need:

Prepared frame (painted, with top and bottom rings bound).
Fabric as for detachable Tiffany cover.
Sewing thread.
Trimming (fringe or braid); you will need the measurement of the circumference of the bottom ring plus 1·5 cm ($\frac{5}{8}$ in) for seam allowance.
For coordinating braid, you will need the measurement of the circumference of the top ring, plus 1·5 cm ($\frac{1}{2}$ in) for seam allowances.
Clear adhesive.

Fitting the cover

Cut out the fabric to the required measurements. If you are using one piece, fold it in half with the shorter edges together and mark the fold with basting. If you are using two pieces, join them down one side as for detachable Tiffany shade.
Place the fabric on the frame with the right side facing outward so that the seam or line of basting is level with one of the bound struts. Center the fabric on the length of the strut so that 4·5 cm ($1\frac{3}{4}$ in) extends at the top

183

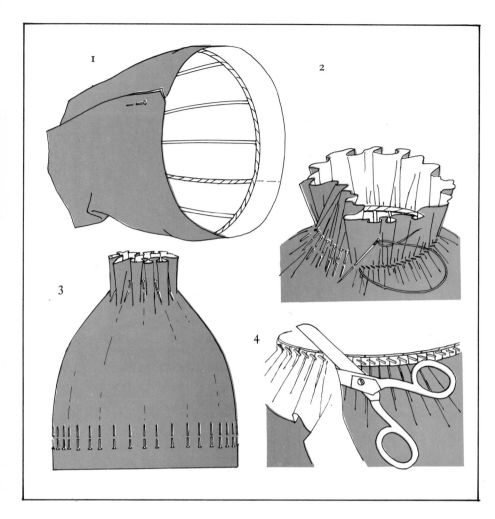

For a semi-fitted Tiffany shade:
1. Fit fabric around frame to fit snugly at widest part.
2. Pin fullness into tiny pleats between the struts.
3. Stitch fabric to ring bindings working in a clockwise direction.
4. Trim away surplus fabric.

with the rings as you progress. When you reach the other end, fold it under to meet the first fold exactly and glue it down. Secure with a pin.

The braid is attached to the top ring in the same way, but the outer edge should be pinched up slightly with your fingers so that the inner edge will lie flat.

If you prefer you can hand-sew the trimming in place.

Lined lampshades

The cover for tailored, lined lampshades is made in two sections, one for each half of the frame. One of the sections is fitted and shaped on the frame itself and then used as a template for the other section. The pieces are then seamed together and the whole cover replaced on the frame and stitched to the rings.

Usually you have a choice of whether to fit the cover on the straight or the bias grain. Of the two methods, fitting on the bias grain is easier because the fabric is more pliable, but it is more wasteful and some patterned fabrics do not look right when used this way. Straight drum shapes should always be fitted on the straight grain because it helps to maintain the correct shape. Very waisted shapes – where the circumference is less in the middle of the frame than at the top – must be fitted on the bias grain so that the fabric will be stretched at the top ring when it is replaced on the frame.

The fabric for the lining can be cut on the bias grain, but if you use a pliable fabric, such as crêpe-backed satin, it can easily be fitted on the straight grain which is less wasteful.

Instructions in this section are for a bias grain cover with a straight grain lining. To fit a straight grain cover, follow the instructions for fitting the lining but mark and stitch the two sections as for the bias grain cover. The complete instructions for a drum shape shade are given at the end of this section.

and bottom. Pin the seam or basting line to the bound strut in one or two places in the middle.

Wrap the fabric around the frame and pin the edges together in line with the opposite bound strut so that the cover fits tightly at the widest part of the frame but does not distort the fabric (fig. 1). Remove the fabric from the frame and baste along the straight grain, even with the pin.

Join the fabric as described for the detachable Tiffany shade.

Stitching the fabric to the frame

Place the cover on the frame as before, with the right side facing out, and pin it to the binding along the bottom ring. Place the pins so that the points face into the body of the lampshade so that you are less likely to scratch yourself. Smooth the cover up the line of the struts, keeping the grain straight and pin at the top of each strut.

Fold away the fullness between the struts into tiny pleats and pin them (fig. 2). Repeat along the bottom ring if this is narrower than the widest part of the frame.

Start stitching the fabric to the binding on the outside of the rings using a small overcasting or hemming stitch. Work in a clockwise direction around the ring, making sure that you catch the gathers firmly in position. Use double thread and begin and fasten off securely, using several small back stitches (fig. 3).

Turn the surplus fabric back over the stitching so that the fold is even with the edge of the rings, and stitch through all thicknesses. Trim the surplus fabric close to stitching (fig. 4).

Fringe edging Fold under one end of the fringe for 6 mm ($\frac{1}{4}$ in) and glue it down with a spot of adhesive. Place the fold on the bottom ring so that it is even with a seam and the top edge of the fringed section is even with the edge of the ring. The braided or solid section along the top edge of the fringe must cover the binding on the ring, the raw edges and the stitching of the fabric.

Apply adhesive for about 10 cm ($\frac{1}{4}$ in) along the underside of the braided section and place it in position on the ring, stretching it slightly. Secure with a pin. Apply adhesive to the next 10 cm (4 in) and glue down as before. Keep checking that the braid is even

The lining

This type of lampshade should always be fitted with an internal lining, which hides the struts and gives it a professional finish. Internal linings are known as balloon linings because although they are fitted onto the outside of the frame, in the same way as the cover, when they are stitched in place inside the frame they "balloon" away from the struts.

You will need:

Fabric to required measurements.
Lining to required measurements.
Prepared frame (with bound rings and two bound struts).
Sewing thread.
Trimming.
Clear adhesive, soft pencil.

Measuring and cutting fabric (see Fabric requirements for tailored cover).

Fitting the cover

In order to achieve a really smooth, taut cover, it is essential to fit the fabric carefully to the frame, to keep the grain of the fabric straight without distortion and to place the seams exactly over the struts of the frame.

Fold one of the fabric squares in half diagonally with the wrong side facing out and press the fold lightly with your fingers at each end.

Place the frame on your work surface with the bottom ring facing you and the two bound struts to the left and right. Place the fabric on the frame so that the fold is even with the center of the top half; if the frame has eight struts, place the fabric on it so that the fold is in line with the center strut (fig. 1): if the frame has six struts, place the fabric on it so that the fold is in the center of the two top struts.

Open out the fabric, keeping the fold in line with the center strut or in the center of the two top struts. Pin it to the rings at the top and bottom of the crease, keeping it taut but without stretching it.

Smooth the fabric out to the bound struts with your fingers to mold it to the shape of the frame. Pin it to the tops and bottoms of the bound struts, so that the pins are pointing inward. Place more pins at about 1.5 cm ($\frac{1}{2}$ in) intervals down the left-hand strut, easing out any fullness in the fabric. Place the pins at right-angles to the strut with the points inward. Starting at the top of the left-hand strut, follow the grain line of the fabric diagonally across the frame. Keeping the line completely straight and tight, pin it where it meets the right-hand strut or the bottom ring (fig. 2).

Go back to the next pin down on the left-hand strut and follow the grain down in the same way. Tighten fabric and pin. Continue in this way, pining and tightening the fabric away from the left-hand strut diagonally across to where it naturally falls on either the right-hand strut, or the bottom ring (fig. 2a).

Working upward along the grain in the opposite direction, tighten the fabric from the left-hand strut to the top ring and pin at the top of the intermediate (unbound) struts (fig. 3). Remove the pin at the top of the right-hand strut, tighten the fabric in the same way and replace the pin.

Complete the pinning down the right-hand strut and along the remaining part of the bottom ring, smoothing out any remaining fullness or wrinkles with your finger by running it in the direction of the grain. Never run your finger along the bias grain or you will distort the fabric and possibly stretch it out of shape.

Using a pencil. lightly draw down the fabric in between the pins over the outer bound struts. Draw lines about 1.5 cm ($\frac{1}{2}$ in) long inward from the bound struts along the top and bottom rings. Mark a dot on the rings at the top and bottom of each intermediate strut.

Remove all the pins and remove the fabric from the frame.

Marking the second section Place the marked section on the second section with right sides together so that the edges are even and the grain, pattern or slub is running in the same direction on both pieces. Pin the sections together along the penciled strut lines. Work tailor's tacks at the

1. Placing the fabric on the frame.
2. Following the grain line across.
2a. Tightening the fabric onto the bottom ring.

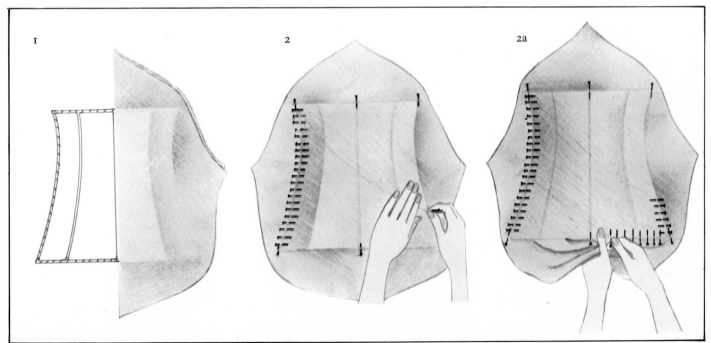

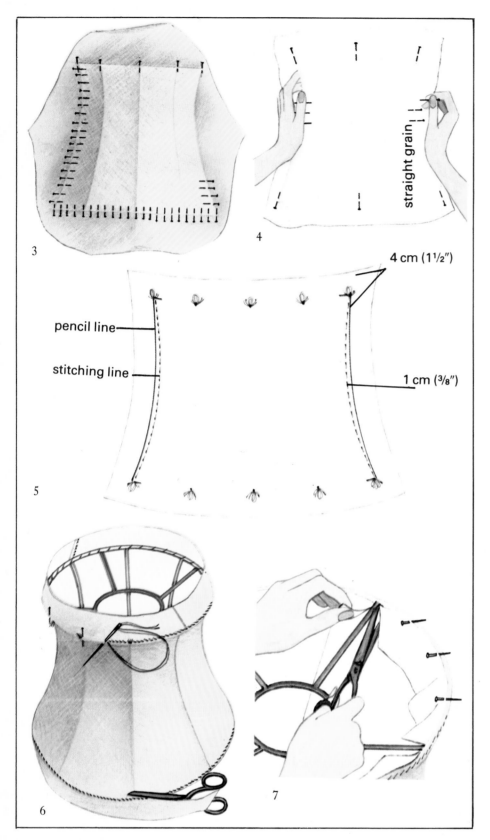

open lightly with your fingers. Spread adhesive along the seam allowances, then press them together so that they adhere and trim to within 3 mm ($\frac{1}{8}$ in) of the stitching.

Put the cover to one side while you fit the lining.

Fitting the lining

Fold one of the lining pieces in half lengthwise along the straight grain and crease the ends of the fold lightly with your fingers. Open out the fabric and place it on the frame with wrong side facing upward (with crêpe-backed satin this is usually the crêpe side) so that the crease is even with the center of the frame. Pin the fabric at each end of the crease to the rings and then smooth out to the side struts and pin at the tops and bottoms. Do not overtighten at these points or the fabric will not keep to the shape of the frame. Pin the fabric halfway down the left-hand strut. Tighten along the grain and pin halfway down the right-hand strut.

Working up from these points, pin up to the top ring, tightening the fabric horizontally by pulling from the left and right, and working first on one strut and then on the other (fig. 4).

Work downward to the bottom ring in the same way.

When the sides are pinned, pin the fabric to the rings, tightening only enough to remove any wrinkles. Check that the grain line is completely square and avoid overtightening vertically or you will lose the shape.

Mark the fabric as for the main fabric and remove from the frame.

Mark the second section of the lining in the same way and stitch the two pieces together down the sides so that the stitching starts 3 mm ($\frac{1}{8}$ in) in from the marked line at the top and bottom and curves in to about 1 cm ($\frac{3}{8}$ in) from the line in the middle (fig. 5). This forms the balloon shape of the lining.

Finish as for the cover.

Remove the binding from the struts.

Attaching the cover

Turn the cover right side out and place it on the frame so that the seams lie over the struts which were originally bound, and the tailor's tacks line up with the ends of the struts and are on the rings. Pin the fabric to the rings

3. *Tightening fabric onto top ring.*
4. *Tightening lining horizontally between struts.*
5. *Basting curved stitching line to form the balloon lining.*
6. *Stitching the cover to the rings and trimming the excess fabric.*
7. *Slitting the lining to fit it around the light fitting.*

outer ends of the short pencil lines and at each dot.

Cut around the shape adding about 4 cm (1$\frac{1}{2}$ in) all around.

Machine stitch the pieces together down the penciled strut lines and fasten off securely.

Cut through the tailor's tacks and open out the fabric. Press the seams at the tops and bottoms of the intermediate struts. Do not put any pins into the fabric down the length of the struts – they must be placed in the rings only.

Check that the seam allowances are lying flat over the struts and are not twisted, and make any adjustments needed. Working alternately on each side of one of the seams, start tightening the cover on the frame by adjusting the pins. When you make one alteration to one side of the seam go to a similar place on the opposite side and make the same alteration. Keep checking the seam and grain lines. Insert more pins into the rings between the struts so that the cover is lying taut against the frame.

Stitching the cover to rings When you are satisfied with the fit of the cover, it can be stitched to the rings. The most comfortable way of doing this is to sit with the frame on your lap with a pad of fabric beneath it to prevent your legs from being scratched.

Start stitching at a strut and work toward your free hand so that you can hold the fabric taut onto the frame with your fingers as you stitch.

Use each length of thread doubled and start and finish with two or three backstitches. Work in a close, firm hemming stitch, placing the stitches on the outer edge of the ring.

When you have stitched around both rings, cut off the excess fabric close to the stitching (fig. 6).

Attaching the lining

Place the lining into the frame and align the seams with those of the cover. Position the tailor's tacks correctly on the bottom ring and pin. Draw the fabric up the shade and pin on the inside of the ring at the top of each strut. Roll back the excess fabric at the

top inside ring and clip into it in line with the arms of the light fitting and at intervals in between if the fabric seems tight (fig. 7). Roll the fabric over the top ring, fold under the fabric at each side of the slits for the fitting, and pin all around to the outside edge so that the pins are over the previous stitching.

Stand the frame upside down (with the top ring at the bottom), check that the seams are over the struts and pull the fabric on both sides of the seams to tighten it over the bottom ring. Working alternately on each side of the seams, pin the fabric to the ring.

Stitching the lining to rings Stitch the lining in the same way as the cover, placing the stitches on the outside of the ring (fig. 8). Cut off the excess fabric close to the stitching.

Finishing the slits To finish the slits for the light fitting, cut a bias strip for each one, 5 cm (2 in) long by 2·5 cm (1 in). Fold in the raw edges so they meet in the middle and then fold the strip in half again.

Slip-stitch the folds together lightly. Place each strip loosely around a fitting so that it covers the slit and pin the ends on the ring (fig. 9). Secure with a few stitches and trim off any surplus fabric even with the raw edges of the lining.

Trimming the shade Finish the shade by trimming with braid, velvet ribbon or a bias strip.

Trimming with self bias strip Cut 3 cm (91¼ in) wide bias strip equal in length to the circumference of each ring plus 1·5 cm (½ in) for seams. Fold each strip in half lengthwise with the wrong side facing out. Place the strip around the appropriate ring so that the raw edges are even with the turned back edges of the fabric and the

bulk of the strip extends beyond the frame. Stretch the strip around the ring slightly if the struts bow inward. Pin the short ends together along the straight grain so that the strip fits tightly. Remove the strip, open it out and stitch with right sides together along the pinned line. Press seam open. Re-fold the strip with the right side facing out and place it on the frame as before. Overcast the double strip in place firmly all around, making sure that the outer edges of the stitches come to the outer edge of the ring. Fasten off securely and turn back the strip on to the frame so that the fold is even with the rings and the stitches and raw edges are covered. If necessary, press strip lightly with your fingers, and slip-stitch neatly along the inner edge.

Straight drum shapes

A straight drum frame is one which has top and bottom rings of the same size – the rings can be circular or oval. Both the cover and lining fabric should be fitted on the straight grain.

The method is similar to that previously described, but it is essential that the tightening is done vertically and not horizontally, in order to maintain the correct shape.

To do this, place the fabric on the frame and pin it to the top and bottom rings so that it is really tight (fig. 10). Then pin it to the side struts, pulling only enough to remove any wrinkles. Finish the shade as for other shapes, but without shaping the seams on the lining.

8. Stitching the lining to the outside of the rings.
9. Pinning the fabric strip to hide the slits in the lining.
10. Tightening cover for a drum shade.

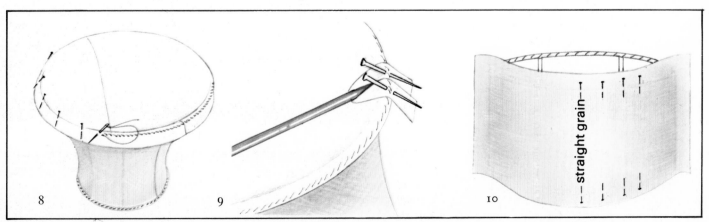

Sewing Snips

Lined picnic basket
You will need:
Wicker hamper.

Calculated amount of printed cotton fabric for lining.

Remnants of printed cotton fabrics for pockets.

2·5 cm (1 in) wide contrasting bias binding.

2·5 cm (1 in) wide contrasting ribbon or braid.

Sewing thread to match fabric.

Buttons for pockets (optional).

Making the pattern and estimating fabric requirements
Take the measurements of the inside of the basket – base, sides and lid. Add 1·3 cm (½ in) seam allowance to each measurement, and make a paper pattern for each section. Test the paper patterns against the basket to check that they fit correctly.

Take rough measurements of your set of picnic plates (allowing plenty of ease to accommodate them) measure Thermos flask, and so on, and note the measurements of the individual compartments accordingly.

The lining is made double, so you will need two of each piece. For the ties you will need 14 strips of fabric, each 6·5 by 76 cm (2½ by 30 in). Work out a cutting plan to find the quantity of fabric needed. Quantities for pockets and ties will depend on individual requirements. Plan each pocket and flap on paper, then measure all around to find quantity of binding needed.

Cutting out
Cut out the pieces of lining fabric using the paper patterns.

Cut two pieces for each section.

Making the lining
Placing right sides together, stitch each pair of fabric pieces together taking 6 mm (¼ in) seams and leaving an opening to turn through. Turn each section right side out, and slip-stitch openings.

Plate pockets Cut out a rectangle of fabric to required dimensions; as the edges are bound, seam allowances are

not needed. Bind the edges with contrasting binding. Position each pocket as required on the lining section and topstitch in position along the side and bottom edges, leaving a little slack in the fabric between the two sides in order to make sufficient room for plates.

Button-down pockets These can hold paper napkins and can be made in exactly the same way as the plate pockets. Cut out a flap section to fit each pocket, bind all edges, and stitch the flap to the lining fabric just above the top edge of the pocket. Sew a little loop of binding to the center bottom of the flap and a button in the corresponding position on the pocket itself for fastening.

Ties Use for matches, condiment

Right. Small button-down pockets and ties made of bias binding or ribbon serve to hold even the smallest of picnic condiments and accessories, so that they do not get lost in a muddle.

Below. Pockets are made to measure to hold plates, knives and forks securely so that they do not rattle about loose, reducing the risk of breakage.

Left. A wicker picnic basket fitted with a colorful lining that has pockets, ties and loops to hold picnic gear is as attractive to look at as it is useful for keeping things neat.

containers, corkscrew, can opener, and Thermos flask. They are made from two lengths of ribbon with one end stitched to the lining fabric. The distance between each piece depends on the width of the item to be secured. Hold it in position against the lining fabric for a rough guide.

Flatware pockets Cut out a long rectangle of fabric about half the depth of a knife and bind the edges as for a plate pocket. Sew on strips of binding vertically at intervals, where you wish to divide the pockets into individual compartments. Stitch pocket to lining fabric along side and bottom edges, and stitch along vertical strips of binding through all fabric layers to make compartments.

Fastenings Make these from strips of lining fabric. Fold each strip in half lengthwise with right sides facing and stitch together, leaving end opening for turning. Turn right side out and slip-stitch opening. Alternatively, use binding.

Stitch ties to corners of each lining section. The lining sections are attached to the basket by looping the tabs through the holes in the wickerwork and tying securely.

No kitchen should be without potholders, and they need not be the usual square of padded fabric. By raiding your sewing basket and saving gloves that have lost their mates, you can make a bright, imaginative collection of an everyday household article. The potholder below is made of simple patchwork triangles cut from scraps of fabric.

Potholder ideas

Make sure you always have a pot-holder within easy reach by pro-viding yourself with a collection of them in all shapes and sizes. Hang them up in convenient places where they will also provide decorative touches of color to brighten up your kitchen.

Choose washable fabrics and synthetic stuffing which does not shrink. The details are very much up to you. The simplest method is probably to sand-wich two pieces of fabric together with stuffing in between layers and then to bind the edges. Add a loop in cord or ribbon with which to hang up the potholder.

There are innumerable possible vari-ations.

You could make a patchwork holder using a variety of printed fabrics, combining flowers, dots, checks, stripes – the more variety of fabrics the jollier the finished effect.

The edges can be finished with bind-ing or ribbon, or stitched in a contrast-ing color.

You might even try recycling an old woolen glove by protecting the right side of the palm and inside thumb with a layer of stuffing, held in place with a piece of fabric, cut to the right

size and shape and sewn on with the edges turned under to keep them from fraying.

Similarly, patch an old sock with colorful fabric and insert a layer of stuffing into it so that it lies flat. Work buttonhole stitch all around, both to close the open edge and to finish the other edges.

Chair covers and windbreak

If you have some old deckchairs which are unused because they have torn or shabby canvas, why not give them a new lease of life? With gaily printed deckchair canvas (available from large stores) and a coat of col-ored paint on the woodwork, they can be smartened up easily and cheaply – and made more comfortable if you pad the seat at the same time. All you need is your sewing skill and some simple handyman's equipment.

Deck chair cover
You will need:

Ripping chisel, mallet, hammer.
Paint, polyurethane varnish, paint-brush, woodworking adhesive, med-ium grade sandpaper.
Calculated length of 40 cm (15 in) wide deckchair canvas.
14 to 16 1·5 cm ($\frac{5}{8}$ in) upholstery tacks.

Cross-stitch an appropriate kitchen motif, or quilt a plaid potholder.

Strong needle and thread.

To prepare the deckchair

Carefully remove the tacks holding old canvas with a ripping chisel (or an old blunt wood chisel) and a mallet. To do this, place the tip of the chisel under the head of the tack and tap the handle of the chisel with the mallet. Always work in the direction of the grain of the wood – in this case it is along the length of the rail – in order to avoid splitting the wood. When the tack is loosened, lift it out with the claw section of a hammer. As you work, note how the canvas is wrapped around the rails. Stick any splintered wood in place with adhesive. Prepare, paint and varnish frame. Leave to dry.

To calculate the length of the new canvas

Lay the chair out flat and measure from the rail to which the canvas was attached at the top to the rail to which it was attached at the bottom. Keep the tapemeasure taut between the two. Add 15 cm (6 in) allowance for seams and for wrapping the canvas around the rails.

Attaching the canvas

Fold under one end of the canvas for 2·5 cm (1 in). Lay the deckchair flat, with the notches facing up. Tack the folded edge of the canvas to the inside face of the rail on the notched section of chair (fig. 1, p. 194), using seven to eight tacks placed at 5 cm (2 in) intervals. Avoid putting the tacks in exactly the same position as before. Bring the canvas right around the bar and up to the other end of the un-notched section of the chair. Pull the canvas taut and take it right over the rail, fold under the excess fabric and tack it to the underside, again using seven to eight tacks at 5 cm (2 in) intervals (fig. 2).

Padded deckchair

You can make the deckchair more comfortable by padding the canvas with foam rubber.

You will need:

Twice the calculated amount of 40 cm (15 in) wide canvas.
Sheet of 1·3 cm (½ in) thick foam rubber, 2·5 cm (1 in) narrower and 10 cm (4 in) shorter than basic length of canvas.

To make the padded deckchair

Cut the canvas into equal lengths. Place the foam rubber on the wrong side of one canvas piece, leaving a 1·3 cm (½ in) border on each side and 5 cm (2 in) border at the top and bottom. Baste in position all around the edges and at intervals across the width.
Put the canvas pieces together with right sides facing and stitch them down the long sides taking just less than 1·3 cm (½ in) seams so that you clear the foam rubber. Use strong thread, a heavy needle and a medium-length stitch.
Turn the canvas right side out and press the seams. Machine stitch across the top and bottom of the canvas 5·5 cm (2¼ in) from each end to catch in the foam, and then at 23 to 25 cm (9 to 10 in) intervals in between through all thicknesses.
Attach the padded canvas to the frame in the same way as for a standard cover.

Make yourself comfortable with deckchair and protective windbreak.

Incorporating a head pillow

A bolster neck cushion can be incorporated easily by adding to the length of canvas needed for recovering the deckchair. The filling for the bolster can be made from a sheet of foam rubber.

You will need:

Calculated length of 40 cm (15 in) wide deckchair canvas, plus 45 cm (18 in).
Sheet of 1·3 cm (½ in) foam rubber 30 by 45 cm (12 by 18 in).
21 to 24 1·5 cm (⅝ in) upholstery tacks.

To make the head pillow

Start to cover the chair in the same way as for a standard cover, but at the top bring the excess under the top rail. Bring the canvas up tautly and tack to the top rail.
Set the chair in its upright sitting position and bring the excess canvas over the top rail. Roll up the foam to make a bolster 30 cm (12 in) wide and secure with a few stitches. Wrap the excess canvas around the foam and try it out for size and comfort, adjusting it if necessary (fig. 3). Tack the end enclosing the foam roll to the top rail, in the same way as for the first row of tacks. Fold in the sides of the canvas neatly and stitch down

Windbreak

On breezy days, a windbreak can make all the difference to the comfort of a picnic. The simple version shown here is easy to transport and erect. However, although you can make it as long as you like, it should not be more than about 122 cm (4 ft) high unless the stakes are driven a long way into the ground, or it might be blown over. If you are going to be using it as a windbreak for a barbeque, remember to cook well away from the windbreak as a precaution against fire.

You will need:

Calculated length of 90 cm (36 in) wide deckchair canvas.
Stakes (either 2·5 cm [1 in] diameter dowel rod, broom handles or 1 cm [⅜ in] aluminum tubing) at least 26 cm (10 in) longer than the height of the windbreak; sufficient for one each end and at about 45 cm (18 in) intervals in between.
Rubber caps for stakes (the kind

193

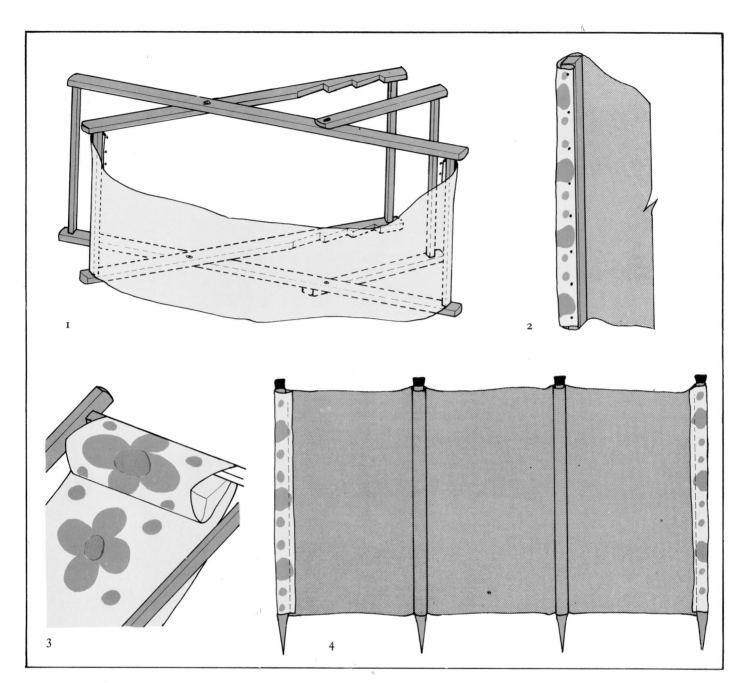

1

2

3

4

generally used for furniture feet).

Making the casings

The canvas is used sideways so that the selvages form the top and bottom of the windbreak and do not need hemming.

To make the casings for the stakes, turn under and make double hems at each side edge (fig. 4). Check that the stakes will slip easily into casings.

Divide the fabric between the end casings into equal sections, about 45 cm (18 in) wide. Make a fold at each section, bringing the right sides of the fabric together. Measure from the fold the size of the casing and machine stitch through the doubled canvas along this line. Make all the casings in the same way.

1. Tack folded edge of canvas to the inside face of the rail on the notched section of the chair.

2. Pull the canvas to the un-notched section, fold and tack in place.

3. Make a head pillow from extra fabric tacked to the top rail and then tucked around a foam pillow.

4. For the windbreak, make casings at each end and stitch evenly spaced pleats in the center to take the stakes.

Preparing wooden stakes Taper off one end of each with a chisel or handyman's knife to make a fairly thick point. This makes them easier to bang into the ground. Insert the stakes into the casings (the points should be at the bottom) and fit a rubber cap over the top of each stake.

Bathroom set

This bathroom set is made from a graph pattern. There is a matching toiletry bag and quilted sponge bag. The shower caps come in two sizes and have a pretty lace trim. Both caps and bags are lined with a waterproof fabric.

Making the pattern

Draw up the pattern to scale from the graph pattern given here. One square represents 2·5 cm (1 in) square.

This bathroom set would be a welcome present for a travelling friend.

You will need:

For mother's cap and bag:
90 cm (36 in) wide fabric, 70 cm

(¾ yd) for cap.
90 cm (36 in) wide quilted fabric, 50 cm (½ yd) for bag.
2·30 m (2½ yd) lace trimming.
Two cards bias binding.
Sewing thread to match fabric.
Two large snap fasteners.
90 cm (36 in) wide waterproof fabric for lining both cap and bag, 80 cm (⅞ yd).
60 mm (¼ yd) elastic.
For daughter's cap and bag:
90 cm (36 in) wide fabric, 60 cm (⅝ yd) for cap and bag.
18 cm (7 in) square of quilted fabric for base of bag.
1·40 m (1½ yd) 6 mm (¼ in) wide ribbon to tone with fabric.
Sewing thread to match fabric.
2·70 m (3 yd) lace trimming.
70 cm (¾ yd) round elastic.
90 cm (36 in) wide waterproof fabric for lining both cap and bag, 60 cm (⅝ yd).

Cutting out

A seam allowance of 6 mm (¼ in) has been included on all edges.

1. Putting lace trimming on shower cap.
2. Sewing binding to gusset seam.
3a. Fold raw edges to center. 3b. Put these edges together and slip-stitch.

To make the caps

For each cap, cut one piece of the appropriate size from fabric and one from lining.
Place the lining on the wrong side of the fabric and baste together. Make two rows of machine stitching around the lines indicated on the pattern to form the casing for the elastic. Zigzag stitch the outer edges together to finish.
Place the lace trimming on the right side of the cap edge and machine stitch in place as close to the edge of the cap as possible (fig. 1). Overlap the raw ends of the lace and finish. Work a row of zigzag stitching over the row of straight stitching to hold the lace secure and flat. Press the cap flat on the right side only with a cool iron. (Test waterproof fabric first.)
Cut a small hole in the lining only, between the two rows of machine stitching, and insert the round elastic using a bodkin. Pull up to fit head and secure the elastic.

Mother's bag

Cut out bag and gusset sections from quilted fabric and lining. Baste lining fabric to the wrong side of quilted fabric bag section and the two gusset sections.

Sew bias binding to the upper short edge of each gusset section. Sew bias binding to the upper straight edge of the bag. Press flat on the right side only. Clip into seam allowance of the bag section as indicated on the pattern for gussets. Placing wrong sides together, stitch the gusset sections to the bag, matching the clips on the bag to the corners of the gusset sections. Commencing from the bound straight edge, sew bias binding around the gusset seams and the curved flap edge of the bag (fig. 2).
Press with a cool iron on the right side of the fabric. (Test waterproof fabric first.)
Sew snap fasteners in positions marked on bag and bag flap to close.
Cut a strip of fabric measuring 58·5 by 7·5 cm (23 by 3 in). Fold the raw edges to the center as shown (fig. 3a) and baste. Turn in the seam allowance on the short ends and baste. Fold the outer fold edges together, baste and slip-stitch around the entire edge (fig. 3b). Press flat.
Sew handle to bag in position as indicated on the gusset pattern piece.

Daughter's bag

Cut out one bag section from fabric and one from lining. Cut out base in quilted fabric and in lining. Cut two casings in fabric.
Baste the lining to the wrong side of the bag side and base sections.
Placing right sides together, stitch the side seam. Finish the seam edge by sewing the raw edges together with a row of zigzag stitching. Turn under the seam allowance on all edges of the casing sections, baste and press flat. Place in position as indicated on the pattern and topstitch in place, leaving the short ends open, with gaps on either side of bag for the ribbon ties. Finish the upper edge of the bag with a row of zigzag stitches. Sew on the lace trimming as instructed for the hat. Placing right sides together, pin the bag to the base, easing in any fullness. Stitch and finish the seam.
Cut ribbon into two lengths. Starting at A, thread one length of ribbon through the casings completely around bag and sew the ends securely together. Starting at B thread other ribbon through in same way. Pull the ribbon out at each side of the casing as shown to close (fig. 4).

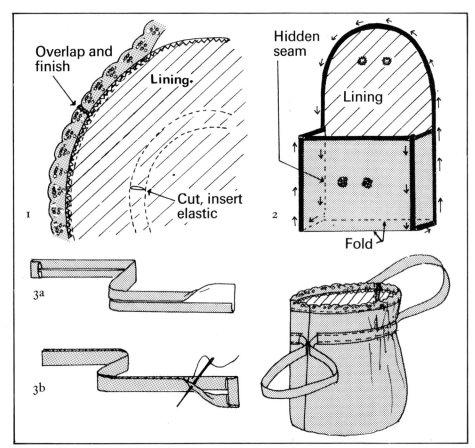

Graph pattern for sponge bags and mob caps

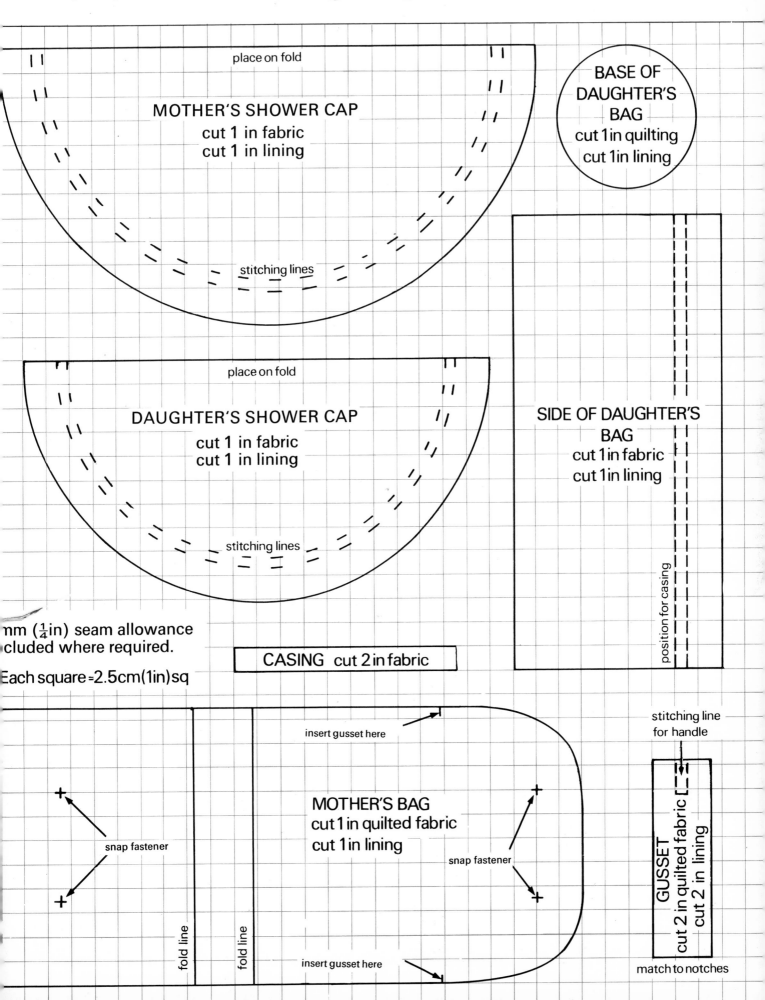

place on fold

MOTHER'S SHOWER CAP
cut **1** in fabric
cut **1** in lining

stitching lines

BASE OF DAUGHTER'S BAG
cut **1** in quilting
cut **1** in lining

place on fold

DAUGHTER'S SHOWER CAP
cut **1** in fabric
cut **1** in lining

stitching lines

SIDE OF DAUGHTER'S BAG
cut **1** in fabric
cut **1** in lining

position for casing

nm (¼in) seam allowance
cluded where required.

Each square = 2.5cm(1in)sq

CASING cut **2** in fabric

insert gusset here

stitching line for handle

MOTHER'S BAG
cut **1** in quilted fabric
cut **1** in lining

snap fastener

snap fastener

GUSSET cut **2** in quilted fabric
cut **2** in lining

fold line

fold line

insert gusset here

match to notches

Basic Equipment Check List

Here is a list of the basic items you will need in sewing garments and making accessories for the home. They can be found in the notions departments of department stores and furnishing fabrics departments.

For Pattern making
Yardstick (meter stick)
Pattern paper
Household scissors for cutting paper
Tapemeasure
Tracing wheel

For cutting out and marking
Tailor's chalk
Tracing paper
Dressmaker's carbon paper
Marker pencils
Pins
Dressmaker's fabric shears

For sewing
Hand-sewing needles
Machine needles (see machine needle and thread chart)
Pincushion
Embroidery scissors for fine work
Thimble
Thread (Cotton, silk and synthetic or various weights; see needle and thread chart)

Notions
Bias binding
Buttons
Button-covering kit
Drapery hooks
Drapery rings
Elastic
Hooks and eyes
Interlining (sew in and iron on)
Grosgrain belting
Piping cord
Snap fasteners
Seam binding tape
Shirring elastic
Trimmings such as beads, braids, fringe and ribbon
Nylon touch-and-close fastening tape (Velcro)
Zippers (nylon and metal, also concealed zippers)

Index

A

Armholes 50, 54
Alterations 50, 51, 52, 106, 107, 108
    see also Patterns (alterations),
      Hemming, Shortening, Lengthening
Aprons, mother and daughter 40, 41,
    42, 43, 44

B

Back measuring *see* Measurements
Balance marks 11
Basting 13, 14
    stitches 16, 17
    slip 17
    diagonal 17
Bedspreads
    eiderdown covers 175, 176, 177
    flounced 173, 174, 175
    throw-over 169, 170, 171, 172, 173
Belts 60, 61
Bias 11
    binding 123
    strips 12, 71, 128
Binding 18
Blouse 81, 82
    see also Blouson, Shirts
Blouson, jersey 72, 73, 74, 75
Buttonholes 24
    bound 99
    handworked 24
    machine-made 24
Button loops 71
Buttons 24

C

Chair covers
    deck chair 191, 192, 193
    padded 193
Chalk, tailor's 6, 15
Clip 20
Collars 22, 45, 46, 54, 55
Corners
    pressing 22
    round 171
    shirt 88
    square 171
    with neck facing 45
Cuffs 46

Curtains
    cafe 158, 159, 160, 161, 162
    see also Draperies, Headings for
      curtains
Cushions 126, 127, 128, 129, 130, 131,
    132, 133, 134
Cutting out 12, 15
    round tablecloths 119, 120, 121
    special directions 15, 16
    see also Patterns

D

Darts 21, 49, 54
Draperies
    glass 149
    hanging 147
    lined 150, 151, 152, 153, 154, 155,
    156, 157
    reversible 155
    sheer 149
    unlined 143, 144, 145, 146, 147
    see also Curtains
Dress 45, 46, 47, 48
    long evening 52, 53, 54, 55, 56
    see also Sundress

E

Ease 11, 33
Eiderdown cover 175, 176, 177

F

Fabric
    knitted 66, 67, 68, 69, 70, 71, 72, 73, 74
    lampshades, for 180
    lining 150
    machine needle chart 7
    metric widths 8
    patterns 93, 94
    pile 16
    preparation 11, 119
    sheer 149
    testing 11
    thread chart 7
Facings 21, 30
    preparation of 28, 29
Fastenings 24, 25, 26, 55, 140, 141, 190
    see also Buttons, Zippers
Finishing 36, 55

    see also Pressing
Fitting, preparation for 16
Flaps 16
Flower prints, cutting 15, 16
Fraying 123

G

Gathering 33, 34
    see also Shirring
Gathers, pressing 22
Grading *see* Layering
Grain 11
Graph patterns, using 9, 10

H

Ham, tailor's 6
Heading for curtains 159, 160
    ruffled 160
    scalloped 159, 160, 161
Hems 22, 30, 36, 55
    finishing 30, 31, 32, 33
    lengths 30
    plain 30, 31
    types of 30, 31, 32, 33
Herringbone *see* Stitches
Hooks
    and bars 25
    and eyes 25

I

Interfacing 30
Iron 6
Ironing *see* Pressing
Ironing board 6

J

Jacket, unisex 99, 100, 101, 102, 103,
    104, 105
Jersey
    machine needle, thread for 6, 7
    making up 66

L

Lampshades 179, 180, 181, 182, 183,
    184, 185, 186, 187
    lined 184, 185, 186, 187
    preparing frame 182
    Tiffany cover 183, 184

trimming 180
Layering 20
Lengthening items 50
Linings
   detachable 153
   for curtains 150, 151, 152, 153, 154, 155
   for lampshades 185, 186, 187
   for picnic basket 189
   see also Fabric
Locking in lining *see* Draperies

M
Measurements
   metric 8
   taking 8, 9, 49, 137, 143, 144, 145, 169
Metric stick 8, 9
Mitering 123

N
Nap 11, 16
Napkins 124
Neatening hems 30
Needles, machine 6, 7
Nightshirt 76, 77, 78, 79
Notches 11, 20

O
One-way 11
Overalls 113, 114, 115, 116
Overcasting 18

P
Patterns
Pants 106, 107, 108, 109, 110, 111, 112, 113
   slim fitting 113
   alterations to 49
   for aprons 42, 43, 44
   for bathroom set 195, 196, 197
   for blouson 75
   for dress 48
   for nightshirt 78, 79
   for separates 84, 85
   for shirts 69, 70, 90, 91
   laying 10, 11, 12
   marking 15
   sizes 8
   testing 49, 50
Picnic basket, lined 189
Pile fabrics *see* Fabrics
Pillows *see* Cushions
Pillowcases 178
Pinking shears 8
Pins 6
   positioning 12
Piping 128, 129, 131
Piping foot 129
Place mats 124
Plaids, cutting 15, 16
Pleater tape 147, 153
Pleats 92, 93, 94, 95, 96, 97, 98

box 94
   construction of 95, 96
   finishing 96
   hemming 96
   pinch pleats 155, 156
   types of 94
Pockets 16, 41
   button down 189
   flatware 190
   gathered 83, 86
   patch 36
Potholder 191
Pressing
   cloth 6, 11, 66
   rules 21, 22
   shrinkage 22

R
Rouleau 71
Ruffles 38, 40, 41, 137, 141, 160
   dust 178

Scissors 6
Seams 17, 21, 22, 146
   channel 19
   double topstitch 19
   finishes 17, 18
   flat fell 19
   French 20
   grading 20
   layering 20
   patterned fabrics 146, 147
   understitching 20
Selvage 11
Separates 80, 81, 82, 83
Sewing machine 6
   needles for 6, 7
Shirring 33
Shirt
   classic 87, 88, 89, 90, 91
   men's 66, 67, 68, 69
   raglan sleeved 81, 82, 83
   see also Blouson
Shortening 50
Shower cap 196, 197
Shrinkage 22, 31, 32
   by pressing 22
   testing for 11
Skirt
   A-line 65
   flared 61, 62, 63
   pleated 96, 97, 98
   separate 83, 84, 85, 86
Slash 20
Sleeves 46
   openings 88
   Raglan 81, 82, 83
Slipcovers 134, 135, 136, 137, 138, 139, 140, 141, 142
Snaps
   metal 24

nylon 25
Stitch ripper 6
Stitches
   backstitch 17
   basting 16, 17
   blanket 17
   blind 30
   halfback 26, 30
   hemming 17, 18, 30
   herringbone 18
   overcasting 18
   prick 18
   reinforcing 17
   running 18
   slip 17, 18
   stay 16
   topstitch 20
   zigzag 18
Stripes, cutting 15, 16
Sundress 34, 35, 36, 37

T
Tablecloth
   rectangular 121, 122, 123, 124
   round 118, 119, 120, 121
Tabs 16, 54
Tacks, tailor's 14
Tacking 13, 14
   thread 14
   trace 14
Tapemeasure 6
Thimble 6
Thread 6, 7
Tie-backs 162, 163
Toiletry bag 196, 197
Touch and close fastener 25, 26
Tracing wheel 6

U
Underlining 54
Understitching 20

W
Waistbands 57, 58, 59, 60, 64
Windbreak 192, 193, 194
Window shades 163, 164, 165, 166, 167, 168

Z
Zipper foot 129
Zippers 26, 27
   concealed 28
   decorative 27
   guards 29
   invisible 29, 30
   length required 26
   methods of sewing 27, 130
   open ended 28
   seams 26, 27
   slipcover 140, 141
   types 26

Pictures Contributed by:

Steve Bicknell: 126/7, 128T, 168, 176, 195.
Camera Press: 159, 188, 189.
Heidede Carstensen: 148.
John Carter, 14, 73, 77, 100, 110, 114.
Bob Davidson: 47.
Alan Duns: 121, 124/5.
Jenny Franklin: 23.
Geoffrey Frosh: 157.
Nelson Hargreaves: 172/3.
Courtesy Harrison Drapes: 151, 152L.
Paul Kemp: 156TL.
Peter Kibbles: 154.
David Levin: 165.
Chris Lewis: 132L, 119T&B.
Bill Maclaughlin: 182.
Stuart Macleod: 67TL, 81.
D. Marsden: 161.
Nigel Messett: 181.

Illustrators

Suzanne Bowen-Morris 37; Michael Boyes 124BL; Rosemary Chanter 17TC/TR/BC, 20T&B, 21T; Lynette Colbert 112; Marta Czok 78/9, 117; Victoria Drew 128B, 129R, 130TL; E. Embleton/B. Firth 92R, 93BR&T, 94/5; Terry Evans 72, 74, 80, 82, 83, 84; Barbara Firth 11, 16, 17TL, 18, 19, 24, 26, 27, 28, 29, 30, 31, 32, 33, 34TR, 38, 4, 40, 41, 42, 43, 44, 49, 50, 51, 54, 55, 57, 58, 59, 60, 61, 63, 64, 66, 89, 97, 99TL, 106/7, 108/9, 136, 137, 138, 179, 180, 185, 186, 187; Angela Fishburn 132; John Hutchinson 69, 70; Janet Kirkwood 75; Janine Kirwan 134; Brian Mayors 56, 65, 86, 90, 91, 96, 98; Janet Smith 111; Lynette Stock 196; Paul Williams/B. Birth 44, 115; Paul Williams/ Chris Legee 76; Paul Williams 103, 104, 105, 139, 140, 141, 142, 160, 177B, 178.